An
E. M. Forster
Dictionary

by
Alfred Borrello

The Scarecrow Press, Inc.
Metuchen, N.J.   1971

ISBN 0-8108-0392-5

Library of Congress Catalog Card Number: 72-151091

To

J. M. J.

and

Anne and Dominick Borrello

for their years of

patience.

Table of Contents

Preface

In the forenoon of Sunday, June 7, 1970, as I was
working on the final draft of this volume, the news of the
death of E. M. Forster was broadcast. The report came not
as a special bulletin, but as part of the regularly scheduled
news program which was sandwiched between periods of light
music appropriate to the time of the day and the day of the
week. It was noted that he had died quietly, at the age of
ninety-one, in his sleep. Thus his life had ended as the
greater part had been lived: unobtrusively, without fanfare.
He wrote little--perhaps too little in the estimation of some
critics--but of the five novels he produced few will deny that
two, A Passage to India, and Howards End, are to be counted
among the greatest contributions in their form produced in
this century. The remaining three, albeit less totally successful works, are remarkable in their own striking
individualities.

The manner of his death suggests that aspect of his
work which first attracted me to his novels and is the prime
motivation for the production of this volume. His works
present a surface of controlled calm and peace which, upon
deeper concentration of one's aesthetic sensibilities, reflects
an essentially artistic economy of word, phrase, and internal
structure. As one reads, one becomes increasingly aware
that he is in the presence of a master artist who is all the
greater for not flaunting the perfection of his art. Subtlety
is his trademark. It is my hope to reveal in part through
this volume the bare bones of his art in order to contribute
to a finer and a broader understanding of that art. All too
often, commentators have restricted their investigations of
his work to the two most successful of his novels. They forget that he has also written a large number of essays, two
volumes of biography and other works which, when examined,
reveal a great deal about Forster and the art he practiced in
his novels.

The genesis of this volume does not rest solely upon
my personal interest in Forster. The work also owes its
life to Thomas Hurley, a long-time friend, and the discussions

we had on <u>Howards End</u> and <u>A Room with a View</u>. We spoke of many aspects of these works: their richly allusive prose, their surface serenity, their balance. Though these conversations ranged far and wide they always came to rest on the fact that, while commentary on Forster's masterpieces abounds, little has been done to examine or comment upon the lesser works. This volume was designed in part to fulfill that need.

I must also thank Mr. Hurley for the help he gave in proofreading the manuscript. It was a long and tedious job accomplished during the greater part of an impossibly hot and busy New York summer.

I should also like to extend my thanks to Mrs. Rhona Silverman for the help she gave me in assembling the data for this volume.

Mrs. Adele Schneider has also earned my gratitude. In her capacity as technical and special services librarian at Kingsborough Community College, she located and procured for me one of Forster's more elusive pamphlets without which this volume could not have been completed. I must note that she worked under an almost impossible deadline. My thanks also go to the generous people at the Library of the University of North Carolina from whom she obtained a copy of the work. They hastened to answer her call with a speed I thought was not possible in the academic world.

I cannot end my list of thanks without including the librarians at the New York Public Library's Information Division. I do not know their names, nor, I am certain, do they know me, yet they never ceased offering help when I called for it; nor can I omit to thank the very charming young lady at St. John's University's Library who proved invaluable in tracking down an elusive bit of information, but whose name I failed to take. She might recall, however, if she chances to read this, that I did remember to thank her as I had promised.

A. Borrello

Brooklyn, New York
August, 1970

viii

Introduction

This volume is the first of three projected works designed to serve as basic tools of reference for the scholar as well as the student and the general reader interested in the works of E. M. Forster. The other volumes, now in preparation, include: An E. M. Forster Glossary which intends to clarify the allusions (geographical, historical, literary, mythological, etc.) which serve as the warp of his art; and An Annotated Bibliography of Works About E. M. Forster which will identify and summarize the books, pamphlets, and articles which constitute the corpus of critical commentary on his writings.

This volume, though conceived and created in the tradition of the Austen, Thackeray, Dickens, and Faulkner dictionaries, is nevertheless more uniform and more inclusive. Included in this volume are the following:

1. Summaries of all of E. M. Forster's novels, short stories, collected essays, biographies, pageants, and pamphlets. Essays, book reviews, letters, introductory messages, etc. not collected in his three volumes of essays (Abinger Harvest, Pharos and Pharillon, and Two Cheers for Democracy) have generally been omitted from this dictionary for a variety of reasons, chief of which is their relative unavailability. Almost all of the essays in Forster's collections have been reprinted several times and most under different titles. Each variant has been noted and elaborate cross-references have been constructed to aid the researcher. In addition, full publication data have been provided for each essay summarized as well as for each work summarized. An attempt has also been made in these summaries to suggest, whenever possible, the general tone of the original.

2. Forster's biographies (Marianne Thornton, Goldsworthy Lowes Dickinson), his volume of criticism (Aspects of the Novel), and his Indian reminiscences, (The Hill of Devi) have been summarized chapter by chapter.

3. Forster's guide book, Alexandria, has been

described in detail, but no summary of its sections has been attempted. A detailed summary of the data Forster gives would almost equal the original in size.

4. A listing of all titles of chapters and sections, acts and scenes. The chapter titles assigned to the first American edition of Howards End by Forster's American publishers have, however, not been included since Forster objected to them. They were dropped from later printings.

5. Descriptions of all of Forster's characters. Exceptions have been made for those appearing in "The Abinger Pageant" since all save Dr. Riccabocca and the Woodsman, who are included, are shadowy figures rather than characters.

All too often, Forster gives no name to his minor characters. Rather, he identifies them by means of sharp and pithy descriptions (e. g. the chinless curate with the dampest hands). While this method produces apt designations of these figures, it does create a difficulty in the construction of an alphabetical list. Generally, the problem has been solved by listing the individual by the first adjective in the phrase which Forster chooses to describe him (i. e. two he-baby papists is listed under "two"). When a character has no first name but does have a title (e. g. Mr. , Mrs. , Lady, Major) the title is considered the first name for the purposes of alphabetizing.

6. A list compiled from the novels and the short stories of key geographical locations (e. g. Chandrapore from A Passage to India), sites (the Marabar Caves, etc.), houses (Howards End, etc.), titles of books and short stories written by characters (e. g. The Eternal Moment, a novel written by Miss Raby, the central figure of "The Eternal Moment"), shops (e. g. Alinari's in Florence, etc.), hotels (e. g. The Bertolini), inns (e. g. The George) alluded to or frequented by the characters. No attempt, however, has been made to identify their counterparts, if any, in the real world. This function will be performed by the forthcoming An E. M. Forster Glossary.

7. No separate section has been established for the characters. Their names have been arranged alphabetically with the summaries and the other information offered.

8. As an aid to a more satisfactory utilization of the material in this volume, two appendices have been compiled; the first lists all of Forster's characters in terms of

the works in which they appear; the second is a list of all of his works summarized in this dictionary.

9. A list of abbreviations used. These serve as identifications of the work in which the character appears. The abbreviations in parentheses follow the description of the character.

Despite the exhaustive effort which has been made to eliminate errors from this work, it would be foolhardy to claim that it is absolutely free of fault. Should the reader encounter errors or discover omissions, I should be grateful to hear of them.

A List of Abbreviations Used

AB	"The Abinger Pageant"
AH	Abinger Harvest
AS	Arctic Summer
Celest	"The Celestial Omnibus"
Collect Ta.	The Collected Tales
Co-ord	"Co-ordination"
Curate	"The Curate's Friend"
England's	England's Pleasant Land
Eternal	"The Eternal Moment"
HE	Howards End
LJ	The Longest Journey
Machine	"The Machine Stops"
Mr.	"Mr. Andrews"
Mrs. G.	"Mrs. Grundy at the Parkers"
My Own	"My Own Centenary"
Other	"Other Kingdom"
Other Side	"The Other Side of the Hedge"
Our Graves	"Our Graves at Gallipoli"
PI	A Passage to India
Point	"The Point of It"
Road	"The Road from Colonus"
RWV	A Room with a View
Siren	"The Story of the Siren"
Story	"The Story of a Panic"
Voters	"A Voter's Dilemma"
WAFT	Where Angels Fear to Tread

AN E. M. FORSTER DICTIONARY

A

ABINGER HARVEST--1st edition, London, Edward Arnold and Co., 19 March 1936; 1st American edition, New York, Harcourt Brace and Co., 30 April 1936. Reprints of about eighty articles, essays, reviews, etc. arranged in the order of their subjects rather than in the order of their composition. There are five sections: 1) Commentaries on passing events; 2) Literary criticism; 3) The past; 4) The East; and 5) The text of The Abinger Pageant. The title of the collection derives from the fact that relatives of Forster have been connected with the village of Abinger, in Surrey, for nearly sixty years, and he knew the place all of his life. The collection contains the following works: Part I, The Present--Notes on the English Character; Mrs. Grundy at the Parkers'; "It is Different for Me", My Wood; Me, Them and You; a Voter's Dilemma; Our Graves in Gallipoli; Happiness!; Roger Fry: An Obituary Note; Our Diversions (1. The Scallies, 2. The Birth of an Empire, 3. The Doll Souse, 4. Mickey and Minnie, 5. Chess at Cracow, 6. The Game of Life, 7. My Own Centenary); Liberty in England. Part II, Books--A Note on the Way; Forrest Reid; Ibsen the Romantic; T. S. Eliot; Proust; Word-Making and Sound-Taking; The Early Novels of Virginia Woolf; Ronald Firbank; Howard Overing Sturgis; Sinclair Lewis; Joseph Conrad: A Note; T. E. Lawrence; Jane Austen (1. The Six Novels, 2. Sanditon, 3. The Letters). Part III, The Past--The Consolations of History; Macolnia Shops; Cnidus; Gemistus Pletho; Cardan; Voltaire's Laboratory (1. How They Weighed Fire, 2. Troublesome Molluscs); Captain Edward Gibbon; Trooper Silas Tomkyn Comerbacke; Mr. and Mrs. Abbey's Difficulties; Mrs. Hannah More; Battersea Rise. Part IV, The East --Salute to the Orient!; The Mosque; Wilfrid Blunt (1.) The Earlier Diaries: 1888-1900, 2. The Later Diaries: 1900-1914); For the Museum's Sake; Marco Polo; The Emperor Babur; Adrift in India (1. The Nine Gems of Ujjain; 2. Advance India!, 3. Jodhpur, 4. The Suppliant, 5. Pan); Hickey's Last Party; Two Books by Tagore (1. Chitra, 2. The Home and the World); The Mind of the Indian State; Hymn before

Action. Part V--The Abinger Pageant. (For summaries and publication information see: individual titles.)

"ABINGER NOTES"--See: "The Last of Abinger"

"ABINGER PAGEANT, THE"--First published in Abinger Harvest, 1936. The "Pageant" is "rural" rather than historical and tries to show the continuity of country life. It consists of a short prologue and six episodes linked together by a narrator, a woodsman. The episodes are 1: From Briton to Norman; 2: The Middle Ages; 3: The Hammer Forge (The year of the Armada); 4: The Days of John Evelyn; 5: Smugglers and Other Gentry (18th century); and 6: Towards Our Own Time. The Epilogue concludes with the thought that the fate of the land is in the hands of the people. (See also: England's Green and Pleasant Land another pageant treating a similar subject.)

ABBOT, CAROLINE--A tall, grave, rather "nice-looking" young lady who accompanies Lila Herriton to Italy. Since she is "charming" and "sober, " and is seeking a companion for a year's travel, the Herritons hope that Lila's going with her would save Lila from a disastrous re-marriage. Their hopes, however, are dashed. Lila meets and marries Gino Carella. Caroline later tries to take Lila's child by Gino back to England. She confesses to Philip Herriton that she has fallen in love with Gino. In the meantime, Philip realizes that he is in love with Caroline, but she ultimately rejects him. (WAFT I)

ABBOT, MR. --Caroline's father a "good, quiet, dull" man. He is first introduced to the reader when he comes to see Lila and his daughter off to Italy. Later, he meets Harriet on her way home with the bank notes her mother has sent her to draw from the bank for Philip's trip to Italy to rescue Lila's child from Gino. Harriet is annoyed and tries to shake him off. [It is interesting to note that both Gino Carella's father and Mr. Abbot are dentists.] (WAFT I)

ABERDEEN, MRS. --Rickie Elliot's bedmaker in his lodgings at Cambridge. (LJ I)

"ABOUKIR AND ROSETTA"--Title of Sect. viii (Part II), Alexandria.

ACHILLES--On Mt. Olympus, Achilles asks the boy to stand upon his shield. The boy declines in favor of Mr. Bons. (Collect--Celest)

ADAM--Michael's third child and second son, who, unlike
Henry and Catherine, his other children, caused his father
some anxiety. Michael could never understand Adam in spite
of careful observation. As a result, they never became real
friends. (Collect Ta - Point)

ADAM'S BOY--Son of Adam, grandson of Michael. He tells
his cousin, Catherine's boy, that they should leave the room
of their grandfather who is ill even though their parents have
told them to remain. He argues, in the manner of his father,
that they ought not to do what old people tell them to do.
(Collect Ta - Point)

"ADRIFT IN INDIA"--1. The Nine Gems of Ujjain--1st
published in New Weekly, I (21 March 1914), p. 10; reprinted
in Abinger Harvest, 1936. The author gives a description of
his visits to the ruins, concluding that there is no point in
differentiating among them. 2. Advance, India!--1st published in New Weekly, I (11 April 1914), p. 106; reprinted in
Abinger Harvest, 1936. Forster is invited to attend the public
wedding of a Mohammedan and his bride who is "emancipated."
He finds the wedding "almost heartrending" because it reveals
the problem of India's future: the mélange of India's tradi-
tions and those of the West. 3. Jodhpur--1st published as
"Adrift in India: In Rajasthana, " in New Weekly, I (16 May
1914), pp. 269-270. reprinted as "Adrift in India, 3:\
Jodhpur" in Abinger Harvest, 1936. The author visits Jodhpur which he discovers has a civilization still "alive. " 4: The
Suppliant--1st published as "Adrift in India: The Suppliant"
in New Weekly, II (25 July 1914), p. 166. Forster describes
how a suppliant insinuates himself into the home of his Indian
friend as a result of the Indian's excessive sense of hospitality. [See: Mohammed Latif.] 5: Pan--1st published as
"Pan, " in Criterion, I (July 1923), pp. 402-408. The
pleasures, origins, and habit of chewing pan [betel] are
described.

"ADVANCE, INDIA!"--See: "Adrift in India, (2.) Advance,
India. "

AENEAS--The horse Stephen chooses when Aunt Emily (Mrs.
Failing) tells him to take Rickie for a ride. Rickie's horse
is called Dido. [In naming the horses, Forster intimates the
ironically similar relationship which grows between Rickie
and his half-brother, Stephen. Like Dido who dies for the
love she bears Aeneas, Rickie is to give his life for
Stephen.] (LJ XII)

AGATHOX LODGE--The home of the boy who has discovered the celestial omnibus. It is at 28 Buckingham Park Road, Surbiton. (Collect Ta - Celest)

AHAB--The name of one of Evie Wilcox's puppies. The other, Jezebel. Evie liked to name animals after the "less successful" characters of Old Testament history. (HE XVI)

AHMED--The son of Aziz, and brother to Karim. (PI II)

ALAN, MISS CATHERINE--See: Two little old ladies. (RWV II)

ALAN, MISS TERESA--See: Two little old ladies. (RWV II)

ALBERT--See: Cissie and Albert.

ALEXANDRIA, THE--The hotel Henry Wilcox suggests to Margaret Schlegel for their wedding reception. It is located off Curzon Street. (HE XXVI)

ALEXANDRIA: A HISTORY AND A GUIDE--1st edition, Alexandria, Egypt, Whitehead Morris, Ltd., 1922. 1st American edition, Garden City, New York, Anchor Books (Doubleday and Co.), 1961. The text was written while Forster was stationed in Alexandria during the First World War as a volunteer for the Red Cross and is divided into two sections: "The History," which details the history of the city from the Greco-Egyptian period to the modern period; and "The Guide" which offers an orderly description of the city and its environs. Also included are maps, appendices offering information on the modern religious communities, etc.

"ALEXANDRIA VIGNETTES: EPIPHANY"--See: "Epiphany"

"ALEXANDRIA VIGNETTES: LUNCH AT THE BISHOP'S (A.D. 310)"--See: "St. Athanasius," Part I, in Pharos and Pharillon.

"ALEXANDRIA VIGNETTES: THE RETURN FROM SIWA"--See: "The Return from Siwa"

"ALEXANDRIA VIGNETTES: THE SOLITARY PLACE"--See: "The Solitary Place"

ALI, MAHMOUD--A friend of Aziz and Hamidullah who dislikes the British intensely. He makes a passionate defense of Aziz during the trial. (PI II)

"AMERICA, INDIA, CHINA"--Title of Chapter XI, Goldsworthy Lowes Dickinson. For summary see: Goldsworthy Lowes Dickinson.

AMERICAN GIRL NEW TO THE COUNTRY, AN--A guest at the Grand Hotel des Alpes. She interrupts the conversation of Miss Raby and Feo Ginori with a request that Ginori decipher the value of a handful of coins. (Collect Ta - Eternal)

AMERICAN LADY--A guest at the Albergo Biscione in Vorta who thinks that she sees saints in the fresco on the wall of the dining room. (Collect Ta - Eternal)

AMERICAN LADY'S FATHER, THE--With his daughter, he is a guest at the Albergo Biscione. He murmurs "superstition" when his daughter remarks that she thinks she sees saints in the fresco on the wall of the hotel's dining room. He and his daughter are a "lugubrious couple" lately returned from the Holy Land, where they had been shamefully cheated. Consequently, their attitude toward religion has suffered. (Collect Ta - Eternal)

AMERICAN MISSIONARY, AN--On her way back to England, Adela Quested's ship stops at Port Said. She goes ashore with an American missionary whom she had met on board. He asks her to what she is returning because, he notes, "Every life ought to contain both a turn and a return." He has an empty mind which has no genuine idea of what he means by "turn" and "return." [Forster's treatment of him is typical of almost all the clergymen in his fiction. They are generally in possession of great ideas the dimensions and/or meanings of which elude them. As a result, they are more often than not ineffectual.] (PI XXIX)

AMRITRAO--Hamidullah, the leading barrister of Chandrapore and holder of a Cambridge degree, suggests that a Hindu lawyer be in charge of the case to defend Aziz against Adela Quested's accusation. He believes the move would make a wider appeal. He mentions one or two names--men from a distance who would not be intimidated by local conditions. However, he prefers Amritrao, a Calcutta barrister, who had a reputation professionally and personally, but who

was notoriously anti-British. Amritrao accepts the commission.   (PI XIX)

"ANDANTE PASTORALE"--The title of Rickie's short story
which was singled out for special praise by the publishers
who rejected it along with the entire collection in which it
appeared, Pan Pipes. Rickie, however, did not care for it,
considering it too sentimental.   (LJ XV)

ANDERSON, MR. --Lives in the same lodgings in Cambridge
as does Rickie, but below him. His teacups, as Mrs. Aberdeen, Rickie's bedmaker, notes, are difficult to wash.   (LJ
I)

ANDERSON'S--On returning to his college, Rickie makes tea
and eats the biscuits which Mrs. Aberdeen has brought for
him from Anderson's, a bake shop.   (LJ VI)

"ANDRE GIDE: A PERSONAL TRIBUTE"--See: "Gide's
Death"

ANDREWS, MR. --He is recently deceased. He was kind,
upright, religious, broad church, middle class. He was educated at Winchester and Oxford, was married at thirty-two
and had four children, two of whom died.   (Collect Ta - Mr.)

"ANGEL OR APE"--An essay in "The Clarion," a publication Stephen Wonham reads regularly and from which he gets
most of his ideas. The article is by Mrs. Julia P. Chunk.
(LJ X)

ANGELO--Henry Wilcox's Italian chauffeur who drove Margaret about Shrewsbury and "dearly loved making her late."
(HE XXV)

ANNA--Mrs. Worter's sister and houseguest and ultimately,
one of the party in Evelyn's wood.   (Collect Ta - Other)

ANNE--The Honeychurch maid. Cecil Vyse says she has
two faults: she begs your pardon when she hears you per-
fectly and kicks the chair-legs with her feet.   (RWV VIII)

ANNIE--The Sclegel's maid who opens the door to the woman
who comes asking for her husband.   (HE XIII)

ANNISON, MR. --The senior member of the staff at Sawston
School.   (LJ XVI)

"ANONYMITY: AN ENQUIRY"--1st published in Calendar of
Modern Letters, II (November 1925) pp. 145-156; reprinted
as "Anonymity: An Inquiry" in Atlantic Monthly, CXXXVI
(November 1925), pp. 588-595; reprinted as a pamphlet,
London, Hogarth Press, 1 December 1925; reprinted in Two
Cheers for Democracy, 1951.

Forster asks, "does ignorance or knowledge of author-
ship signify anything to the reader?" In so far as words convey information, they ought to bear a signature, but if the words
create atmosphere, no signature is needed. All literature
(words which convey atmosphere) tends toward a condition of
anonymity. So far as words are creative, a signature merely distracts from their true significance. To forget its creator is one of the functions of a creation. The desire to
know who wrote a piece of literature is modern. Good literature tends to make one forget the writer. The demand
that literature should reflect a personality is modern. Literature should not be an "expression" but a "discovery."
The study of a creative subject like literature is dangerous
and should never be attempted by the immature. Newspapers
are pernicious caricatures of literature because the anony-
mous articles in them take on a universal air, an air of "absolute truth."

ANOTHER GUEST--On the way from Shrewsbury to Oniton,
Evie Wilcox's wedding party picks up another guest. (HE
XXV)

ANSELL'S BEDMAKER--Is less interested in work than is
Rickie's, Mrs. Aberdeen. She says "Oh Dang!" when she
discovers that she has to lay Ansell's table cloth. (LJ I)

ANSELL, MARY--Stewart's sister. Mr. Ansell, their father,
notes when Stewart is deciding upon a career, that there is
enough money to get her and her sister, Maud, good hus-
bands. (LJ III)

ANSELL, MAUD--Stewart Ansell's sister. See: Mary Ansell (LJ III)

ANSELL, MR.--The father of Stewart, Mary, and Maud. He
is a provincial draper of moderate prosperity and a man of
some education who has the great gift for detecting what is
important. He welcomes Rickie into his home. [Forster
creates him in the Dickens-Wells tradition. He is very
much like a Wellsian hero gone good.] (LJ III)

ANSELL, STEWART--The son of a provincial draper and a
close friend of Rickie. Like him, he is a student at Cambridge. He bitterly opposes Rickie's marriage to Agnes
Pembroke, whom Rickie marries, nevertheless. He is more
successful when he persuades Rickie to accept Stephen Wonham. Stephen is the illegitimate son of Rickie's mother.
(LJ I)

ANSTEY, LADY--The year of the publication of Miss Raby's
most successful work, The Eternal Moment, saw Lady Ans-
stey, Mrs. Heriot, and the Marquis of Bamburgh and many
others visit Vorta, the scene of the novel. They returned
enthusiastic. Lady Anstey exhibited her water colors of it;
Mrs. Heriot wrote about it in The Strand, and Nineteenth
Century published an article about Vorta by the Marquis. As
a result, Vorta became popular. (Collect Ta - Eternal)

ANTELOPE, THE--The country inn near Aunt Emily's home.
(LJ XXXIV)

ANTONIO--A character in Miss Lavish's book about Florence. In the novel, he steals a kiss from the heroine, Leonora, much as George Emerson did from Lucy. (RWV XV)

ANTONY--Adele Quested and Mrs. Moore's Goanese servant.
They take him along on the expedition to the Marabar Caves.
The trip was planned by Aziz. Antony was hired at Bombay
and does well in an hotel or among smart people but as soon
as his employers consort with anyone whom he thinks second
rate, he leaves them to their disgrace. (PI XIII)

APPLEBLOSSOM, MISS--Mr. Ansell's cashier in his provincial drapery establishment and later his housekeeper.
(LJ III)

"ARAB PERIOD"--Title of Section IV (Part II), Alexandria.

ARCHDEACON, THE--He confides to Inskip his belief that
Evelyn Beaumont has eloped with Ford. (Collect Ta - Other)

ARCTIC SUMMER--1st published in Tribute to Benjamin
Britten on His Fiftieth Birthday, ed. by Anthony Gishford,
London, Faber and Faber, 1963. There is a newspaper rec-
ord of a public reading by Forster of the fragment "A Novel
that 'Went Wrong': Author Gives First--and Only--Public
Reading at Aldeburgh Festival," Manchester Guardian, (13

June 1951), p. 3. [A fragment of an unfinished novel.
Forster indicates that more of the fragment exists, but indicates that it will never be published.]

Martin Whitby, his wife Venetia, and his mother-in-law Lady
Borlase, are on their way to Italy for a much needed vacation. Martin is in the Treasury and his work has exhausted
him. At Basle Station, he is almost killed in the rush for
train, but is saved by a young man whom he later learns is
C. P. March. After they are safely aboard the train, March
asks about Tramonta where he has heard there are paintings
of Pietro Modenese. The fragment breaks at the point when
Martin has promised to meet March in Milan's Galleria Vit-
torio Emanuale the next day at six with a permesso to visit
Tramonta.

"ARNOLD IN ITALY, AN"--See: "William Arnold"

"ART IN GENERAL"--Section title of Part II, Two Cheers
for Democracy.

"ART FOR ART'S SAKE"--1st published in Harper's Magazine, CIC (August 1949), pp. 31-34; reprinted in Two Cheers
for Democracy, 1951.

[The essay incorporates much of the material from
"The New Disorder."] Forster believes in art for art's sake.
His position does not mean that he holds that art is the only
thing that matters. Art, he notes, not only exists in spe-
cific forms, but it is "pertinacious." Works of art are the
only objects in the material world which possess internal order and that is why he believes in art for art's sake.

"ART OF VIRGINIA WOOLF, THE"--See: "Virginia Woolf"

"ARTS IN ACTION, THE"--Section title of Part II, Two
Cheers for Democracy.

ARYAN BROTHER, THE--When invited to the Turton's garden party, he appears wearing a topi and spats. (PI V)

"ASCENT OF F.6, THE"--1st published as "Chormopuloda,"
in The Listener, Supp. (14 October 1936), p. vii, reprinted
in Two Cheers for Democracy, 1951 as "The Ascent of F.
6."

Essentially, the essay is a review of the play The As-

cent of F. 6, by W. H. Auden and Christopher Isherwood. The
play, Forster finds, is not easy "to focus." It is short and
straightforward, yet "at least four pairs of spectacles are
necessary" before it can be examined properly. As a play
about heroism it is not entirely satisfactory. Viewed as a
politico-economic outlook, it becomes a satire of a familiar
type. Ransom, the central figure, suffers from the last in-
firmity of noble minds: the pursuit of real power. The
final focus, however, is Freudian. Mother-love becomes a
"nasty customer." The play is a tragedy in the modern
mode. It is not an entertainment.

ASPECTS OF THE NOVEL--1st published, London, Edward
Arnold and Co., 20 October 1927; 1st American edition, New
York, Harcourt, Brace and Co., 20 October 1927.

The volume originated as a series of lectures (the
Clark lectures) delivered under the auspices of Trinity College, Cambridge, in the Spring of 1927.

I.   Introductory--remarks concerning the nature of
novels and a good-natured denunciation of "pseudo-scholars"
in the field. Novels must not be considered chronologically.
The success of a novel lies in its own sensitiveness, not in
its subject matter.

II.   The Story--the fundamental aspect of a novel.
Story is a narrative of events arranged in their time-se-
quence. It converts the reader to a listener. The story is
essentially primitive; it generates intolerance. Fiction cannot be divorced from time.

III.   People--Their nature is conditioned by what the
novelist guesses about other people and about himself and
modified by other aspects of his work. The function of the
novelist is to reveal the hidden life at its source. We can
know more about a fictional character than we can about a
real person because the creator of fiction is also its narrator. A character in a novel is real when the novelist knows
everything about him.

IV.   People (Continued)--Characters do not coincide
as a whole with people in real life. They only parallel
people in the real world. If characters are given complete
freedom, they "kick the book to pieces;" if they are kept too
sternly in check, they die and destroy the novel by "intesti-
nal decay." To avoid these problems, the novelist uses flat

characters (caricatures) and round characters. The test of
a round character is whether he is capable of surprising in
a convincing way. The point of view in a novel is not as
important as a proper mixture of characters.

V. Plot--Is a narrative of events with the emphasis
falling upon causality. It demands intelligence and memory.
Mystery is essential to plot. Plot is the novel in its logical, intellectual aspect.

VI. Fantasy--The novel of fantasy has an impro-
vised air: this is its charm.

VII. Prophecy--Is a tone of voice in the novel. It
may imply any of the faiths of man or the "mere raising of
human love and hatred." The prophetic aspect of the novel
demands of the reader humility and the suspension of the
sense of humor. Prophecy is not like fantasy because its
"face is towards unity" whereas "fantasy glances about."
A prophet does not reflect. Forster can think of only four
prophetic writers: Melville, D. H. Lawrence, Dostoevsky,
and Emily Brontë.

VIII. Pattern and Rhythm--Spring out of plot. Rigid
patterns "shut the door on life." Rhythm is the interrela-
tionship of the parts.

IX. Conclusion--The change in the subject matter of
the novelists of the future will be enormous, but they will
not change. If the novelists of the future see themselves
differently than those in the past, they will see their characters differently and "a new system of lighting will result."

ASTROLOGERS--Two brothers who live opposite Aziz in an
unfurnished house. (PI X)

"AUNT 1852-1879"--Section title in Marianne Thornton: A
Domestic Biography. For summary see: Marianne Thornton.

"AUNT 1852-1879, 1: EAST SIDE"--Section title in Marianne Thornton: A Domestic Biography. For summary see:
Marianne Thornton.

"AUNT 1852-1879, 2: EDUCATIONAL"--Section title in
Marianne Thornton: A Domestic Biography. For summary
see: Marianne Thornton.

"AUNT 1852-1879, 3: MILTON BRYON"--Section title in
Marianne Thornton: A Domestic Biography. For summary
see: Marianne Thornton.

AUNT JULEY'S NURSES--These ladies think that Aunt Juley's
concern for the comforts of her nieces and her nephews during her illness is natural. Margaret Schlegel, however,
senses the approach of "Death" in that concern. (HE
XXXIV)

AUSTINSON--The director of the Nottingham and Derby Railway whom Martin Whitby had met. (AS)

AVERY, MISS--An old neighbor of the Wilcoxes who lives
near Howards End. She has a row with Evie Wilcox when
Evie returns the wedding present she had sent: an expensive pendant. Despite Margaret's insistence that she leave
her furniture alone, Miss Avery unpacks it and arranges it
in Howards End. She also mistakes Margaret for the first
Mrs. Wilcox. (HE XXIII)

"AYLWARD INCIDENT"--See: "Great Aunt 1879-1887, 3:
The Aylward Incident."

AZIZ, DR. --A young, sensitive, amiable Moslem doctor in
Chandrapore, India. Though largely snubbed by the English
colony, he becomes friendly with Mr. Fielding and subse-
quently with two English women, visitors to India. Without
intending it as a real invitation, he asks the ladies to come
with him on a visit to the Marabar Caves. Miss Quested,
the younger, becomes separated from the party and later,
because of an unintentional error, accuses him of attempted
rape. He is jailed and humiliated. Miss Quested finally
withdraws the charge and he, now anti-British, wants to
press her to pay damages, but Fielding dissaudes him. Suspicious of Fielding's motives, he breaks off the friendship.
The two men meet once again after two years. Both realize,
though they enjoy the meeting, that their friendship is impossible because of their racial differences. (PI II)

AZIZ'S MATERNAL GRANDFATHER--Aziz tells Fielding that
his maternal grandfather, who was a poet, fought against the
British in the Mutiny. (PI XXXI)

AZIZ'S WIFE--Has died leaving him with two children: Ahmed and Karim. Aziz shows a photograph of his wife to
Fielding as a supreme act of friendship. (PI VI)

B

BABY--Helen Schlegel's child by Leonard Bast. (HE XLIV)

"BAD FARIES, THE"--See: "Our Diversions, 3: The Doll Souse"

BAMBURGH, MARQUIS OF--See: Lady Anstey. (Collect Ta - Eternal)

BANNISTER, HUGH--The son of the Rev. and Mrs. Bannister, friends of Hamidullah. He is a leather merchant at Cawnpore. Hamidullah longs to see him, recalling how the Bannisters had entrusted their children to him and had treated him as a member of their family. He also recalls holding the young Hugh in his arms during the funeral of Queen Victoria. He uses his relationship to the Bannisters as an example that all Englishmen are not the same in their attitudes toward the Indians. (PI II)

BANNISTER, MRS. --See: Hugh Bannister. (PI II)

BANNISTER, REV. --See: Hugh Bannister. (PI II)

BARONCELLI, CONTESSA--A "dear friend" of Miss Lavish who, when a maid is unavailable to conduct her children to school, dresses them with sailor-hats. Everyone takes them for English. As a consequence, they are safe in the streets of Florence. (RWV II)

BARTLETT, CHARLOTTE--The cousin of Lucy Honeychurch who serves as Lucy's chaperon on their trip to Italy. She is poor and obsequious. (RWV I)

BAST, JACKY--See: Jacky (HE VI)

BAST, LEONARD--"A young man, colorless, boneless, who had already the mournful eyes above a drooping moustache that are so common in London, and that haunt some streets of the city . . . One guessed him as the third generation, grandson to the shepherd or ploughboy whom civilization had sucked into the town; as one of the thousands who have lost the life of the body and failed to reach the life of the spirit. Hints of robustness survived in him, and more than a hint of good looks." He stood at the extreme verge of gentility. He knew that he was poor, but would have died before he

confessed any inferiority to the rich. Nevertheless, he is
not as courteous, intelligent, lovable, as the average rich
man. His mind and body have been underfed because of
poverty. He loses his job as a result of acting on information Henry Wilcox gives. His life then becomes entangled
with that of the Schlegels. Helen has a child by him. He
dies of a heart attack brought about by a beating adminis-
tered by Charles Wilcox, Henry Wilcox's elder son. When
Forster first introduces him to the reader, he is known as
"Margaret's new young man." (HE VI)

BATTERSEA RISE--1st published as a pamphlet, New York,
Harcourt, Brace and Co., 2 December 1955. Later it be-
came the first chapter in Marianne Thornton: A Domestic
Biography. [No English edition.]

        Essentially, a short history of the home and the
Thorntons who owned it. Forster was a descendant of the
Henry Thornton who enlarged the small Queen Anne building.
The library was designed by William Pitt. The house was
razed in 1907 despite efforts to preserve it.

"BATTERSEA RISE"--See: "Daugher 1797-1815, 1: Battersea Rise"

"THE BAY OF THE FIFTEEN ISLES"--The title of a short
story by Rickie Elliot, an aspiring writer. The scene of
the story is set on St. John's Eve off the coast of Sicily.
A party of tourists land on an island which the boatmen
tell them is not usually there. The boatmen warn them not
to set foot on it. They pooh-pooh their warnings. When
they land, the island begins to rock and so do the minds of
its visitors. They start to quarrel and jabber. Suddenly,
fingers burst up through the ground. They are black fingers
of sea devils. The island begins to tilt. The tourists go
mad with fear. But just before the final catastrophe, one
man sees the truth. Here are no devils. Other muscles,
other minds are pulling the island to its subterranean home.
(LJ VI)

BAYS, THE--Aunt Juley's (Mrs. Munt) home in Swanage.
Margaret and Helen go there for their annual visit without
having secured a new house as they had promised themselves
they would. (HE XVIII)

BEARDED PORTER, A--A station official who angers Charles
Wilcox when he is slow in giving him a parcel for which he

has called at the station.   His anger is displayed to Aunt
Juley.   Despite Charles's anger, as he and Aunt Juley leave for
Howards End, the porter looks after them with admiration.
"Life is a mysterious business."   (HE III)

BEAUMONT, EVELYN--An exquisitely beautiful but naïve
girl who is Harcourt's fiancée.   She is an unsophisticated,
sensitive young lady whom he has met in Ireland.   As a
gift, he offers her the copse, Other Kingdom, which he has
purchased to complete his property.   He wants to fence the
property in, but she wishes it to be left in its natural state.
When she disappears, he believes that she has eloped with
his ward.   (Collect Ta - Other)

BEEBE, MINNIE--A young girl of thirteen, the niece of Mr.
Beebe.   (RWV X)

BEEBE, MR. --A stout but attractive clergyman.   Lucy
Honeychurch and Charlotte Bartlett meet him at the Pensione Bertolini in Florence and learn that he is to be the
vicar of Lucy's parish church.   They soon become friends.
He is also friendly with the Emersons who move into the
neighborhood.   (RWV I)

BEEBE, MRS. --Mr. Beebe's mother after whom Cecil Vyse
asks effusively though he has no particular regard for her.
(RWV VIII)

BEETHOVEN--Inquires in Heaven who Miss Haddon is.
When told, he decrees that all in her house should hear a
perfect performance of his A Minor Quartette.   (Collect -
Co-ord)

"BEOMONDS (1874-1876)"--Title of Chapter IV, Goldsworthy
Lowes Dickinson.   For summary see: Goldsworthy Lowes
Dickinson.

BERTHA--The daughter of a friend whom Mrs. Wilcox meets
at the stationery department in the Haymarket Stores.   Mrs.
Wilcox learns that Bertha is motoring as are Evie and Mr.
Wilcox.   (HE X)

BERTOLINI, SIGNORA--The proprietress of the Pensione
Bertolini.   She is a Cockney who has attempted to "rival the
solid comforts of a Bloomsbury boarding house" in her hotel
on the Arno in Florence.   Her success has caused Lucy
Honeychurch and Charlotte Bartlett, her guests, to wonder

if they are in Florence or London.   (RWV I)

"BERTOLINI, THE"--Title of Chapter I, A Room with a
View.

"BETWEEN THE SUN AND THE MOON"--Title of an essay
in Pharos and Pharillon.   For summary see: Pharos and
Pharillon.

"BEYOND GOG AND MAGOG"--See: "Wilfrid Blunt"

BHATTACHARYA, MR. --One of the Indians invited to the
Turton's garden party.   (PI V)

BHATTACHARYA, MRS. --Wife of Mr. Bhattacharya and one
of the more Westernized ladies invited to the Tuton's garden
party.   She is identified by her husband as the taller of two
ladies who addressed Adela Quested in English; the shorter
is Mrs. Das.   She and her husband invite Miss Quested and
Mrs. Moore to visit them.   Mr. Bhattacharya promised to
send his carriage for them.   When the day in question arrives, no carriage appears.   (PI V)

BIDDER, SIR JAMES--A friend of Mr. Henry Wilcox who
would be present at Evie's wedding.   Henry Wilcox feels
that the affair is a splendid opportunity for Margaret Schlegel to meet his "set" of which Sir James is an important
member.   (HE XXV)

"BIRTH OF A BABY"--See: "Letters of 1921: Birth of a
Baby"

"BIRTH OF AN EMPIRE, THE"--See: "Our Diversions, 2:
The Birth of an Empire."

BISCIONE, THE--The hotel in which Miss Raby stays in
Vorta.   Nothing has changed since her last visit.   (Collect
Ta - Eternal)

BISHOP, A--A guest at the Grand Hotel des Alpes.   The
Concierge helps him select postcards.   He buys more than
he wants.   (Collect Ta - Eternal)

"BISHOP JEBB'S BOOK"--1st published as "The Blessed
Bishop's Book" in New Statesman and Nation, N. S. (7 De-
cember 1940) pp. 563-564; reprinted as "Bishop Jebb's
Book" in Two Cheers for Democracy, 1951.

In 1804, John Jebb, later Bishop of Limerick, Ard-
fert, and Aghadoe, bought a folio-size note-book which Forster later inherited. The book was used by the Bishop as
a "common-place" book. He began entries on Nov. 11,
1804. The book came to Forster from his grandfather, who
was Jebb's friend. They came to know each other when
Jebb was "hanging around the Archbishop of Cashel" and
Forster's grandfather was a student at Trinity, Dublin.
When Jebb became a bishop, Forster's grandfather became
his chaplain, courier, and "trumpeter." The Bishop helped
with negotiations for his marriage and, when he died, left
the couple his silver shoe buckles and his common-place
book.

The first two pages of the book are its index. It is
beautiful rather than effective. He wrote very little in the
book, filling only eighteen pages. Forster, who came to
use the volume as his common-place book [see: "The last
of Abinger"] has filled over one hundred pages. There are
some two hundred blank pages remaining.

The Bishop had a beautiful handwriting. He came
from a good family and was a scholar, and a gentleman.
He also was efficient at church business.

While not keeping up the Bishop's index, the book
progresses in Forster's hands. Keeping the Bishop's style,
Forster underlines the first word of every entry and, again,
in the manner of the Bishop, the entries are "non-intimate."
The book, were it to fall into the wrong hands, would do the
reputations of the Bishop and of Forster no harm.

BLAKISTON, MRS.--A brainless but most beautiful girl who
has come to the club with her baby for refuge from the
troubles which came on the heels of the announcement of
Aziz's trial. Her husband is away in the district, and she
dared not return to her bungalow in case the "niggers attacked." Her husband is a relatively unimportant railway
official. In untroubled times she was snubbed officially, but
because of the uproar, she becomes a symbol of all that is
worth fighting for. (PI XX)

BLANCHE--The sister of Leonard Bast to whom he turns for
financial aid after losing his position. She sends him money
out of her dress allowance but does not tell her husband for
fear of his anger. (HE XLI)

BLANCHE'S HUSBAND--Moved by his brother-in-law's financial difficulties, he offers him (Leonard Bast) work. Leonard, however, finds some pretext to avoid it. (HE XLI)

"BLESSED BISHOP'S BOOK, THE"--See: "Bishop Jebb's
Book"

BOB--The father of the boy who discovered the celestial omnibus. He is constantly laughing at his son and will not
take him seriously. (Collect Ta - Celest)

BONS, MR. SEPTIMUS--He was serious and kind. He had
a beautiful house and loaned books. He was a churchwarden
and a candidate for the County Council; he had donated to
the free library enormously; he presided over the Literary
Society, and had members of Parliament to stop with him.
In short, he was possibly the wisest person alive. He accompanied the boy on the celestial omnibus and, as a result,
died. (Collect Ta - Celest)

"BOOK THAT INFLUENCED ME, A"--1st published as
"Books in General" in New Statesman and Nation, N. S. (15
July 1944), p 43; reprinted as "A Book That Influenced Me"
in Two Cheers for Democracy, 1951.

        The book in question is Samuel Butler's Erewhon.
As a book it is difficult to classify. It influenced Forster
because it "took him unawares." He found what Butler had
to say was "original." The book influenced him also because of its technique: "muddling the actual and the impossible until the reader is unsure which is which." While
Erewhon influenced him positively, there are books which
have had a negative influence on him: St. Augustine's Confessions, Machiavelli's The Prince, Swift's Gulliver's Travels, and Carlyle's On Heroes and Hero Worship.

"BOOKS IN GENERAL"--See: "A Book That Influenced Me"

"BOOKSHELVES OF A LOVER OF WORDS"--See: "In My
Library"

BORLASE, LADY--Mother of Venetia Whitby. She is a
large, languid woman, very clever, very good natured and
good hearted and devoted to Martin, her son-in-law. (AS)

BOY, THE--The young boy who discovers the celestial omnibus near his home and travels on it to Mt. Olympus. His

parents will not believe him when he tells them of his discovery. Mr. Septimus Bons does, however, and agrees to
accompany him on his next trip only to die as a result.
(Collect Ta - Celest)

BRACKNELL--Margaret Schlegel has taken an "unemployed"
by that name to clean knives and boots.   When Helen, her
sister, comes in to announce that a woman has been asking
for her husband, Margaret suggests that it might be Bracknell the woman is after.   (HE XIII)

BRAHMAN, A--During the festival of the birth of the god in
Mau, a Brahman brings forth a model of the village of Go-
kul [equivalent to Bethlehem in the Christian tradition.]
(PI XX)

BROWN, MR.--A candidate for election to Parliament who is
very much like his opponent, Mr. Grey.   Both are pleasant.
Both are rich.   Each has a wife, two daughters and a motor
car.   They are alike except that Mr. Brown is a conserva-
tive.   See: Mr. Grey. (AH - Voter's)

BROWNE, MR. THOMAS--See: The Driver (Collect Ta -
Celest)

BRYCE, HAMAR--The tenant at Howards End.   He is an invalid who leaves without giving notice.   (HE XV)

BUMBLE--A permanent official who is first met in Act I
(1760) and reappears in all other acts.   He is in favor of
only what is legal, "strictly legal," even though the legalities
he upholds tend to destroy the countryside.   (England's)

BURTON--Mr. Wilcox's butler at Oniton.   He is handsome
and Margaret Schlegel finds herself attracted to him.   (HE
XXVI)

"BUT . . ."--See: "Voltaire and Frederick the Great"

BUTTERWORTH, MRS.--An old neighbor of the Honeychurches on whom Mrs. Honeychurch, Lucy, and Cecil Vyse
are going to call when they come across George, Freddy,
and Mr. Beebe bathing in the pool in the wood.   (RWV II)

BYSTANDER, A--Asks the little boy whose trap Stephen
tries to hire if he heard Stephen's offer of a railway ticket
and sixpence for the trap.   (LJ XXXIII)

C

"C MINOR OF THAT LIFE, THE"--1st published in Abinger Chronicle, II (June 1941), pp. 35-39; reprinted in Two Cheers for Democracy, 1951.

Is there any absolute difference between musical keys --a difference that is inherent and not relative? Forster has "battered" his head against this question for years. The problem, if there is one, is connected with a sense of pitch. His own sense of pitch is "shaky" and "feeble." But there may be nothing in "key" and can be nothing unless there is a sense of pitch. The C minor key affected Beethoven and he used it as a medium of expression when he was in a particular mood.

CABMAN--On their honeymoon in Florence, George Emerson and Lucy take a cab, the driver of which tells them: "Signorino, domani faremo uno giro." (RWV XX)

CADOVER--The home of Rickie Elliot's Aunt Emily Failing. It was not a large house. It was built in 1800 and favored the architecture of ancient Rome chiefly by means of five large pilasters which stretched from the top of it to the bottom. Between the pilasters was the glass front door. To the right were the drawing-room windows; to the left, the windows of the dining-room and above them was a triangular area which had in its middle a small, round hole according to the usage of Palladio. Eight gray steps sustained the classical note. These led from the building down to the drive and a formal garden on the adjoining lawn which ended in an ha-ha. (LJ III)

CAHILL, PERCY--Several days after her and her father's visit to the Schlegels, Evie Wilcox, for whom the "net of matrimony was being prepared," becomes attracted to Mr. Percy Cahill. She later marries him. (HE XVI)

CALLENDAR, MAJOR--The civil surgeon and Aziz's superior. He cares little for Aziz and his countrymen and displays that lack of care on every possible occasion. (PI II)

CALLENDAR, MRS.--The wife of Major Callendar, the civil surgeon. Like her husband, she has little regard for Indians. She snubs Aziz when he greets her and Mrs. Lesley as they climb into the tonga which takes them to Major Callendar's home.   (PI II)

"CAMBRIDGE"--The title of Part I of The Longest Journey.

"CAMBRIDGE"--1st published, New Statesman and Nation,
N. S. (29 March 1941), pp. 328, 330; reprinted in Two
Cheers for Democracy, 1951.

     [Originated as a review of Cambridge by John Steeg-
man.] It is difficult to meditate on one's "dear old university" without falling into snobbery or priggishness. Hard-
ship of life at Cambridge is vanishing and so is style. Oxford, sister to Cambridge, is so "distended by endowments
as to be unrecognizable." Cambridge, on the other hand,
keeps her shape; no "idealistic millionaire has yet raped
her." The selective Cambridge cannot possibly survive, except as a museum piece. But the "Cambridge-open-to-all,"
the "in-accordance-with-national-needs-Cambridge" will only
be a technical finishing school--"a degree monger."

"CAMBRIDGE (1881-1884)"--Title of Chapter VI, Goldsworthy
Lowes Dickinson. For summary see: Goldsworthy Lowes
Dickinson.

"CAMERA MAN, A"--See: "Sinclair Lewis"

CANTÙ, SIGNOR--Owner of the Grand Hôtel des Alpes. He
is the son of Signora Cantù and also her business rival. She
claims that he is out to ruin her and her hotel, the Biscione.
(Collect Ta - Eternal)

CANTÙ, SIGNORA--The owner of the Biscione. She was an
inflexible aristocrat. Because she was old, she liked to
meditate on the fairness of Fate which had not spared her
contemporaries and had often not spared her juniors. (Collect Ta - Eternal)

"CAPTAIN EDWARD GIBBON"--1st published as "Incongruities: Captain Gibbon" in New York Herald Tribune, Sect. 11,
Books, (16 August 1931), pp. 1, 4.; reprinted as "Incongruities, Captain Edward Gibbon" in Spectator (29 August and 5
September 1931), pp. 264-265; 288-289; reprinted as "Captain Edward Gibbon" in Abinger Harvest, 1936.

     A description of a period of Gibbon's life before he
began his Decline and Fall of the Roman Empire. Forster
concludes that "he was a genius who read, dreamed, and al-

so knew . . . by direct contact a fragment of the rough
stuff of society, and extended his knowledge through the
ages."

"CARDAN"--1st published in Independent Review, V (April
1905), pp. 365-374; reprinted in Abinger Harvest, 1936.

     A commentary on the life of Girolamo Cardano (1501-
1576) as seen through his autobiography.   Forster holds
that if Cardano escapes the oblivion he so much dreaded, it
will not be because he was a doctor and a mathematician, but
because of his autobiography.   It is his sentimentality which
gives him value.   Truthfulness was his one virtue.

CARELLA, GINO--An Italian who marries Lila Herriton, a
widow who is older than he.   He is the son of a dentist and
is somewhat vulgar but has a splendid physique.   When Lila
first meets him, he is twenty-one, twelve years younger than
she, and has just completed his military service in the Ber-
saglieri.   He has no profession and lives on Lila's money.
Lila cannot understand him and, consequently, a rift grows
between them.   Lila dies in childbirth leaving Gino a son.
Gino becomes completely devoted to the son she gives him
and is crushed when the child dies in an accident.   (WAFT
II)

CARRUTHERS--The head boy at Dunwood House, Sawston
School.   (LJ XVI)

CARRUTHERS, A. P.--A friend of Gerald Dawes.   He is the
secretary to the college musical society at Cambridge and a
possessor of a "socker [sic] blue."   (LJ III)

"CATASTROPHE"--Section title in The Hill of Devi.

"CATASTROPHE: PONDICHERRY"--Section title in The Hill
of Devi.

"CATASTROPHE: THE YUVRAJ"--Section title in The Hill
of Devi.

CATHERINE--Michael's second child and only daughter who
"took after her mother," Michael's wife, Janet.   (Collect
Ta - Point)

CATHERINE'S BOY--He comes into his grandfather's (Mi-

chael) bedroom to ask after his health.   (Collect Ta -
Point)

"CAVES"--Title of Part II of A Passage to India.

"CECIL AS A HUMORIST"--Title of Chapter X in A Room
With a View.

CEDAR VIEW--The boarding house at Sawston School which
is the rival of Dunwood House.   Rickie Elliot once confused
it with Dunwood House.   (LJ XVII)

"CELESTIAL OMNIBUS, THE"--1st published in Albany Review, II (January 1908), pp. 459-475; reprinted in The Celestial Omnibus and Other Stories, 1911; The Collected
Tales, 1947.

[A short story.]   One day, a young boy discovers
that the station of a very special omnibus line is near his
home.   His parents, he knows, will not believe him when he
tells them of the trip he takes to "heaven" on the line.   The
driver of the omnibus is Sir Thomas Browne.   When the boy
returns home in the evening, he is caned and called a liar.
His father's friend, Mr. Bons, also does not believe him,
but promises to come along with him the next evening.   He
is shocked to see the omnibus of which the boy had spoken.
This time, however, the driver is Dante.   Bons becomes increasingly uneasy.   When the passengers reach their destination, Mt. Olympus, Mr. Bons screams in terror that he
wants to return to his own world.   Achilles, whom they
meet, asks the boy to stand upon his shield, but the boy declines, saying that Mr. Bons should because he is more
learned.   Mr. Bons, totally unnerved by the experience,
calls to Dante to return him to his own world.   Dante refuses.   Mr. Bons falls.   A piece appears in the local paper
noting the death of Mr. Bons.   His mangled body, as if
dropped from a great height, is discovered in a mutilated
condition near the gas works with two omnibus tickets in his
pocket.

CELESTIAL OMNIBUS AND OTHER STORIES, THE--1st
published, London, Sidgwick and Jackson, Ltd., 11 May
1911; 1st American edition, New York, Alfred A. Knopf, 11
July 1923.

Contents: "The Story of a Panic,"   "The Other Side
of the Hedge,"   "The Celestial Omnibus,"   "Other Kingdom,"

"The Curate's Friend," "The Road from Colonus." These
stories were reprinted with those in The Eternal Moment
and Other Stories as The Collected Tales, 1947.   For publication data and summaries see: individual title.

"CENTENARY OF THE LONDON LIBRARY, THE"--See:
"The London Library"

CERTAIN POOR WOMAN, A--Rickie Elliot meets a certain
poor woman whose child Stephen had saved at the level-
crossing of the railroad. She had decided, after some de-
lay, to thank the kind gentleman in person. (LJ XV)

CHAKELEY--Charles Wilcox tells his sister, Evie, that he
must speak to Chakeley about the pollarding of the churchyard elms during their mother's funeral. Evie encourages
him to complain noting that Chakeley is responsible though
he denies it. (HE XI)

"CHALLENGE OF OUR TIME, THE"--1st published in The
Listener (11 April 1946), pp. 451-452; reprinted as "The
Point of View of the Creative Artist" in The Challenge of
Our Time, London, Percival Marshall, 1948; reprinted as
"The Challenge of Our Time" in Two Cheers for Democracy,
1951.

        Victorian liberalism and idealism are dead and the
world is in a "mess." If we are to answer the challenge of
our time successfully, we must combine the new economy
and the old morality. The doctrine of laissez-faire will not
work in the material world, yet it is the only doctrine which
will work in the world of the spirit. We must desire planning for the body not the spirit. There is a difficulty, however. Where does the body end and the spirit begin?
Should the individual be favored over the community? Forster can see the need sometimes for the community to be
favored over the individual, but he cannot free himself from
the conviction that something irreplaceable is lost when this
occurs. He is nevertheless convinced that a planned change
must take place if the world is not to disintegrate. He is
hopeful, however, that in this planning there may be a
sphere for human relationships and for art. The artist and
writer ought to express what they want and not what they are
told to express by the planning authorities.

CHAND, RAM--An Indian friend of Aziz. Generally, he
likes to foment trouble. He tells the Nawab Bohadur that he

will be cheapened if he goes to the "at home" of the Collector. He also visits Aziz while he is ill to stir up trouble. (PI IV)

CHANDRAPORE--The scene of the major part of A Passage to India. (PI I)

CHAPLAIN, THE--Is with the narrator boating off Capri when the narrator's book is lost overboard and the boatman volunteers to dive for it. (Collect Ta - Siren)

CHAPLAIN'S SISTER, THE--She accompanies the Chaplain, the narrator, the aunt of the narrator, and the Colonel on the boating party off Capri during which the narrator's book is lost overboard. (Collect Ta - Siren)

"CHARTERHOUSE (1876-1881)"--Title of Chapter V, Goldsworthy Lowes Dickinson. For summary see: Goldsworthy Lowes Dickinson.

"CHESS AT CRACOW"--See: "Our Diversions, 5: Chess at Cracow."

CHI-BO-SING--See: Enicharmon (Collect Ta - Machine)

CHILD, A--Tells Giuseppe and his brother that Maria has been thrown off the cliff. (Collect Ta - Siren)

CHILD, THE--Stephen's daughter to whom he has given his mother's name. (LJ XXXV)

CHINLESS CURATE WITH THE DAMPEST HANDS, THE--Philip tells his mother, Mrs. Herriton, that Lila, widow of his brother Charles, was setting her cap for the chinless curate with the dampest hands. He tells her that he had come upon them in the park. They were speaking of the Pentateuch. This incident convinces Mrs. Herriton that Lila should visit Italy to save her from marriage. (WAFT I)

CHINLESS SUNBURNT MEN, THE--Helen Schlegel sees two chinless, sunburnt men go into the Wilcox apartment. These may have been Dolly's brother, Albert Fussell, and her father, the Colonel. (HE VII) See: Col. Fussell, Albert Fussell.

CHITRA--See: "Two Books by Tagore, 1: Chitra."

CHORLY-WORLY--Dolly Wilcox's affectionate name for one

of her children.   (HE XXXIII)

"CHORMOPULODA"--See: "The Ascent of F. 6"

"CHRISTIAN PERIOD"--Title of Section ii (Part I), Alexandria.

CHUNK, MRS. JULIA P.--The author of "Angel or Ape,"
an essay which Stephen reads in The Clarion, and by which
he is much moved.   (LJ X)

CISSIE AND ALBERT--The semi-detached villas near Windy
Corner, the Honeychurch home, and opposite the church.
They were bought by Sir Harry Otway from Mr. Flack.
Cissie was rented to the Emersons.   (RWV VIII)

"CLEMENT OF ALEXANDRIA"--Section title, Pharos and
Pharillon.   For summary see: Pharos and Pharillon.

"CLOUDS HILL"--1st published in The Listener, (1 September 1938), pp. 426-427; reprinted in Two Cheers for Democracy, 1951.

    A description of Clouds Hill, the home of T. E.
Lawrence (author of Seven Pillars of Wisdom,) which Forster visited when Lawrence was alive. Though not a "show
place" and "not much to see"--it was only a tiny, four-room
cottage hidden away in a four-acre dell of rhododendrons in
the Devonshire heathland--Forster found it "charming," "unusual," and "magical." Forster first visited the place in
1924. In those days the bottom rooms (two) were filled with
firewood and lumber and the top two were used for living.
Forster recalls the happy "casualness" of his visits and how
he "ate out of tins" and drank out of "pretty cups of black
pottery." Lawrence was careful of the comfort of his visitors. The "harder he lived himself, the more anxious he
was that others should fall soft."

"CNIDUS"--1st published in Independent Review, II (March
1904), pp. 278-282; reprinted in Abinger Harvest, 1936.

    A description of Forster's visit to the site of the ancient city during a rainfall. He saw one or two temples,
an agora, and the theatre, where he fell off the stage into
its orchestra. On the whole, he found the episode of his
visit "absurd."

COATES, MR.--Next in seniority at Sawston School after Mr.
Annison, he is passed over for the headmastership of Dunwood House. (LJ XVI)

COLLECTED TALES, THE--1st edition, New York, Alfred
A. Knopf, 10 July 1947; 1st English edition, London, Sidgwick and Jackson, Ltd., 18 March 1948.

    Forster's introduction indicates that these "fantasies"
were written at various dates, but all previous to the first
world war. He also maintains that they represent all that
he has written in "a particular line." He also describes the
genesis of the first story, "The Story of a Panic," which was
written after he "came down in [his] boyhood from Cambridge" and "travelled in Italy for a year." The first chapter came to him while he was sitting in a valley several
miles above Ravello. Contents: From The Celestial Omnibus and Other Stories: "The Story of a Panic," "The Other
Side of the Hedge," "The Celestial Omnibus," "Other Kingdom," "The Curate's Friend," "The Road from Colonus;"
From The Eternal Moment and Other Stories: "The Machine
Stops," "The Point of It," "Mr. Andrews," "Co-ordination," "The Story of the Siren," "The Eternal Moment."
[For summaries and publication information, see: individual
titles.]

"COLONEL WILSON"--See: "Letters of 1921: Colonel Wilson"

"COMMENT AND DREAM: JEW-CONSCIOUSNESS"--See:
"Jew-Consciousness"

"COMMENT AND DREAM: ON A DEPUTATION"--See: "Our
Deputation"

CONCIERGE, THE--See: Feo Ginori (Collect Ta - Eternal)

"CONCLUSION"--The title of Chapter IX of Aspects of the
Novel.

CONDER, MISS--A friend of Aunt Juley. She could enter a
picture gallery, look at the pictures, and "say straight off
what they all feel, all round the wall." Aunt Juley could not
do that, but she could do that about music. Aunt Juley sug-
gets Miss Conder to Margaret Schlegel as a walking companion in the absence of Helen. (HE V)

CONFESSIONS OF A MIDDLE AGED MAN--The title of a
book by Michael in which he pays tribute to youth but demonstrates that "ripeness is all." (Collect Ta - Point)

COOK, THE--She cries when Agnes Pembroke tells her that
Gerald Dawes is dead. (LJ V)

COOK AT HOWARDS END, THE--Evie Wilcox, trying to assume her mother's place in Howards End, speaks to the
cook. (HE XI)

COOK AT ONITON, THE--While preparing the wedding
dishes for Evie Wilcox's wedding, one of them boils over
and the cook throws cedar shavings to hide the odor. (HE
XXVI).

"CONSOLATIONS OF HISTORY, THE"--1st published in
Athenaeum, (16 January 1920), pp. 69-70; reprinted in
Abinger Harvest, 1936. A student of history can enjoy the
study because "there is no passion that cannot be gratified in
the past." Further, the past is devoid of all dangers: social and moral; one can meet kings and courtesans. One
can satisfy one's vanity as well as one's sensuality.

"CO-OPERATION"--See: "Co-ordination"

"CO-ORDINATION"--1st published as "Co-operation" in English Review, XI (June 1912), pp. 366-372; reprinted as "Co-
ordination" in The Eternal Moment and Other Stories, 1928;
The Collected Tales, 1947.

[A short story.] Miss Haddon is a piano teacher who
must work under a new coordinative system based essentially on the fact that all of her pupils play the same duet because the school in which she works has only one subject
for the year: Napoleon. At the tea during which the principal explains the system, several of the mistresses are enthusiastic, but Miss Haddon is not. She is growing old and
her teaching is becoming less effective. She wonders when
she will be dismissed. Meanwhile, in heaven, Beethoven inquires who Miss Haddon is. When told, he decrees that all
in her house will, that evening, hear a perfect performance
of his A Minor Quartette. At the same time Napoleon, also in heaven, hears of the many references made to him
from members of the school and is pleased. As a result,
he decrees that all should take part in his victory at Auster-
litz. Things occur as they are ordained and, during a lull

in the girls' prep period, the battle breaks out. Miss Haddon decides to quit teaching and learns of an inheritance which makes her retirement possible. The principal and all of the girls are invited to her retirement cottage. Mephitopheles is much put out by what he sees and takes his case to the Judgment Seat. He is intercepted by Raphael to whom he explains the impossibility of the situation. Raphael calls him an "innocent devil" and claims that co-ordination has occurred through melody and victory.

COTTAGE HOSPITAL--The charity to which Caroline Abbot was devoted. She comes to the Herritons for money to donate to it. (WAFT V)

"COTTON FROM THE OUTSIDE"--Section title, Pharos and Pharillon. For summary see: Pharos and Pharillon.

COUSINS OF MISS QUESTED--Miss Quested is to be married to Ronnie Heaslop at Simla in the home of some cousins. Their house looked "straight into Thibet [sic]." (PI XIV)

CRANE--Mr. Wilcox's chauffeur who is as ugly as sin. Charles asks him curtly who has used the new car noticing mud on the axle. He also asks him who had the key to the garage. Crane responds that it is old Penny, the gardener, who had it. Charles insists that it could not have been Penny. Meanwhile, Crane has wiped off the mud leaving Charles vexed and thinking that he had been treated like a fool. (HE XI)

"CREDO"--See: "What I Believe"

"CULTURE AND FREEDOM"--1st published as "Two Cultures: The Quick and the Dead" in The Listener, (26 September 1940), pp. 446-447; reprinted as "Two Cultures: The Quick and the Dead, The Nazi Blind Alley" in Vital Speeches of the Day, VII (15 October 1940), pp. 28-30; reprinted as "Three Anti-Nazi Broadcasts, 1: Culture and Freedom" in Two Cheers for Democracy, 1951.

Forster has a desire that culture prosper all over the world. He is convinced that, if the Nazis win, culture would be destroyed in England and the Empire. Germany has allowed her culture to become governmental. In England, culture is national and grows out of ways of looking at things now and in the past. Freedom is bound up in the

whole question of culture. The writer must feel free or he
may find it difficult to fall into the creative mood. The
artist must have freedom to tell other people what he is
feeling. The Nazis hold for censorship. The public, too,
must be free to read, to listen, to look. Germany, like
England, has a great national culture. The Nazis wanted it
to be governmental. When a national culture becomes governmental, it is always falsified.

CUNNINGHAM, MR. --A neighbor of Leonard Bast who
greets him upon the latter's return from the Schlegels. He
comments upon the declining birth-rate in Manchester about
which he had just been reading in the Sunday paper. (HE
VI)

CURATE, THE--(Harry)--The narrator of the short story,
"The Curate's Friend." See: "The Curate's Friend"

"CURATE'S FRIEND, THE"--1st published in Pall Mall Magazine, N. S. , VI (October 1907), pp. 470-474; reprinted in
Putnam's Monthly, III (October 1907), pp. 43-47; reprinted
in The Celestial Omnibus and Other Stories, 1911; reprinted
in The Collected Tales, 1947.

[A short story.] Harry, the Curate, and his fiancée, Emily, in the company of a "little friend" of Emily's
and Emily's mother, decide to "tea-out" atop an earthwork
which Harry believes Roman but later proves to be Saxon.
While he is preparing the tea urn, attempting to make it
stand on the sloping ground, he hears a cry of pain. Suddenly, the Curate sees what he takes to be a boy who has
been bathing. When he sees the "boy's" tail, he shrieks.
The creature scampers off into the wood. The Curate
chases it and talks to it. The creature, a Faun, tells the
Curate that he is the only one who can see him. The Faun
says that women with tight boots and men with long hair cannot see him, and he talks only to children. He tells the
Curate that he, however, will always see him and shall be
his friend until he dies. He tells the Curate that he will
make him happy. The Curate responds that he must make
others happy and that he must start with Emily. The Faun
touches Emily and her little friend. They fall in love. The
Curate is angry, but the Faun discovers that in his secret
heart he is really happy over such a turn of events. The
Curate's life becomes filled with happiness as he realizes
he has become one with the Faun and the hills and the
stream.

D

DAN (Dante)--The cadaverous driver of the second omnibus in which the boy and Mr. Bons travel to Mt. Olympus. (Collect Ta - Celest)

DANTE--See: Dan (Collect Ta - Celest)

DAPPLE--Dr. Lal's horse. (PI VI)

DAS--Assistant to Ronny Heaslop and judge at the trial of Aziz. He is the brother of Mrs. Bhattacharya and a Hindu, but he becomes friendly with Aziz, a Moslem. (PI XXII)

DAS, MRS. --The wife of Das, the judge, and sister-in-law of Mrs. Bhattacharya. She is present when Mr. Bhattacharya promises to send his carriage for Mrs. Moore and Miss Quested without intending to keep his promise. (PI V)

"DASSERA"--See: "Letters of 1921: Dassera"

DAUGHTER OF MARIA RHOMAIDES--See: Maria Rhomaides (Collect Ta - Road)

"DAUGHTER 1797-1815"--Section title in Marianne Thornton: A Domestic Biography. For summary see: Marianne Thornton.

"DAUGHTER 1797-1815, 1: BATTERSEA RISE"--Section title in Marianne Thornton: A Domestic Biography. For summary see: Marianne Thornton.

"DAUGHTER 1797-1815, 4: THE DEATHBEDS"--Section title in Marianne Thornton: A Domestic Biography. For summary see: Marianne Thornton.

DAUGHTER 1797-1815, 3: ON CLAPHAM COMMON'--Section title in Marianne Thornton: A Domestic Biography. For summary see: Marianne Thornton.

"DAUGHTER 1797-1815, 2: THE PARENTS"--Section title in Marianne Thornton: A Domestic Biography. For summary see: Marianne Thornton: A Domestic Biography.

DAWES, GERALD--The fiancé of Agnes Pembroke. She felt that she dare not tell him of Ansell's rude behavior for

fear that Ansell would be "half-killed." Dawes had the "figure of a Greek athlete and the face of an English one." He
and Rickie Elliot were friends, having met at the public
school they both attended. Unlike Rickie, Gerald was not
successful at Cambridge and dropped out. He was killed
while competing in a football match. (LJ I)

DEALTY, MR. --A fellow clerk whom Leonard Bast meets
while walking near the Houses of Parliament after leaving
the Schlegels. (HE VI)

"DEATH DUTIES, THE"--Title of Act III, England's Pleasant Land. For summary see: England's Pleasant Land.

"DEATH OF HENRY SYKES THORNTON, THE"--See:
"Great Aunt 1879-1887, 2: The Death of Henry Sykes Thornton"

DECCANI BRAHMAN, THE--See: Narayan Godbole. (PI VII)

DEMPSTER'S BANK--Leonard Bast had taken a position in a
bank in Camden Town, a branch of Dempster's Bank. (HE
XXII)

"DEN, THE"--Title of a section in Pharos and Pharillon.
For summary see: Pharos and Pharillon.

DEREK, MISS--A rather selfish young lady who takes advantage of her Indian employer. She is companion to a maharani in a remote Native State and comes to Chandrapore to
visit with the McBrydes. At the last moment, she fills a
gap in the production of Cousin Kate and earns a bad notice
in a local paper. She is genial and gay. She, too, is a
guest on the ill-fated outing to the Marabar Caves. (PI V)

"DESMOND MACCARTHY"--See: "A Tribute to Desmond
MacCarthy"

"DEVELOPMENT OF ENGLISH PROSE BETWEEN 1918 AND
1939"--See: "English Prose Between 1918 and 1939"

DIDDUMS--Dolly Wilcox's affectionate name for her new-
born baby. (HE XXXVIII)

DIDO--The horse Rickie Elliot is given to ride. See: Aeneas. [Dido is the name Virgil gives to the founder and
Queen of Carthage in his epic, The Aeneid. She falls in

love with Aeneas who is driven to Carthage by a storm.
Mercury reminds him of his mission to found Rome.   As a
result, Aeneas leaves Carthage and Dido throws herself upon a funeral pyre.] (LJ XI)

DIMBLEY, MISS ELIZA--A character in the short story,
"The Other Side of the Hedge."   She is identified as the
"great educationalist."   (Collect Ta - Other Side)

"DISASTER WITHIN, THE"--Title of Chapter XV in A Room
with a View.

DOCTOR, THE--Harold's doctor who blames Michael for
Harold's death.   (Collect Ta - Point)

DOCTOR, THE--Mr. Wilcox says that the doctor is not im-
plicated in the note his wife wrote before her death asking
that Howards End be left to Margaret Schlegel.   (HE XI)

"DOES CULTURE MATTER?"--1st published as "Notes on
the Way" in Time and Tide, (2, 9, 16, 23 November 1935)
pp. 1571-1572; 1607-1608; 1657-1658; 1703-1704--the third
contribution was revised and reprinted (omitting the last
paragraph) as the first half of "Does Culture Matter?" in
Two Cheers for Democracy, 1951.   The second half of the
essay in Two Cheers for Democracy comes from "Does
Culture Matter?" in Spectator (4 October 1940), pp. 337-
338.

     Forster uses culture, a "forbidding word," to de-
scribe the various beautiful and interesting objects which
men have made in the past and handed down to us and which
some of us hope to hand on.   Many people despise these objects; nevertheless, they are important.   Forster believes
in culture as a Faith and Faith makes one unkind.   He is
always pleased when culture scores a "hit."   Of course,
many people never cared for the classics.   Up to now these
people have been indifferent, ribald, and good-tempered a-
bout them.   Now, however, the good-humor is vanishing.
As a result, creations from the past are losing their honor
and are on the way to being jetisoned.   In this age of un-
rest, not only must objects be ferried across the river, but
the power to enjoy them must also be ferried.   This power
is acquired through tradition.

     Cultivated people are a drop in the ocean.   The prob-
lem of these people is this: "Is what we have worth passing

on?" The clamor for art and literature which Ruskin and Morris thought they had detected is dead. People today are either indifferent to the esthetic products of the past or are suspicious of them. It is tempting not to recommend culture. The difficulty is that the higher pleasures of culture resemble religion. It is impossible to enjoy them without handing them on. Our chief job is to enjoy ourselves and to spread culture not because we love our fellow men, but because certain things seem unique to us and priceless.

DOLORES--At 4:30, Dolores and Violét come to Miss Haddon for their piano lesson. They play worse than Ellen. (Collect Ta - Co-ord)

"DOMESDAY GARDEN PARTY AD 1899"--Title of Scene i (Act II), England's Pleasant Land. For summary see: England's Pleasant Land.

DORIS--The Parker's maid who "collapses" under the pointed questioning of Mrs. Grundy. (AH - Mrs G)

DRAGOMAN, THE ENGLISH SPEAKING--His arrival with Mrs. Forman, Emily, and Mr. Graham disturbs Mr. Lucas at the khan. (Collect Ta - Road)

DRIVER, THE--The driver of the first celestial omnibus who answers the boy's questions about the vehicle with the words "Omnibus est." He asks the boy to remember him as Sir Thomas Browne. (Collect Ta - Celest)

DRIVER, THE--Interrupts Miss Raby and the Colonel to announce that they had arrived at Vorta. When they do not seem to hear, he repeats loudly, "Vorta! Vorta!" (Collect Ta - Eternal)

DRIVER OF A DILIGENCE, THE--He slows down when he sees Lila walking alone, hoping that she might be on her way to the station. She declines his offer to drive her there, then changes her mind, but he does not hear her cries. (WAFT IV)

DRIVER OF HELEN'S CAB, THE--Hands Helen Schlegel a note given him for her by Henry Wilcox. (HE XXXVII)

"DUCAL REMINISCENCES"--See: "A Duke Remembers".

DUCIE STREET--The Wilcoxes have taken a house in Ducie

Street after leasing Howards End because, as Mr. Wilcox
puts it, Howards End is impossible to live in.   (HE XV)

"DUKE REMEMBERS, A"--1st published as "Ducal Reminiscences" in The Listener, Supp. #38 (8 December 1937)
p. xix; reprinted as "A Duke Remembers" in Two Cheers
for Democracy, 1951.

A review of Men, Women and Things, memoirs of
the Duke of Portland. Forster finds the autobiography a
"very good-tempered book" and "self-assured." The writer,
he notes, is a man of energy, good humor, and natural
sense. He does not like the present day.

DULBOROUGH, THE DEAN OF--A character Forster invents
who preaches on Forster's centenary as reported in The
Times (London) A. D. 2077. (AH - My Own)

DUNWOOD HOUSE--The largest and most lucrative of the
boarding houses at Sawston School. (LJ XVI)

"DUTY OF SOCIETY TO THE ARTIST, THE"--1st published
in The Listener, (30 April 1942), pp. 565-566; reprinted in
Two Cheers for Democracy, 1951.

[A broadcast talk in the Overseas Service.] The
artist never quite fits in. Hence, if he is to work in a
more controlled society in the future, officials should be
able to rely on advisory bodies to guide them in giving com-
missions and be educated to respect art.

E

"E. K. BENNETT (FRANCIS) (1887-1958)"--1st published in
The Caian [publication of Caius College, Cambridge Univer-
sity] LV (Michaelmas Term, 1958), pp. 123-127; also is-
sued in pamphlet form for private distribution, May 1959.

Forster knew Bennett for nearly fifty years. They
first met at the Working Men's College, Crownsdale Road,
London. At that time, Bennett was very poor. He saw in
his poverty an experience which might help him to help others. His father was a baker and his mother a "highly educated and gifted woman." In 1914 he received a scholarship to
the Working Men's College. Then he went to Caius College,
Cambridge and was elected a scholar in Modern Languages.

He knew Romain Rolland, Lowes Dickinson and others with whom he worked to avert World War I.   When the war began, he was drafted.   After the war, he returned to Caius and, in time, became Fellow, Tutor, Senior Tutor, and for some years, President.   He also published.   All this and more, Forster notes, is in his obituary notice in The Times (London).

Music was Bennett's ultimate refuge.   His musical inclincations were German and "nineteenth century."   He liked some moderns (Benjamin Britten, Peter Pears).   His politics were Tory.   He had no sympathy for "earnest left-wingery or with organized Humanism."   He followed much of the Christian code but was "anti-ascetic."

He founded the Shadwell Society--a "mixture of literature and gaiety."   He never forgot that books are intended to be read, plays to be seen, music to be heard.   The Society reflected this faith.

He is said not to have been a good lecturer, but he was "unequalled at supervision."   His sympathy was combined with practical generosity.   He had "Dignity" and "Style:" qualities Forster finds "not easy to define."

EAGER, REV. CUTHBERT--The rector of the English church in Florence whose notice Lucy sees posted in the dining room of the Pensione Bertolini where she is staying with Miss Bartlett.   Later, he takes a party, including Lucy and Miss Bartlett, on a carriage trip to Fiesole.   (RWV I)

"EARLY NOVELS OF VIRGINIA WOOLF, THE"--1st published as "The Novels of Virginia Woolf," New Criterion, IV (April 1926), pp. 277-286; reprinted in Yale Review N. S., XV, pp. 505-514; reprinted as "The Early Novels of Virginia Woolf," Abinger Harvest, 1936.

"So near and yet so far" is what Forster feels about her work.   It is far more difficult to "catch her" than it is for her to "catch what she calls life."   She is capable of conveying the actual process of thinking.   She has made a definite contribution to the novelist's art.   Other so-called innovators are merely "innovators innovating subject matter. They do not advance the art."

EARNEST GIRL, AN--One of the members of the dinner party attended by Margaret and Helen Schlegel.   The group discusses what a fictional millionaire should do with his money. The earnest girl objects to the suggestion that he dispose of his wealth by giving three hundred pounds a year to as many poor people as possible. She rests her objection on the conviction that such a bequest would not help them but tend to "pauperize" them. (HE XV)

"EAST SIDE"--See: "Aunt 1852-1879, 1: East Side"

EDITOR OF THE HOLBURN, THE--A tall, neat man of forty, slow of speech, "slow of soul" and extraordinarily kind. He rejects the story Rickie submits to him "because it does not convince." (LJ XV)

EDSER, LADY--An Anglo-Indian [an Englishman living in India] Lady who attends Evie Wilcox's wedding at Oniton. (HE XXV)

"EDUCATIONAL"--See: "Aunt 1852-1879, 2: Educational"

"EDWARD CARPENTER"--1st published as "Edward Carpenter: A Centenary Note" in Tribune, (22 September 1944), pp. 12-13; reprinted as "Edward Carpenter" in Two Cheers for Democracy, 1951. Forster also contributed "Some Memories," to Edward Carpenter in Appreciation, ed. by Gilbert Berth, London, George Allen and Unwin, Ltd., 1931, pp. 74-81.

Edward Carpenter was born at Brighton (1844) and is relatively unknown. Those who know him probably dismiss him as a crank. Forster considers him a "lovable, charming, energetic, courageous, possibly great" individual. He was also once "an inspiration in the world of Labour." Of respectable upper-middle class parentage, he grew up with no conception of the lives of the poor. He went to Cambridge and had the religious doubts common to his period. After he became a clergyman, they increased. He left the Church. He was not happy in the class into which he was born. He wanted to live and work with manual laborers. As a result, he settled in Sheffield. His action was considered revolutionary, but his socialism was that of Shelley and Blake. He strove to destroy existing abuses such as landlordism and capitalism. He was not interested in efficiency or organization. He believed in Liberty, Fraternity, Equality. His faith rested on a love of the individual and the beauty of nature. He worked for a socialism which would be non-industrial, un-organized, and rooted in the soul.

"EDWARD CARPENTER: A CENTENARY NOTE"--See:
"Edward Carpenter"

"EDWARD GIBBON"--See: "Gibbon and His Autobiography"

"EDWARD GIBBON, THE HISTORIAN"--See: "Gibbon and
His Autobiography"

EDWARDS, SIR VINCENT--Voices his opinion of Forster's
work during the latter's "Centenary." He finds that work
"lofty." (AH - My Own)

EGYPT--1st published as a pamphlet, London, Labour Research Department, 1920. [No American edition.]

        The remarks of Forster trace the history of Egypt
from the Turkish conquest (16th century) through the British
occupancy, World War I, and the post-war rebellions. Forster also discusses the Egyptian administration, notes special problems including that of foreign residents in whose
hands lie most of the business, banking, and industry, though
numerically small; the Suez Canal; and the religious factors.
He also offers suggestions for solving the entire problem of
Egypt. The pamphlet was intended to "state facts" rather
than a "case." Some of the information Forster gives comes
from Milner's England in Egypt and Cromer's Modern Egypt.

ELEGANT GRANDSON OF THE NAWAB BAHADUR, THE--
Debauched and effeminate, Nurredin, the elegant grandson,
had to be left behind when the Nawab offers to take Ronnie
Heaslop and Miss Quested for a drive. Aziz does not like
to talk to him. During the disturbances which follow in the
wake of Aziz's trial, he is "rescued" by a crowd from the
hospital because a rumor has been spread that the English
are committing atrocities against the Indian patients. (PI
VIII)

"ELIZA IN EGYPT"--Section title in Pharos and Pharillon.
For a summary see: Pharos and Pharillon.

ELIZABETH--Miss Raby's maid. A bit impertinent, she
tries to persuade her mistress to stay at the Grand Hotel
des Alpes because her friend's lady is staying there. Colonel Leyland's sister does not think her a fit chaperone.
(Collect Ta - Eternal)

ELLEN--One of Miss Haddon's pupils who complains that the

music she has been given to play is impossible.   Her complaint follows Miss Haddon's warning not to thump the piano.
(Collect Ta - Co-ord)

ELLIOT, AGNES--See: Agnes Pembroke

ELLIOT, MR.--Rickie's deceased father.   He was a barrister and as weak and lame as his son.   Early in his marriage, he left his wife.   He had not one scrap of genius, but
passed for cultured because he knew how to select things
properly.   Basically, he was cruel.   (LJ II)

ELLIOT, MRS.--Rickie's deceased mother.   She was a beautiful woman possessed of a beautiful voice but there was "no
caress in it."   She had no gift of making her home beautiful.   She had an illicit affair and, as a result, gave birth to
Stephen Wonham, Rickie's half-brother.   She died soon after
her husband leaving Rickie and orphan well-supplied with
money but not with the commodity he most needed--love.
(LJ II)

ELLIOT, RICKIE (FREDERICK)--A sensitive, slightly lame
young man who received his familiar name from a cruel re-
mark of his father on his lameness.   Because of that lameness and the lack of love between his parents, Rickie grows
up in loneliness.   He finds a measure of peace and contentment in Cambridge among the friends he meets there, but
he longs for love.   His emotions center on Agnes Pembroke,
who is engaged to Gerald Dawes.   Gerald's death frees Agnes to marry him.   During their engagement, he learns that
Stephen Wonham is his half-brother.   Rickie's marriage
turns out to be an unhappy one.   Meanwhile, Agnes contrives
to have Stephen turned out of Aunt Emily's house so that
Rickie can inherit her wealth.   Stephen confronts Rickie and
their fight marks the beginning of Rickie's regeneration.
Rickie, later, is killed in an effort to save his brother's
life.   (LJ I)

ELSES, SOMEBODY--Mr. Eager, the rector of the English
church in Florence, is avid to show off his knowledge of the
foreign residents to Lucy Honeychurch.   He points out the
home of the Somebody Elses farther down the hill from the
home of Mr. Someone Something.   Mrs. Else has just published the monograph, "Medieval Byways," and her husband
is working at "Gemistus Pletho."   (RWV VI)

"E. M. FORSTER LOOKS AT LONDON"--See: "London is

a Muddle"

EMERSON, GEORGE--a young man who meets Lucy Honeychurch in the Pensione Bertolini when his father offers her
and Miss Bartlett their room with a view.   George falls in
love with Lucy who, when he kisses her during an outing in
the hills of Florence, is shocked by his openess and ill-
breeding.   Nevertheless she is attracted to him.   During the
remainder of her stay in Italy and back home in England,
she tries to stifle her growing love for him.   Finally,
through the efforts of his father, she realizes the foolishness
of the position she has taken and consents to marry him.
(RWV I)

EMERSON, MR. --George's father, an old man of heavy build
with a fair, shaven face and large eyes which have something childish in them.   He says exactly what he means.
He is a Socialist.   He has raised his son to be free of that
hypocrisy which demands that one hide his true self.   His
offer of his room with a view to Lucy Honeychurch and Charlotte Bartlett starts a chain of events which leads to George's
marriage to Lucy.   (RWV I)

EMILY--Harry, the Curate, is engaged to her.   She does not
marry Harry, however, but another, on the instigation of the
Faun whom Harry meets.   Harry admits that she has made
a fine wife and even though she freely corrects her husband's
absurdities, no one else is allowed to breathe a word a-
gainst him.   (Collect Ta - Curate)

EMILY'S MOTHER--Her insistence on "tea-ing" outdoors results in the Curate's encounter with the Faun and her daughter's marriage to another.   (Collect Ta - Curate)

EMMANUELE--The "nice" Italian waiter who speaks English.   (Collect Ta - Siren)

"EMPEROR BABUR, THE"--1st published in Nation and
Athenaeum, (1 April 1922), pp. 21-22; reprinted in Abinger
Harvest, 1936.

[A review of the Leyden and Erskine translation of
The Memoirs of Babur annotated and revised by Sir Lucas
King.]   Babur, a descendant of Tamerlane and Genghis Khan,
inherited Ferghana and proceeded to conquer Samarkand when
he was thirteen.   He soon lost both.   At twenty-one he an-
nexed Kabul and then Delhi where he founded the Mogul Em-

pire. He loved poetry and swimming. He belonged to "the
middle of Asia." His memoirs do not interpret India though
he founded a kingdom there and a great dynasty. He had
small influence with the Indians.

"ENCHANTED FLOOD, THE"--1st published as "The Unbuilt
City" in The Listener, (26 April 1951), p. 673; reprinted as
"The Enchanted Flood" in Two Cheers for Democracy, 1951.

[A review of The Enchanted Flood by W. H. Auden.]
A poet is needed to "arrest" the sea. Auden is such a poet. The Enchanted Flood reprints lectures about the sea.
The first part, "The Sea and the Desert," contrasts and
compares these protagonists. The second, "The Stone and
the Shell," interprets a dream of Wordsworth's with which
the book began. At this point Auden has "much symbolism
on his hands." Forster believes that he "fails to contrive
it." The third and final section, "Ishmael-Don Quixote,"
analyses the two types of heroes. The Enchanted Flood is
a poem. Though its tone is critical, it is not constructed
like a lecture course or a thesis which calls for the "urban
polity," the "new heroism."

"ENCLOSURE A. D. 1760"--Title of Sc. ii (Act I), England's
Pleasant Land. For summary see: England's Pleasant
Land.

"ENCLOSURES, THE"--Title of Act I, England's Pleasant
Land. For summary see: England's Pleasant Land.

"END, THE"--See: "Great Aunt 1879-1887, 5: The End"

"END OF THE MIDDLE AGES, THE"--The title of Chapter
XX of A Room with a View.

"END OF THE OLD ORDER, THE"--Title of Sc. ii (Act II)
of England's Pleasant Land. For summary see: England's
Pleasant Land.

'ENERY--The son of Signora Bertolini, the owner of the Pensione Bertolini. (RWV I)

ENGLAND'S PLEASANT LAND--1st published as a synopsis,
9 July 1938, probably distributed free with the purchase of
a ticket to the performance of the pageant; first published in
full, London, Hogarth Press, 29 April 1940.

The pageant was written for the Dorking and Leith
Hill District Preservation Society and first performed July 9,
1938. It was produced by Tom Harrison with music direct-
ed by Ralph Vaughn Williams. The music was composed by
William Cole, Mary Cowper, D. Moule Evans, Julian Gard-
iner, John Ticehurst, and Ralph Vaughn Williams. It was
first performed on the grounds of Milton Court between Dorking and Westcott, but has no special locale and can be performed anywhere. The subject is the English countryside:
its growth and destruction. The action covers nearly one
thousand years. The scene is the English countryside, close
to a village and a manor house which have grown up together during the centuries.

The play is not about any particular person. The
characters should be thought of as types who are connected
in various ways with rural England. The same actor takes
various roles in different time-periods to emphasize this
point. Only the costumes change, not their characters.

The play has a character who stands outside of the
action: the Recorder. His duty is to interpret events to the
audience and to point the moral. The play has a prologue,
two acts, and an epilogue.

The Prologue (A. D. 1066)--The Recorder offers the
theme of the play: how the countryside has changed as the
centuries have passed, and a moral: will man who made
England and who has nothing to fear but his own soul and his
own strength use that strength to destroy what he has made?
While the Recorder speaks, the pageant begins with a sym-
bolic representation of the Norman period. When the pageant ends, the Recorder announces the passing of seven hundred years and the reign of George III (1760) just as troubles
and changes are about to begin in the countryside.

Act I--"The Enclosures." Sc. i. "Squire George's
Difficulties A. D. 1760"--In which the pros and cons of enclosure are argued. Sc. ii--"Enclosure A. D. 1760"--The
enclosure occurs and the Squire becomes a great landowner.
The villagers become his hired laborers or seek work in the
towns. Sc. iii--"The Labourer's Revolt 1830"--The laborers
are on the point of revolt because of what the Acts of Enclosure have done to them. The capture of a poacher almost
causes a revolution.

Act II--"The Death Duties." Sc. i. "The Domesday

Garden Party 1899. " Squire George is no longer considered
the ogre he once was because of the Acts of Enclosure. The
villagers come to pay their respects to him. Jack, one of
them, points out that the villagers were also at Domesday
and should be part of the Squire's celebration. The Squire
is dying. The young Squire asks Jack to help him to build
the new England. He calls the past cruel; the present,
snobbish. The old Squire dies at the end of the scene.

Sc. ii--"The End of the Old Order. " Young Squire
George notes that the old Squire is dead and, as his first
act to begin the new era, he invites Jack into his house only
to be stopped by Bumble who reminds young Squire George
of the death duties. Young George can pay them only be
selling his house and lands. He points out that one hundred
years ago his family had treated Jack badly and now it is
time for revenge. Jack and Jill despair for the future as
Jerry buys the land for development.

Epilogue--Spoken by the Recorder who points out that
there is still time to save the countryside.

"ENGLISH FREEDOM"--See: "Liberty in England"

"ENGLISH PROSE BETWEEN 1918 and 1939"--1st published
as The Development of English Prose Between 1918 and 1939,
Glasgow, Jackson, Son and Co. , 15 December 1945. Somewhat revised, it re-appeared as "English Prose between
1918 and 1939" in Two Cheers for Democracy, 1951.

The essay originated as the fifth W. P. Ker Memorial Lecture delivered in The University of Glasgow, 27 April
1944. Forster notes that some of the books published during the period look backward and try to record the tragedy
of the past (e. g. Sassoon). Others look forward and try to
avert or explain the disaster which overtook Europe. Even
when not writing directly about a war, they still display un-
rest, disillusionment, or anxiety. The obvious characteris-
tic of the period is that the authors have war on their minds.

The period (Forster calls it the "long weekend") can
be divided into the 20's and 30's. The 20's react after a
war and are carried toward it. The 20's want to enjoy life
and understand it; the 30's want only to understand it in order to preserve civilization. A strong influence in the period is the movement from agriculture to industrialization
which began in the early part of the nineteenth century.

Joined to this was the movement of man to understand himself and to explore his own contradictions. Thus the period
also forms part of larger movements.

New words and phrases crept into the prose of the
period. This popular tendency brought freshness into literature, and informality, and democratic manners, but also
brought vulgarity and flatness. Also there was a movement
on the part of better writers to create something better than
the bloodshed and dullness which had been creeping all over
the world. Forster does not agree with those critics who
consider the period a failure. He assesses its value as high.

ENICHARMON--A commentator who, in the world of the future, comments upon the comments of Urizen who, in turn,
has commented upon Gutch's thoughts on Ho-Yung's thoughts
on Chi-Bo-Sing who has commented upon the thoughts of
Lafcadio Hearn who commented upon Carlyle's thoughts on
Mirabeau's description of the French Revolution. (Collect -
Ta - Machine)

ENID--See: Rose (Collect Ta - Co-ord)

"EPILOGUE"--Section title in the pageant, England's Green
and Pleasant Land. For summary see: England's Green
and Pleasant Land.

"EPIPHANY"--Title of an essay in Pharos and Pharillon.
For summary see: Pharos and Pharillon.

ESMISS ESMOOR--During Aziz's trial, the Indians believe
that Mrs. Moore has been spirited away by the English because her testimony would have cleared Aziz. This news
sets off pandemonium. A chant goes up. "Esmiss Esmoor,"
the crowd screams. Altars are set up to Esmiss Esmoor
whose relationship to Mrs. Moore grows dimmer with time.
Ronny Heaslop is annoyed that his mother has been "traves-
tied into . . . a Hindu goddess." (PI XXIV)

THE ETERNAL MOMENT--The title of Miss Raby's most
famous novel. It was written around the idea that man
does not live by time alone, "that an evening gone may become like a thousand ages in the courts of heaven." The
idea was expounded more philosophically by Maeterlinck.
(Collect Ta - Eternal)

"THE ETERNAL MOMENT"--1st published in Independent Review, VI (June, July, August 1905), pp. 206-215; 86-95; 211-223; reprinted in The Eternal Moment and Other Stories, 1928; The Collected Tales, 1947.

[A short story.]   Miss Raby, a famous novelist and authoress of The Eternal Moment, is reminiscing [with Col. Leyland] about her past.   He is accompanying her on her trip northward in Italy.   After they pass the Italian border to Vorta, the scene of The Eternal Moment, which she had not visited in years, the Colonel suggests that the Alpes would be a good hotel in which to stay.   Miss Raby counters with the Biscione, where she had stayed on her first visit years ago, owned by Signora Cantù the mother of the owner of the Alpes.   Miss Raby likes things Italian, while the Colonel admires Teutonic efficiency.   Miss Raby proceeds to the Biscione where she meets the proprietress who is an aristocratic gossip.   Signora Cantù tells Miss Raby the gossip of the region ending with a complaint that her son, with the help of his wife and Concièrge are out to ruin her.   The Concièrge, Feo Ginori, is the handsome Italian porter who had declared his love for Miss Raby some twenty years before.   When she leanrs of the true identity of the Concièrge, she goes to the Alpes ostensibly to visit Col. Leyland who, it appears, has gone to the Biscione to see her.

Miss Raby soon finds herself alone with the Concièrge. He did not remember her.   She finds him changed: physically, he is inclining to fat, and emotionally, he has become worldly, the fault she finds in her own class.   She tries to remind him that they have met before.   He pretends to remember, but does not.   She tells him not to be polite.   He was not polite when they first met.   She describes the incii- in detail.   He gapes at her in horror.   At that moment, the Colonel comes in.   She tells him that the Concièrge is the man of whom she spoke the day before.   The Concièrge denies it.   He tells them the incident had occurred before he had learned "manners."   He fears for his job.   Col. Leyland, in order to end the embarrassing situation, asks Miss Raby if she will walk before dinner.   The Concièrge's alarm begins to fade.   He smiles and winks at her.   She tells him that he mustn't think that she is still in love with him.   But, for all her denials, she had been and had never loved so greatly again.   She asks the Concièrge to give her one of his children.   He tells her his wife would never permit it.   Col. Leyland is shocked and tries to limit the scandal by touching his finger to his forehead implying that Miss Raby is mad.   Like the good servant he is, the Concièrge takes the cue.

THE ETERNAL MOMENT AND OTHER STORIES--1st edition,
London, Sidgwick and Jackson, Ltd. , 27 March 1928; 1st
American edition, New York, Harcourt, Brace and Co. , 19
April 1928. Contents: "The Machine Stops," "The Point of
It," "Mr. Andrews," "Co-ordination," "The Story of the Si-
ren," "The Eternal Moment." These stories were reprinted
with those in The Celestial Omnibus and Other Stories as The
Collected Tales, 1947. For summaries see: Individual titles.

ETHEL--The youngest daughter of Mr. Lucas. She was un-
married, unselfish, and affectionate. It was generally understood that she was to devote her life to the comfort of her father. Mrs. Forman always referred to her as "Antigone." She
cannot understand her father's longing to remain in the uncomfortable inn in Greece. Ultimately, she marries and Mr. Lucas prepares himself to live with his sister whom he fears.
(Collect Ta - Road)

EUPHEMIA--A servant of the Honeychurchs who will not chop
the suet "sufficiently small." (RWV VIII)

EUSTACE--Is an "undescribably repellent" fourteen year old.
He neither played hard nor worked hard. His carving and
playing pan-pipes causes a strange manifestation which almost results in his death. (Collect Ta - Story)

"EXPERIENCE DU BONHEUR, L' "--See: "Happiness"

                                   F

FAILING, ANTHONY--The husband of Aunt Emily, a landowner and an amateur essayist. Aunt Emily writes a mem-
oir of him after he dies. (LJ X)

FAILING, AUNT EMILY--Rickie Elliot's aunt and the sister
of his father. She is lame like her brother and nephew.
For a time she took care of Rickie after the death of his
parents. She also took the illegitimate Stephen Wonham, son
of Rickie's mother, into her home. She is a domineering woman whom Agnes Pembroke believes, at first, can push
Rickie along in his career as a writer. (LJ I)

"FAMILY"--Title of Chapter I of Goldsworthy Lowes Dickinson. For summary see: Goldsworthy Lowes Dickinson.

"FANTASY"--Title of Chapter V of Aspects of the Novel.

For summary see: <u>Aspects of the Novel.</u>

FAUN--Has all the carefree qualities of the classical Faun
and, as the Curate (Harry) muses at the beginning of the
story, may have been left behind when the Romans were
forced to leave England. Only Harry can see him. (Collect
Ta - Curate)

FEMALE ATTENDANT, A--The woman on the airship to
whom Vashti would have to announce her wants if necessary.
She was a relic of the past when direct utterance was the
vogue. Her exceptional duties--she had often to address
passengers with direct speech--had given her a certain rough-
ness and originality of manner. (Collect Ta - Machine)

"FERNEY"--1st published as "Happy Ending," <u>New Statesman</u>
<u>and Nation,</u> N.S. (2 November 1940), p. 942; reprinted as
"Ferney," in <u>Two Cheers for Democracy,</u> 1951.

        A description of Forster's visit in June, 1939 to Fer-
ney, the house built by Voltaire. The chapel, small and
simple, looked a trifle "<u>moisi</u>" [Fr. moldy, musty]. The
chateau itself was quiet: shutters closed, doors locked. It
is a small building. It brings to mind Voltaire's humanity
which was not a "platform gesture."

FIELDING, CECIL--The principal of the little government
school in Chandrapore. He knew little of the district and
thus had less against the inhabitants than most of the English. He was, therefore, less cynical than other Anglo-Indians. He was athletic and cheerful and popular with the parents of his pupils. He did not get along with Anglo-Indians
because they feared the ideas he had. He defends Azis a-
gainst them and is ostracized for his pains. Aziz, too,
doubts his friendship when Fielding offers Adela Quested, his
enemy, protection after the close of his trial. Almost in
despair over the whole situation, Fielding sails for home,
marries Mrs. Moore's daughter, Stella, and returns to India
only to discover that he can no longer be close and friendly
with Aziz. (PI III)

FIELDING'S BEARER--An Indian, helps Fielding dress while
Aziz waits in the other room. (PI VII)

FIELDING, STELLA--See: Stella

FIRST GRAVE--One of the two graves which senses and

voices its beliefs on the futility of war.   (AH - Our Graves)

FLACK, Mr. --The real-estate agent who built and sold the semi-detached villas (Cissie and Albert) to Sir Harry Otway. (RWV VIII)

FLACK, MRS. --A bedridden old lady, "so very vulgar" as Sir Harry Otway describes her, who occupies one of his villas (Albert) rent-free.   She is the aunt of the Mr. Flack who built and sold the villas to Sir Harry Otway.   (RWV IX)

FLEA THOMPSON'S GIRL--Stephen Wonham is interested in her.   He meets her in Salisbury and asks her why her lover had broken faith with him (Stephen) in the rain.   He warns her of approaching vengeance.   (LJ XII)

FLOYD, MR. --The friend of Freddy Honeychurch who is coming on a visit to Windy Corner.   (RWV XIII)

"FOR THE MUSEUM'S SAKE"--1st published as "The Objects" in Athenaeum, (7 May 1920), pp. 599-600; reprinted as "For the Museum's Sake" in Two Cheers for Democracy, 1951.

[Review of By Nile and Tigris, by Sir Wallis Budge.] After the Treaty of Vienna, every progressive government felt it a duty to amass old objects and to exhibit a fraction of them in a building called a museum.   These objects were called "National Possessions."   Forster details the underhanded methods used to acquire these possessions by relating the history of "B. M. 10470" or the "Papyrus of Ani" acquired illegally by Sir Wallis Budge.   The remainder of the essay is a review of Budge's book, By Nile and Tigris, which Forster finds is the "most fascinating travel book that has appeared for years."

FORD, JACK--The ward of Harcourt Worters.   He is in love with Harcourt's fiancée, Evelyn Beaumont.   When Harcourt discovers some insulting remarks about himself which Jack has written in his notebook, Harcourt sends him away. Shortly after, Evelyn disappears.   Harcourt is certain that she has eloped with Jack.   He goes to his ward's rooms certain that he will find Evelyn there, only to be disappointed in his hopes.   (Collect Ta - Other)

FORMAN, MRS. --A lady who travels with Mr. Lucas's party in Greece.   It is she who sends the present to his daughter

wrapped in the Greek newspaper announcing the death of the
inhabitants of the khan [inn] in which Mr. Lucas had hoped
to remain. (Collect Ta - Road)

"FORREST REID"--1st published as "The Work of Forrest
Reid" in Nation (London), (10 April 1920), pp. 47-48; reprinted as "Forrest Reid" in Abinger Harvest, 1936.

[A review of Pirates of the Spring by Forrest Reid.]
Reid believed that a man's great decisions and experiences
occur in boyhood, and that his subsequent career is little
more than a recollection. This belief is significant in
Reid's own development. His novels fail when considered as
transcripts of human activities because they cover too small
a field. His characters are all young. His scene is the
North of Ireland. His books must be classified as "visions"
before they can be appreciated. His best novels are The
Bracknels and Following Darkness. Uncle Stephen is his
masterpiece.

"FORREST REID"--1st published as "Forrest Reid: 1876-
1947" in The Listener (16 January 1947), p. 120; reprinted
as "Forrest Reid" in Two Cheers for Democracy, 1951.

[Written on the occasion of the death of Forrest
Reid.] Reid was the most important person in Belfast. He
was partly a Mediterranean and Celtic dreamer who did not
appreciate England. He had a passionate feeling for Northern Ireland. He was revered by Henry James and thought,
for a time, that all women novelists, saving Jane Austen,
are bad.

"FORREST REID: 1876-1947"--See: "Forrest Reid" in
Two Cheers for Democracy, 1951.

FÖRSTMEISTER, HERR--In order to win Helen Schlegel back
to Germany, her cousin, Fraülein Mosebach, encourages
Herr Förstmeister to propose to her. She rejects him.
(HE XII)

"FOURTH CHAPTER"--The title of Chapter IV in A Room
with a View.

"FRAULEIN MOSEBACH'S YOUNG MAN"--Can remember
nothing but Fraulein Mosebach while at the concert of Beethoven's Fifth Symphony at Queen's Hall which is also attended by the Schlegels and Aunt Juley. (HE V)

FRENCH LADY, A--Spreads among the guests of the Grand Hôtel des Alpes the agreeable news that an Englishman had surprised his wife making love to the Concièrge. (Collect Ta - Eternal)

FRIEND OF MRS. WILCOX, A--Mrs. Wilcox discovers her friend in the stationery department of the Haymarket Stores bent on the same errand: the purchase of Christmas cards. They briefly discuss the motor trip of Mr. Wilcox and Evie and discover that Bertha, the friend's daughter, is also motoring. (HE X)

"FROM MYSTICISM TO POLITICS (1887-1893)"--Title of Chapter IX in Goldsworthy Lowes Dickinson. For summary see: Goldsworthy Lowes Dickinson.

"FROM THE SQUARE TO MEX"--Title of Section vi (Part II) of Alexandria.

"FROM THE SQUARE TO NOUZHA"--Title of Section iv (Part II) of Alexandria.

"FROM THE SQUARE TO RAMLEH"--Title of Section v (Part II) of Alexandria.

"FROM THE SQUARE TO RAS-EL-TIN"--Title of Section ii (Part II) of Alexandria.

"FROM THE SQUARE TO THE RUE ROSETTE"--Title of Section I (Part II) of Alexandria.

"FROM THE SQUARE TO THE SOUTHERN QUARTERS"-- Title of Section iii (Part II) of Alexandria.

FUSSELL, ALBERT--The brother of Dolly, the girl who marries Charles Wilcox. Fussell belonged to the same club as Charles and was as devoted as he was to golf. It was in a mixed foursome that Charles met Dolly. (HE VIII)

FUSSELL, COLONEL--The father of Dolly and Albert. He recalls, during the trip to Evie Wilcox's wedding, a handsome girl who jumped overboard in the harbor of Gibralter on a bet. The incident occurred when he was young and on his way to a tour of duty in India. (HE VIII)

FUSSELL, DOLLY--The young lady who marries Charles Wilcox. Her mother is dead; her father is in the Indian

Army--retired; the brother, Albert, is also in the army.
Margaret Schlegel thinks that they may have been the "chinless sunburnt men" whom Helen had seen going into the Wilcox flat.   Dolly is very pretty with one of those "triangular
faces" that "often proves attractive to a robust man."   Despite her physical attractiveness, she was a "rubbishy little
creature and she knew it."   (HE VIII)

G

"GAME OF LIFE, THE"--See: "Our Diversions, 6: The
Game of Life"

"GEMISTUS PLETHO"--1st published in Independent Review,
VII (October 1905), pp. 211-223; reprinted in Abinger Harvest, 1936.

        A summary of the life and accomplishments of the
philosopher-scholar, and neo-pagan, Georgius Gemistus Pletho, best remembered for his work on Florence.   Forster
holds that "the Renaissance can point to many a career which
is greater but to none which is so strangely symbolical."

GENNARO--The "stop-gap" waiter, clumsy, impertinent, who
had been had "up from Minori" in the absence of the nice,
English-speaking Emmanuele.   (Collect Ta - Story)

GEORGE, MISS--The daughter of Squire George.   She is as
outspoken as her mother.   The Squire finds it necessary to
remind her that she is speaking to guests and is not to be
sharp with them even if she does disagree with Squire Jeremiah.   She calls Parliament "wicked" to pass the Enclosure
Acts.   (England's)

GEORGE, MRS. --The wife of Squire George.   She is blunt
and outspoken against enclosure.   After Squire Jeremiah
leaves, however, she tells her husband that Jeremiah was
sensible in what he had to say for enclosure.   (England's)

GEORGE, SQUIRE--A country landowner.   He is sober,
sensible, polite and loves his village and his land.   He does
not go along with enclosing his land because he sees such a
deed as dishonorable.   Yet, through his wife's persuasion,
he gives in and manages to secure from Parliament an Enclosure Bill.   As a result, he is turned into a rich landowner.   (England's)

GEORGE, THE--The inn in Oniton where Margaret Schlegel
wants Helen to take Jacky and Leonard Bast after they have
appeared unasked and unannounced at the home of Henry Wilcox.   (HE XXVI)

GEORGE, YOUNG--The son of Squire George.   In later
scenes, he is known as the young Squire.   He is against enclosure as is his father, but sees the point about England's
need for more corn which is raised by Squire Jeremiah as
an argument for enclosure.   He suffers the consequences of
enclosure by having the villagers turn against him.   Ultimately, he too, is turned out from the land because of high
death duties.   (England's)

"GEORGE CRABBE AND PETER GRIMES"--1st published in
Two Cheers for Democracy, 1951.

[A lecture given at the Aldeburgh Festival of 1948.]
Forster describes Aldeburgh and the incursions the sea has
made reducing its five streets to three.   It is intersected by
the river Alde, the estuary of which is the scene of the
Crabbe poem, "Peter Grimes."

George Crabbe was born in Aldeburgh in 1754.   He
disliked his native town and grew up in "straitened" circumstances, afraid of his father and with a hatred for his life
as apprentice to an apothecary.   In 1779, he decided to leave
the town to seek his fortune in London as a poet.   He nearly died of starvation, but was rescued by Edmund Burke who
recognized his genius.   He turned to the church for his profession, took orders and returned to Aldeburgh three years
later.   He was again unhappy there.   He was appointed domestic chaplain to the Duke of Rutland and he was happy in
that position.   His antipathy to Aldeburgh continued though it
did not play an essential part in the creation of "Peter
Grimes."   He married money and ended up as a "West country pluralist."

The poem, "Peter Grimes," has its origin in an old
fisherman of the Aldeburgh area who had a succession of ap-
prentices from London and a sum of money for each.   They
tended to disappear and the fisherman was warned, as a consequence, that he would be charged with murder the next
time it occurred.   Crabbe changed the fisherman's name,
Tom Brown, to Peter Grimes.   He finished the poem in
1809.   It is clear that Crabbe, in writing the poem, was ob-
sessed by the notion of the unkindness of two generations of

males to each another and of punishing that unkindness vi-
cariously.   There is another "motive" in the poem: "at-
traction-repulsion."   Peter tries to escape from certain
places only to drift back to them like Crabbe.

Peter Grimes, the opera, was written by Benjamin
Britten who, while in the United States, read the Crabbe po-
em with feelings of nostalgia.   He was commissioned by
Koussevitsky, the American conductor, to write an opera.
The opera, however, is not Crabbe set to music.   There is
in it an indication of a social problem not to be found in
Crabbe.   Crabbe "satirized society;" he did not "criticize
it."

"GEORGE ORWELL"--1st published in The Listener, (November 1950), p. 471; reprinted in Two Cheers for Democracy, 1951.

[A review of Shooting an Elephant and Other Essays
by George Orwell.]   Despite the fact that George Orwell's
originality has been recognized in England along with an appreciation of his "peculiar blend of gaiety and grimness,"
there is still a tendency to shy away from him.   America
has clasped 1984 to its heart, but England has "eluded it"
for a variety of reasons.   Some say it is too bourgeois, or
too much to the left, or that it is not a novel but a treatise,
or because he is a "nagger."   Forster believes he is a nagger bdcause he has found much to discomfort him in this
world.   He is, nevertheless, a "true liberal."   He held that
all nations are "odious," but some are less odious than others.   His works encourage no slovenly trust in the future.
He believes in kindness, good-temper, and accuracy.   He also believes in "the people."   He does not explain how they
are going to survive.   He was passionate over the purity of
prose.   He held that liberty is connected with prose.   Bu-
reaucrats who want to deny liberty tend to write and speak
badly and to use pompous, wooly, or portmanteau phrases
in which true meaning disappears.   He does not define liberty, but he feels we need more of it.

"GERALD HEARD"--1st published as "The Trigger" in The
Listener, (14 September 1939), p. 542; reprinted as "Gerald
Heard" in Two Cheers for Democracy, 1951.

[A review of Pain, Sex and Time by Gerald Heard.]
Forster examines Gerald Heard's theories of salvation for humanity.   Man's physical evolution is at an end; his evolu-

tion, however, can continue through the psyche if he chooses.
Heard contends that man's capacity for sex and for pain are
symptoms of unused energy. If man could "detonate" his
powers, he would be capable of "blowing away" the economic and political horrors now surrounding him. This Forster
contends is the old doctrine of "change of heart," but in a
"violent and earthly form." The trigger needed to explode
the power within the human being is easily discovered in the
"unexplored forces in the human heart." Forster holds that
the "bomb of the spirit" could explode, but its direct action
"seems no stronger than a paper bag's." "Mr. Heard's analysis works" but, "his remedy would fail."

GERMAN WAITRESS, THE--Suggests to Miss Raby that she
find a better place to sit other than outside the inn where
only the lower classes eat. (Collect Ta - Eternal)

GERRISH--A friend of Gerald Dawes at Cambridge, presum-
ably an athlete. Gerald asks Rickie Elliot if he knows him.
Rickie does not. (LJ III)

"GIBBON AND HIS AUTOBIOGRAPHY"--1st published as "Edward Gibbon, The Historian" in London Calling, #151 (30
July 1942), pp. 14-15; reprinted with some revisions as
"Edward Gibbon" in Talking to India, London, Allen and Unwin, 1943; revised and reprinted as "Gibbon and His Autobiography" in Two Cheers for Democracy, 1951.

        The essay originated as a broadcast talk in the BBC's
Overseas Service. Even as a little boy in Putney, Gibbon
was not playful or friendly. His work has the majesty, the
precision and reliability of a well-built ship. He never fuss-
es. He is still the leading authority on the period covered
by his Decline and Fall of the Roman Empire. His success
was paid for by the curtailment of his passions. We could
not have a Gibbon today; our conditions forbid it. His autobiography is one of the minor masterpieces of the century:
intelligent, dignified, and often amusing. Forster concludes
his remarks with a précis of the autobiography.

"GIDE AND GEORGE"--1st published as "Humanist and Authoritarian" in The Listener, (26 August 1943), pp. 242-243;
reprinted as "Gide and George" in Two Cheers for Democracy, 1951.

        Gide and George are two modern European writers
who offer contrasted reactions to the present chaos (World

War II). Gide refused to collaborate with the Nazis or Vichy when his country collapsed. Finally, when Hitler advanced into Vichy, he escaped to Tunis. When the Allied Armies captured it, they found him there (Spring 1943). Yet, Forster does not present Gide as a hero. He is a humanist. He has the four leading characteristics of a humanist: curiosity, a free mind, a belief in good taste, and a belief in the human race. He reacts to the European tragedy as a humanist.

Stephan George, a "fine lyric poet," a sincere man of high ideals and of an iron will, died in 1933 after Hitler came into power. He was well-bred and, by nature, a recluse. He ruled his disciples almost as a priest. He taught them to despise the common man, to prefer instinct to brains, and to believe in good birth and state organization. George was a natural aristocrat and Gide, a natural democrat. His poems spoke of a "Fuehrer" and a "New Reich." He saw in authority a cure for the evils of his age. The Nazis "embraced him," but "it was more than he could stand." In 1937, he went to Switzerland to die. Creative writers are always greater than the causes they represent. Forster makes no attempt to interpret either Gide or George in terms of the causes they represent.

The essay originated as a broadcast talk in the BBC's Indian Service.

"GIDE'S DEATH"--1st published as "André Gide: A Personal Tribute" in The Listener, (1 March 1951), p. 343. A Letter; reprinted as "Gide's Death" in Two Cheers for Democracy, 1951.

Forster did not know Gide well. They first met in Paris in 1935 during an international writers' conference. Gide was as "slippery as a trout." He saw Gide again in Provence, but Gide did not see him. Gide was a hard worker. He taught thousands to mistrust façades. In many ways, he had a pagan outlook, yet he had also a Puritanical and a religious outlook. He did not have a great mind, but he had a free one.

GINO'S COUSIN--Gino Carella's cousin is a lawyer in Rome. Lila makes much of his position to indicate to Philip Gino's social rank. (WAFT II)

GINO'S FATHER--is a dentist. (WAFT I)

GINO'S UNCLE--is a priest. Lila mentions this to Philip
to indicate Gino's social rank. (WAFT II)

GINORI, FEO--The Conciêrge of the Grand Hôtel des Alpes.
A competent European of forty or so who speaks all languages fluently and some well. He is still active and had,
evidently, once been muscular, but either his life or his
time of life has been unkind to his figure; in a few years he
will be fat. His face is less easy to decipher. In his
youth, he declared his love for Miss Raby, who now reminds
him of his declaration. He is upset. Fortunately, Col. Leyland saves the situation. (Collect Ta - Eternal)

GIRL WHO HAD BEEN TYPING THE STRONG LETTER,
THE--Both Charles and Mr. Wilcox, his father, are in-
censed that Bryce would attempt to sublet Howards End without permission. Mr. Wilcox settles the matter by deciding
to write a strong note to him. The entrance of the girl
with the finished note signals an end to the matter and the
beginning of Charles's, Margaret's, and Mr. Wilcox's drive
to Howards End. (HE XXIII)

GIUSEPPE--The twenty year old brother of the unknown Sicilian. He saw the Siren and, after seeing her, he "did no
work, he forgot to eat, he forgot whether he had his clothes
on. His family tried to make him into a beggar, but he
was too robust to inspire pity," and, "as for an idiot, he
had not the right look in his eyes." (Collect Ta - Siren)

GOANESE SERVANT--See: Antony (PI XIII)

"GOD ABANDONS ANTHONY, THE"--Section title in Pharos
and Pharillon. For summary see: Pharos and Pharillon.

GODBOLE, NARAYAN (PROFESSOR GODBOLE)--A teacher
at the Government College and an assistant to Fielding. His
name means trunk, stem, swelling out of God. A friend of
Aziz, Fielding invites him to take tea with him, Aziz, Mrs.
Moore and Miss Quested. He is a Deccani Brahman and,
as such, suggests the mystical aspects of India. (PI VII)

GODBOLE'S COLLEAGUE--Assists him at the feast of the
birth of the god, Krishna. Both sing "into one another's
grey moustaches." (PI XXXIII)

"GOKUL ASHTAMI"--See: "Letters of 1921: Gokul Ashtami"

GOLDSWORTHY LOWES DICKINSON--1st edition, London,
Edward Arnold and Co., 19 April 1934; 1st American edition, New York, Harcourt, Brace and Co., 7 June 1934.

Based on the rambling "Recollections" of Goldsworthy
Lowes Dickinson, the authority of which Forster notes, is to
be trusted only in so far as one remembers that they are
written out of a sense of melancholy.   Forster also used
Dickinson's letters for the biography.   Forster had known
Dickinson for some thirty-five years.   He feels qualified to
write about him from the personal and perhaps the literary
point of view.   He cannot, however, discuss Dickinson as a
philosopher or a publicist and therefore admits that these
sections of the book are bound to be unsatisfactory.   Forster further indicates that Dickinson's life was not dramatic
and, therefore, does not divide itself into strongly marked
periods.   Nevertheless, he adopts a chronological approach
to the life interrupted only by Chapter XI and, to some extent, by Chapter VII.

I.   "Family"--Forster outlines the principal members
of the Lowes family indicating that the father's side is essentially Northumbrian.   Goldsworthy Lowes Dickinson was
the son of Lowes Cato Dickinson and Margaret Ellen Williams.   His maternal grandfather was in publishing and was
credited with the discovery of Charlotte Brontë.

II.   "The Spring Cottage (1862-1872)"--Discusses
Dickinson's youth, pre-school days and his early recollections of the Spring Cottage, his first home.

III.   "The Misses Woodman's Morning Class (1872-
1874)"--Dickinson's early education is discussed.   It was not
alarming, only an "extension of his home life."

IV.   "Beomonds (1874-1876)"--Dickinson's preparatory
school.   He was unhappy there.   There was no physical
bullying but he suffered from "moral bullying" and his own
timidity.

V.   "Charterhouse (1876-1881)"--A discussion of Dickinson's further education at Charterhouse, a public school.
He was "worried by sex and the evasion of the subject by
his elders."

VI.   "Cambridge (1881-1884)"--Dickinson went to
Cambridge only by chance.   Thus he began a connection

which was to last over fifty years.

VII. "Shelley, Plato, Goethe"--A brief discussion of Dickinson's interest in these figures and their work. Shelley "gripped me . . . as a visionary about life." He approached Plato as an "adept who was in the possession of absolute truth, which he had concealed in his writing." Goethe's Faust intrigued him for its "rush of music and passion."

VIII. "The World of Matter (1884-1887)"--Dickinson was in an uneasy state during this period. He worried about his vocation. He wanted to help humanity, yet saw the need of supporting himself.

IX. "From Mysticism to Politics (1887-1893)"--In 1887, Dickinson was elected to a Fellowship at Cambridge. The election settled the direction his life was to take. He became interested in politics during this period.

X. "The Socratic Method (1893-1914)"--During this period, Dickinson emerged as a teacher. His studies, his political opinion, his lecturing, his publications, his capacity for friendship, his interest in the young all flow into a single channel: the educational.

XI. "America, India, China"--Describes his visits to these areas.

XII. "The War and the League (1914-1926)"--He had hopes that the war could be averted. When it broke, he worked for the establishment of the League of Nations.

XIII. " 'The International Anarchy' 1926"--The war ended for Dickinson with the publication of his International Anarchy. It was his "truce," the last argument he could give.

XIV. "The Truce (1926-1932)"--Approaching seventy, Dickinson appeared, at a distance, to be old, but his mind had more elasticity than many younger men could claim. He was a "popular don."

XV. "The Last Months June-August 1932"--Dickinson dies as a result of a "severe operation." He was a great teacher, essayist, author.

"Epilogue"--Forster notes that Dickinson was an "indescribably rare being, he was rare without being enigmatic."

GRAHAM, MR.--One of Mr. Lucas's party who is visiting Greece. Graham is always polite to his elders. The Greek children throw rocks at him when they see him taking Mr. Lucas away from the khan (inn). (Collect Ta - Road)

GRAND HÔTEL DES ALPES--One of the principal hotels of Vorta. The owner is the son of Signora Cantù. The Concièrge is Feo Ginori who, when a young man, tried to make love to Miss Raby. (Collect Ta - Eternal)

GRANDSON OF MARIA RHOMAIDES--See: Maria Rhomaides (Collect Ta - Road)

GRANGE, THE--Mr. Henry Wilcox's home at Oniton. It was up towards the Welsh border and so difficult of access that he had concluded it must be something special. A ruined castle stood on the grounds. The shooting was bad and the fishing, indifferent. The scenery was nothing much. In addition, it turned out to be in the wrong part of Shropshire. (HE XXV)

GRANNY--See: Voice 3 (England's)

GRAVEDIGGERS, THE--They dislike Charles Wilcox, but since it was his mother they were burying, they felt it not the moment to speak of such things and they finished their work, piling up the wreathes and crosses above the grave. (HE XI)

GRAY-HAIRED LADY, A--Asks Miss Raby to buy a ticket to a concert in aid of the stained-glass window fund for the English church in Vorta. She feels that the English should have a rallying point. When Miss Raby tells her that she wishes the rallying point were in England, the gray-haired lady becomes angry. (Collect Ta - Eternal)

GRAYSFORD, MR.--A missionary who, like Mr. Sorley, also a missionary, lives out beyond the slaughter houses and always travels third class on the railways. He never comes up to the club. He claims that all should be welcome in "Our Father's House." Mr. Sorley agrees with him but goes a step further to say, when questioned, that even animals ought to be invited. He drew the line, however at bacteria. (PI IV)

GRAYSFORD, MRS. --The wife of the clergyman, Mr. Graysford. Aziz had operated on her appendix and saved her life.
(PI VI)

"GREAT AUNT 1879-1887"--Section title in Marianne Thornton: A Domestic Biography. For summary see: Marianne
Thornton: A Domestic Biography.

"GREAT AUNT 1879-1887, 1: MY ARRIVAL"--Section title
in Marianne Thornton: A Domestic Biography. For summary see: Marianne Thornton: A Domestic Biography.

"GREAT AUNT 1879-1887, 2: THE DEATH OF HENRY
SYKES THORNTON"--Section title in Marianne Thornton:
A Domestic Biography. For summary see: Marianne Thorn-
ton: A Domestic Biography.

"GREAT AUNT 1879-1887, 3: MY RECOLLECTIONS"--Sec-
tion title in Marianne Thornton: A Domestic Biography. For
summary see: Marianne Thornton: A Domestic Biography.

"GREAT AUNT 1879-1887, 4: THE AYLWARD INCIDENT"--
Section title in Marianne Thornton: A Domestic Biography.
For summary see: Marianne Thornton: A Domestic Biog-
raphy.

"GREAT AUNT 1879-1887, 5: THE END"--Section title in
Marianne Thornton: A Domestic Biography. For summary
see: Marianne Thornton: A Domestic Biography.

"GREAT INDIAN POET PHILOSOPHER"[sic]--See: "Mohammed Iqbal"

"GRECO-EGYPTIAN PERIOD"--Title of Section i (Part I),
Alexandria.

GREY, Mr. --A candidate for election to Parliament who dif-
fers from his opponent, Mr. Brown, only in his "fiscal policy" and his claim to "liberalism." See: Mr. Brown (AH -
Voter's)

GRUNDY, MRS. AMELIA--Has nineteenth-century ideas of
"trying to suppress people's pleasures" while, on the other
hand, Edith Parker tries to "spoil them." Mrs. Grundy confesses that, in her youth, she was too impulsive and hurried
too much from vice to vice. (AH - Mrs G)

"GUIDE"--Title of Part II in <u>Alexandria</u>.

GUTCH--See: Enicharmon (Collect Ta - Machine)

GUY--A suitor of Helen whose virtues and vices are weighed
by Tibby, her brother. He talks of the "pitiful business" in
which Guy was involved. He concludes, nevertheless, that
along with Mr. Vyse, he likes Guy best. (HE XIII)

<h2 style="text-align:center">H</h2>

HADDON, MISS-- A piano teacher who must work under a
new coordinative system based essentially on the fact that
all of her pupils play the same duet. She later retires.
(Collect - Co-ord)

HALF A DOZEN GARDENERS--Everything seems normal at
Oniton. So much so that it would appear that Henry Wilcox
had never had an affair with Jacky. Half a dozen gardeners
are clearing up the remains of Evie's wedding. (HE XXIX)

HAMIDULLAH--Dr. Aziz's uncle who is well-to-do. He is
a Cambridge barrister who hates the English. He conducts
Aziz's defense. (PI II)

HAMIDULLAH BEGUM--Hamidullah's wife and Aziz's aunt.
Hamidullah invites Aziz to spend some time behind purdah
with her. She is the only female relative he has in Chandrapore. She is interested in his well-being and asks him
when he is to marry again. He answers, "once is enough."
(PI II)

HANDSOME GIRL, A--See: Colonel Fussell (HE XXV)

"HAPPINESS!"--1st published as "L'Experience Du Bonheur"
in <u>Athenaeum</u> (23 January 1920), pp. 122-123; reprinted as
"Happiness!" in <u>Abinger Harvest,</u> 1936.

        [A review of <u>Macao et Cosmage</u> by E. L. L. Edy-
Legrand.] Forster calls it a "beautiful book" which tells the
tale of a paradise destroyed by those who intend to bring the
"bonheur" [happiness] they believe is implicit in civilization.

"HAPPY ENDING"--See: "Ferney"

HAQ--The police inspector who visits Aziz when he is ill. (PI
IX)

HAROLD--A young man who is sent to a farm to recuperate
and dies from over-exertion when his friend, Mickey, tells
him to row harder. (Collect Ta - Point)

HARRIS, MR. --The Nawab Bahadur's Eurasian chauffeur who
feels uncomfortable in both the Indian and the English worlds.
He is left behind after the accident when Miss Derek picks
up the Nawab, Miss Quested and Mr. Heaslop. (PI VIII)

HARRY--See: The Curate (Collect Ta - Curate)

HASSAN--Aziz's servant. (PI VI)

HAUGHTY NEPHEW, THE--Asks his Uncle Ernest Schlegel,
the German husband of his Aunt Emily and the father of his
cousins, Meg, Helen and Tibby, if he believes the Germans
to be stupid. Ernest answers that Germans use the intellect
but no longer care about it. This he considers stupid.
Ernest then launches into a long discussion of the German
character to which the young Meg (Margaret) listens intently.
This discussion is followed on the other days and serves as
an education for the girls. (HE IV)

HAUGHTY NEPHEW'S WIFE, THE--The wife of Ernest's
German nephew who is concerned as is her husband, that
Germany was appointed by God to rule the world. (HE IV)

HEADMASTER AT SAWSTON SCHOOL, THE--Agrees with
Herbert Pembroke that it was time he was entrusted with a
boarding house. He also agrees with Mrs. Jackson when she
said that her husband also deserved one. (LJ XVI)

HEASLOP, RONALD (RONNY)--The City Magistrate of Chandrapore. He is the son of Mrs. Moore by her first husband.
His mother comes to India with Miss Quested with the hope
that he and Miss Quested will marry. He is a rather self-
righteous young man whose view of religion identifies his
character. He approves of religion as long as it endorses
the national anthem. He wants his mother and Miss Quested
to have nothing to do with the natives whom he does not
trust. (PI II)

HENRY--Michael's oldest son who never gave his father any
trouble. (Collect Ta - Point)

"HENRY THORNTON"--1st published as "Henry Thornton
(1760-1850)" in New Statesman and Nation (U. S.), (1 April

1939), pp. 491-492; reprinted as "Henry Thornton" in Two Cheers for Democracy, 1951.

Henry Thornton, Forster's great-grandfather, was, according to his friend, Sir Robert Inglis, "sober"; his piety was "fervent;" his liberality was "magnificent yet discriminating;" his charity was "large and yet not latitudinarian." He was a successful banker, an extensive philanthropist and a devout Christian. His two claims on the notice of posterity are his Family Prayers and An Essay on Paper Credit.

The prayers were composed from time to time to be read aloud to his family at Battersea Rise, his home. They were published some twenty years after his death. They went through thirty-one editions and are of the usual evangelical type. To us they mean nothing at all. We get from them the aroma of a vanished society.

His treatise on paper money was recently re-edited by Professor Hayek. The original was praised by John Stuart Mill. It was, however, eclipsed by the work of Ricardo, but revived during the second world war by economists in America.

"HENRY THORNTON (1760-1850)"--See: "Henry Thornton"

HERIOT, MRS.--See: Lady Anstey. (Collect Ta - Eternal)

HERMIT, A--His house lay near Howards End. Mrs. Wilcox had known him. He barred himself up, wrote prophecies, and gave all that he had to the poor. (HE LXI)

HERRITON, CHARLES--Lila's husband who is deceased. Ten years before the book opens, he had fallen in love with her because she was "pretty." Mrs. Herriton, his mother, had schemed to prevent the match, but to no avail. (WAFT I)

HERRITON, HARRIET--Lila's sister-in-law. She is as domineering as her mother. She kidnaps Lila's baby by Gino Carella. The child dies when the carriage in which they are riding overturns. (WAFT I)

HERRITON, IRMA--Lila's daughter by her first husband, Charles. When Lila goes to Italy, she is left behind in England to be supervised by her grandmother, Mrs. Herriton. Gino writes to her of her half-brother and it is she who an-

nounces to Sawston the news of her dead mother's Italian
son. (WAFT I)

HERRITON, JOSEPH--The only undesirable member of the
Herriton clan. Lila picks Joseph out as a defense of Gino
Carella to Philip. (WAFT II)

HERRITON, LILA THEOBALD--She is a young English widow
(thirty-three years old) who is unhappy living in the shadow
of her husband's family. She is attractive but not terribly
intelligent. She goes to Italy with Caroline Abbot, meets and
falls in love with Gino Carella, a handsome young Italian,
twelve years her junior. At first she is happy, but slowly
realizes her error in marrying him. She dies in child-birth.
(WAFT I)

HERRITON, MISS--When Miss Orr refuses to marry Herbert
Pembroke, he thinks of Miss Herriton who is her inferior
but would have done as well. He knows that it is, however,
impossible to ask her now that the news of his refusal by
Miss Orr is known in Sawston. (LJ XVI) [It is interesting
to speculate on who this Miss Herriton of Sawston is. There
may be a strong connection between her and Charlotte Herriton of Where Angels Fear to Tread, the novel which The
Longest Journey follows. Charlotte Herriton also lives in
Sawston.]

HERRITON, MRS. --The matriarch of the Herriton family.
She is a domineering woman who controls the lives of her
children, Charlotte and Philip, and her grandchild, Irma.
She would also like to control her daughter-in-law, Lila, by
preventing a second marriage. Hence she agrees to the
Italian trip only, ironically, to have Lila marry Gino.
Though she is a grandmother, she hates the title, "granny."
(WAFT I).

HERRITON, PHILIP--Lila's brother-in-law. He thinks of
himself as worldly. He loves Italy, so he believes, until he
is sent by his mother to prevent Lila's marriage to Gino.
He arrives in Italy only to discover that the marriage has
taken place. After Lila's death, he returns to retrieve her
son by Gino. He falls in love with Caroline Abbot and becomes friendly with Gino. Philip's worldliness evaporates
when the baby dies and he discovers that Caroline is in love
with Gino. He is a tall, weakly-built young man of twenty-
four at the time of Lila's death. His clothes had to be pad-
ded on the shoulders to make him "pass muster." His face

was plain. He had a fine forehead and a good, large nose.
Observation and sympathy were in his eyes. Below the nose,
however, all was confusion. Those people who believed that
destiny resides in the mouth and the chin shook their heads
when they looked at him. (WAFT II) [This is a good description of Forster at that age.]

"HICKEY'S LAST PARTY"--1st published in Calendar of
Modern Letters, II (February 1926), pp. 437-439; reprinted
in Abinger Harvest, 1936.

[A review of The Memoirs of William Hickey, Vol.
IV.] Hickey is not "philosophic or profound." He just
writes "ahead." He is never concerned to discover a "meaning" from his experiences in India or to draw lessons from
his failures or successes. He was a Calcutta attorney and
ended his career as Under-Sheriff and Keeper of the Jail.
He is not pretentious or insincere in his memoirs; nor has
he ever regretted or repented anything. Forster believes
that it would have been pleasant to have met him. He believes that the type is "still with us," though "somewhat
overlaid with newspapers," his kind is to be encountered in
"many an overseas dining club or tenth rate military mess."

THE HILL OF DEVI BEING LETTERS FROM DEWAS SENI-
OR--1st edition, London, Edward Arnold and Co., 15 October 1953; 1st American edition, New York, Harcourt,
Brace and Co., 22 October 1953. "Preface"--Forster explains the genesis of the book. It grew out of two visits to
the Indian State of Dewas, in 1912-13, and 1921 and the letters he wrote during those visits addressed to his mother
and to other relatives.

"Letters of 1912-13"--Describes Forster's first visit,
the sleeping arrangements, entertainments, an elaborate Indian dinner, festivities, and his departure.

"The State and Its Ruler"--Dewas, an Indian State in
the middle of India, was actually two states: the Senior and
the Junior, the territory of which was in many instances co-
extensive. Each had its own ruler. The Senior Branch had
some 446 square miles of territory and a population of some
80,000; the Junior Branch was a bit smaller. The whole
area of the state was divided, by fields and streets, between
the two Branches. The state was divided at the end of the
eighteenth century between two brothers and the division was
confirmed by the English in 1812.

The Ruler of the Senior Branch when Forster visited,
was born January 1, 1888. He succeeded his uncle who
died heirless in 1899 and had intended to adopt him. The
adoption was confirmed by his aunt who was not at all friendly to him. He had a happy childhood and was devoted to his
mother. He grew up in the midst of intrigues and endless
gossip. His close intimates were the Darlings who called
him "Tukky or Tukojii." His full title was Sir Tukoji Rao
III. Forster refers to him as "H. H." His early years
were full of promise. He was a brilliant student at college.
The Government of India appointed Malcolm Darling as his
tutor. He was married to the daugher of the Maharajah of
Kolhapur in March, 1908. The marriage was unsuccessful
though an heir was born [the Yuvraj]. Forster completes
the section with a short description of the new and old pal-
aces.

"Letters of 1921"

"Settling in"--Forster has been asked to serve as secretary to H. H. while Col. Wilson is in England recuperating.
He describes his "settling in" process at the New Palace--
"You would weep at the destruction--much of which was
crumbling before it was finished." He learns of his duties:
"gardens, tennis courts, motors, Guest House, Electric
House" and all the post was to pass through his hands. He
discovers that everything which occurs is said to be one
thing and proves to be another. He is struck by "Oriental
publicity." He meets H. H. 's "Diamond Concubine," and is
oppressed by the ugliness of the New Palace.

"Birth of a Baby"--Describes the rites surrounding
the birth of H. H. 's child by his concubine, Bai Saheba, con-
sisting of fifteen days of music, fireworks, discharge of
rifles, etc. , 1,000 pounds were spent. The amount was
small because the child was a girl. Forster also describes
the troubles H. H. had with his aunt, the Dowager Maharani.
He calls her "Dewas-Nuisance Lady #1."

"Scindhia's Visit"--Scindhia, the Maharajah of Galior,
"a vigorous and vulgar prince," neighbor and uncle to H. H.
is invited to visit Dewas Senior. The visit is an expensive
undertaking and not a success.

"The Rains"--Forster talks of the monsoons: the
first shower is smelly and undramatic. The full monsoon
broke violently, but the temperature was hot between storms.

"The Insult"--An official insult to Forster enrages
H.H. because he sees in it the "AGG's" refusal to recognize
his right to have Europeans serve under him.   "The insult
rumbled on for weeks."   In Dewas, Forster finds the insult
to his advantage.   His colleagues "rallied around him" because he had suffered on their account.

"Gokul Ashtami"--A festival in which few Europeans
have shared.   For ten days nothing may be killed.   No shoes
can be worn in the Old Palace (where the festival is held).
Hymns are sung without stop.   Gods visit each other, take
baths and meals.   They are serenaded by two native bands
and one European one.   Gokul Ashanti is the eight-day feast
in honor of Krishna who was born at Gokul near Muttia.   It
climaxes with the birth of the god and the drowning of a mud
model of Gokul in the tank.   Forster finds "every detail of
the ceremonies in fatuous and bad taste."

"On Tour"--H.H. and his court go to Nagpur in British India to a Maratha Educational Conference.   Mismanage-
ment causes H.H. and his entire suite to be crammed into
one compartment on the train.   Forster visits Chhatarpur
where the Maharajah tries to hire him away from H.H., the
Taj Mahal, Mandu, Khapaho Temples, etc.

"Dassera"--The Great National Festivity.   Forster
discovers that, involved with it, is the worship of coconuts.
In origin it is a military review which turned into the worship of the collective power of the state.

"Colonel Wilson"--At the suggestion of Malcolm Darling, H.H.'s tutor, Wilson became H.H.'s English secretary
in 1920.   He had had a tragic private life.   While on business for Dewas, to which he was devoted, he was crushed
between two railroad cars.   He did not die but was nursed
back to health by H.H. whom he loved.   He went to England
on a rest cure while E.M. Forster took his place.   When
Forster came, the court was filled with Wilson's praises.
In his absence, Forster sent letters explaining the state of
things.   It turned out that Wilson had quarreled with everyone in Dewas.   He believed that Forster was plotting to take
his place permanently, and sent him a "nasty" note.   H.H.
did not want Wilson to return.   The time came, nevertheless, for Forster to leave Dewas.   He was conferred the
Tukojirao III gold medal.   Wilson never did return to Dewas.
As he closes the section, Forster notes that he has "passed
abruptly from Hinduism to Islam and the change is a relief."

"Note on A Passage to India"--Forster began the novel before his 1921 visit to Dewas and took the early chapters with him hoping to continue them. When he confronted the real India, however, they "wilted." He took them up again when he returned to England, but still thought the book "bad." He would not have finished it were it not for the urging of Leonard and Virginia Woolf.

"Catastrophe"

The new constitution planned for Dewas State was a failure. Forster learns that A Passage to India was ill-thought of at the Viceregal Lodge at Delhi.

"The Yuvraj"--The Crown Prince (the Yuvraj) grew into a charming, well-mannered boy. At sixteen he was "fianced" to the daughter of the Chief of Jath. They were married in Dewas at the end of 1926. In 1927, after a misunderstanding, the Yuvraj's wife was sent back to her father and the Yuvraj fled Dewas proclaiming that H. H. intended to poison him. H. H. collapsed. The Government of India became the boy's guardian and, when H. H. died, he became Maharajah of Dewas then Maharajah of Kolhapur, his mother's state.

"Pondicherry"--H. H.'s prestige never recovered from his domestic scandal. The final blow was economic. Dewas was bankrupt and the Government of India refused to help tactfully. On a pilgrimage to Ramesvaram, H. H. became ill. The party turned aside at Pondicherry, the capital of French India and remained there, in exile, until his death. Forster is not concerned with rehabilitating his memory. He offers him as a "subject for study." H. H. had the rare "quality of evoking himself."

HILTON--The station for Howards End. It was one of the large villages along the Great North Road which owed its size to the traffic of coaching and pre-coaching days. It did not share in the rural decay because of its proximity to London. Its long High Street "budded" out right and left into residential estates. (HE III)

HILTON TENNIS CLUB--Dolly forgets her news when she describes for Margaret Schlegel the great row there had been at the Hilton Tennis Club. (HE XXXII)

"HISTORY"--Title of Part I in Alexandria.

HOLBURN, THE--The newspaper to which Rickie Elliot has sent one of his "stray" stories.   (LJ XV)

"HOMMAGE TO WILLIAM BARNES"--See: "William Barnes"

HONEYCHURCH, FREDDY--The brother of Lucy Honey-church.   (RWV I)

HONEYCHURCH, LUCY--The central female character in A Room with a View.   She is a young English woman who is traveling with her cousin, Charlotte Bartlett, in Italy.   They are disappointed with their room in Florence because it has no view.   Mr. Emerson and his son, George, offer to ex-change theirs, which has a view, for Lucy's.   She demurs, but finally agrees.   She regards, however, their offer as ill-bred.   For the remainder of the trip and, on her return to England, she tries to deny her interest in George.   Fin-ally, Mr. Emerson leads her to acknowledge her love for his son.   Ultimately, they marry.   (RWV I)

HONEYCHURCH, MRS. --The mother of Lucy Honeychurch. (RWV I)

HORNBLOWER, MR. --A schoolmate of Rickie at Cambridge. Rickie likes him, but he is not liked by Ansell and Widdring-ton.   (LJ II)

HOSTESS, THE--Margaret and Helen Schlegel attend a dinner party after Leonard Bast leaves them.   At the party a paper is delived.   "How I Ought to Dispose of My Money"--the reader professing to be a millionaire on the point of death who is inclined to leave his fortune to the foundation of local art galleries, but open to "conviction from other sources." All present assume different roles.   The hostess takes the role of "the millionaire's eldest son" and "implores her ex-piring parent not to let the money out of the family."   (HE XV)

HOUSEMAID, THE--Stephen, on returning to Cardover from his ride to Salisbury, sees the housemaid and wonders if he should slip an arm around her waist.   (LJ XII)

"HOW I LISTEN TO MUSIC"--See: "Not Listening to Music"

"HOW LUCY FACED THE EXTERNAL SITUATION BRAVE-LY"--Title of Chapter XIV, A Room with a View.

"HOW MISS BARTLETT'S BOILER WAS SO TIRESOME"--
Title of Chapter XIII, A Room with a View.

"HOW THEY WEIGHED FIRE"--See: "Voltaire's Laboratory,
1: How They Weighed Fire"

"HOWARD OVERING STURGIS"--1st published, in London
Mercury, XXXII (May 1935), pp. 42-47; reprinted in Abinger
Harvest, 1936.

       A review of the novel Belchamber by Howard Overing
Sturgis. Forster calls Sturgis a "domestic author of the
type of Cowper" who wrote to please his friends and, when
he failed to do so, he gave up the practice of literature and
devoted himself to embroidery. He is "a brilliant, sensitive,
neglected writer."

HOWARD, TOM--The brother of the first Mrs. Wilcox
(Ruth). He was the last of the Howards. Dolly Wilcox notes
the significance of this point when she mentions the name of
the home which was to have been his--Howards End. The
house passed to his sister because of his death.   (HE XXIV)

HOWARDS END--The Wilcox home near Hilton. The Wilcoxes came into possession of it through the first Mrs. Wilcox who, in turn, had it from her brother, Tom Howard.
Helen Schlegel describes it in a letter to her sister, Margaret. "It is old and little . . . and red brick." From the
hall one goes on the right into the dining-room and on the
left into the living room. In the hall there is a door which
opens upon stairs going up in "a sort of tunnel" to the first
floor. There are three bedrooms in a row on the first floor
and three attics in a row above. There are nine windows
as one looks up from the garden. There is a very big
wych-elm to the left as one looks up which leans over the
house and stands on the boundary between the garden and the
meadow.   (HE I)

HOWARDS END--1st edition, London, Edward Arnold,
18 October 1910;   1st American edition, New York,
G. P. Putnam's Sons, 11 January 1911.

       Helen Schlegel is invited to Howards End by the Wil-
cox family which she and her sister, Margaret, had met
while vacationing in Europe. While there, she believes that
she has fallen in love with Paul, the younger of two Wilcox
brothers. Both families disapprove of the match. Several

months later, after the match had been broken off, the Wilcoxes move into a flat across the way from the Schlegels
and Mrs. Wilcox and Margaret meet and become friends.

The Schlegels become involved with Leonard Bast, a
poor and half-educated young man they feel has great poten-
tial. They do not know that he has a wife, older than he,
who had trapped him into marriage.

Several months after their acquantance blossoms into
friendship, Mrs. Wilcox dies. Her family is surprised when
they learn, in a note she left, that she had wanted Margaret
to have Howards End. The Wilcoxes decide to disregard the
note. Margaret, not knowing of the bequest, is happy that
the tie between the Schlegels and the Wilcoxes has been brok-
en. She feared that Helen was still in love with Paul and
that contact with the Wilcoxes was painful to her.

Later, they meet Mr. Henry Wilcox in the park. He
tells them that the firm for which Leonard Bast works is
unreliable. The girls, acting on that information, advise
Leonard to change positions. He does so disastrously.

Several weeks later, the lease on the house the Schlegels occupy in London terminates. They have searched for
some time but have found nothing suitable. Hearing of their
problem, Mr. Wilcox, who is in love with Margaret, sends
a letter offering to lease his London house to them. When
she is examining his house, Mr. Wilcox proposes to her.
She asks for a few days to consider his proposal before a-
greeing to marry him.

Before Margaret's marriage, Mr. Wilcox's daughter,
Evie, is married at their country home near Oniton. Helen,
who disapproves of her sister's marriage to Mr. Wilcox, arrives on the scene with Leonard Bast and his wife, Jacky,
who had been Mr. Wilcox's mistress. Helen asks Margaret
to help the Basts, who have been impoverished by Mr. Wilcox's advice. Though she forgives Mr. Wilcox, she refuses
to help the Basts.

Helen, meanwhile, feeling sorry for Bast, falls in
love with him and spends the night with him. She leaves
England shortly after trying to give most of her fortune to
him. He refuses. Margaret is unaware of the relationship
to Bast. She proceeds with her marriage to Mr. Wilcox.
Helen's refusal to attend the ceremony does not surprise

Margaret. However, after eight months, Helen's failure to
return begins to worry her.

Helen finally returns and sends word that she wants
some books which are stored at Howards End. Margaret and
Mr. Wilcox plan to meet her at the house. When they meet,
Margaret understands why Helen is so secretive. She is
pregnant with Bast's child. Helen asks to be permitted to
spend one night with Margaret in Howards End. Mr. Wilcox
refuses. Nevertheless, despite his refusal, the sisters remain in the house overnight. The following morning,
Charles, Wilcox's older son, goes to the house to get them
out only to meet Bast who has come in search of Margaret.
Enraged, Charles beats Leonard with a saber he seizes
from the wall. Shocked by the sight of Helen, whom he does
not know is carrying his child and dazed by the beating, he
has a heart attack and dies.

Charles is tried for manslaughter and sent to prison.
The disgrace is too much for Mr. Wilcox, who becomes an
invalid.

Margaret moves her husband, Helen, and Helen's illegitimate child, a boy, into Howards End. Several months
before Charles's release from prison, Mr. Wilcox gathers
the family together to tell them that he has altered his will.
The money will go to the family, but Howards End will go
to Margaret and, after her death, to Helen's child.

HO-YUNG--See: Enicharmon (Collect Ta - Machine)

"HUMANIST AND AUTHORITARIAN"--See: "Gide and George"

"HYMN BEFORE ACTION"--There is some confusion about
its first publication. B. J. Kirkpatrick in her bibliography
of Forster (p. 12) suggests that it most probably appeared
in a journal before it was printed in Abinger Harvest, 1936.
She has not, however, been able to discover the name of
that journal.

Arjuna, at the beginning of a battle depicted in the
Bhagavad-Gita, asks Krishna in a hymn if it would not be
better to enter the battle unresisting and thus be slain.
Krishna replies that he must fight for three reasons: 1)
death is negligible, 2) duty--his duty is not to save life,
even the lives of his kindred, but to destroy it, 3) the problem of renunciation and attempts to harmonize the needs of

life with eternal truth.

Arjuna is convinced by the Lord Krishna's arguments
and drives into the battle rejoicing.   He wins a great victory.   It is, however, rightly followed by disillusionment
and remorse.   The fall of his enemies leads to his own, because the fortunes of men are bound together.   It is impossible to inflict damage without receiving it.

<u>I</u>

I--See: The Narrator   (Collect Ta - Siren)

"I ASSERT THAT THERE IS AN ALTERNATIVE IN HUMAN-
ISM"--1st published as "A Letter," The Twentieth Century,
CLVII (February 1955), pp. 99-101; reprinted as a pamphlet,
London, The Ethical Union, October, 1955.

Forster has been worried over certain tendencies in
Cambridge and elsewhere.   Humanism is being threatened.
He "disbelieves" in spiritual authority.   He dreads all reli-
gions and places his trust in Humanism which he asserts is
an "alternative" to them.

"IBSEN THE ROMANTIC"--1st published in Nation and
Athenaeum (17 March 1928), pp. 902-903; reprinted in New
Republic (28 March 1928), pp. 186-188; Abinger Harvest,
1936.

Ibsen was a poet at forty because of his romantic in-
clinations and a poet at sixty because of that same inclination.   This inclination is somewhat hidden because he has the
air of a teacher and a depressing view of human relationships.   "To his impassioned vision dead and damaged things,
however contemptible socially, dwell forever in the land of
romance, and this is the secret of his so-called symbolism."
He is haunted by the romantic possibility of scenery.

"IMPRESSIONS OF THE UNITED STATES"--See: "The
United States"

"IN MRS. VYSE'S WELL-APPOINTED FLAT"--Title of
Chapter XI, A Room with a View.

"IN MY LIBRARY"--1st published as "Bookshelves of a
Lover of Words" in London Calling, #105 (26 May 1949),

p. 18; reprinted as "In My Library" in The Listener (7 July
1949), p. 24; reprinted as "On the Meaning of a Man's
Books: E. M. Forster, Looking Over His Library, Finds
Old Friends and Some Strangers" in New York Times Book
Review Section (11 September 1949), pp. 1, 14; reprinted as
"In My Library" in Two Cheers for Democracy, 1951.

Most of Forster's books are in one room. The Library measures twenty-four by eighteen feet. It has a high
ceiling, white wallpaper "ribboned-white--round the walls"
and a dozen wooden bookcases. In the middle of the room
is a bookcase once belonging to his grandfather which contains the works of Barrow, Milton, Evelyn, Arnold, Tacitus,
Homer and works by his own grandfather. Other cases hold
books by France, Proust, Hérédia, Gide; books from his
aunt: Trollope, Austen, Yonge, Malory; books on birds (Be-
wick and Morris), Darwin, Ruskin (Praeterita, Giotto), Rub-
aiyat (which he later gave away to an Oriental friend). He
has brought little to the library himself. Some of those he
has contributed are about India, Indians, modern poetry,
etc. He has no bookplate and no arrangement. He favors
reciprocal dishonesty in lending and returning books. Three
of his favorite authors are Shakespeare, Austen, and Gibbon.

"IN RAJASTHANA"--See: "Adrift in India, 3: Jodhpur"

"IN SANTA CROCE WITH NO BAEDEKER"--Title of Chapter
II, A Room with a View.

"INCONGRUITIES: CAPTAIN GIBBON"--See: "Captain Edward Gibbon"

"INCONGRUITIES: 'COMERBACKE' "--See: "Trooper Silas
Tomkyn Comerbacke."

"INCONGRUITIES: STC"--See: "Trooper Silas Tomkyn
Comerbacke"

"INCONGRUITIES: VOLTAIRE'S SLUGS"--See: "Voltaire's
Laboratory, 2: Troublesome Molluscs"

"INCONGRUITIES: WEIGHING FIRE"--See: "Voltaire's
Laboratory, 1: Weighing Fire"

"INDIA AFTER TWENTY-FIVE YEARS"--See: "India Again"

"INDIA AGAIN"--1st published as "India After Twenty-Five

Years" in The Listener (31 January 1946, 7 February 1946),
pp. 133-134; 171-172. Reprinted as "India Again" in Two
Cheers for Democracy, 1951.

      Originated as broadcast talks in the BBC's Home
Service. Forster left England in October, 1945 for a return
visit to India bound for a conference of Indian writers. The
big change he noticed was the increased interest in politics.
Externally, India had not changed. Industrialization had increased, but it did not dominate the landscape as it did in
the West. In private homes, he noticed the lifting of purdah
and the increasing emancipation of women. For the well-to-
do, life was much easier in India than in England. English
was spoken more widely, but pronunciation was deteriorat-
ing. The debate about why speak English at all was still going on.

      The conference Forster attended was held at Jaipur.
It had been called to discuss literature as a unifying force
of the Indian languages, the Indian copyright act, a scheme
for an encyclopedia, etc. Book production, Forster discovered, was very active. Drama was not prominent.
Criticism was weak. No one alive had the stature of Iqbal
or Tagore. The film industry had become the second
largest in the world with headquarters in Bombay. Forster
saw an interesting experiment in modern architecture: the
new university of Hyderabad. Folk art had a genuine existence among the people. To the tragic problem of India,
Forster could contribute no solution. He did suggest, however, that young people go to India with genuine good will
and affection.

INSKIP, MR. --The narrator of "Other Kingdom." He is a
rather careful individual and the Latin tutor of Harcourt
Worters's ward, Jack, and his fiancée, Evelyn Beaumont.
Inskip is ever ready to agree with his employer. He later
is elevated to secretary to Harcourt. (Collect Ta - Other)

"INSULT, THE"--See: "Letters of 1921: The Insult"

" 'INTERNATIONAL ANARCHY' (1926)"--Title of Chapter
XIII, Goldsworthy Lowes Dickinson. For summary see:
Goldsworthy Lowes Dickinson.

INTERRUPTING STUDENTS--Run after Fielding offering him
honors when Aziz's trial breaks up. They offer him a gar-
land of jasmine and offer to serve as horses pulling his

Victoria. He realizes, however, as they honor him more,
they obey him less. (PI XXV)

"INTRODUCTORY"--Title of Chapter I, Aspects of the Novel.
For summary see: Aspects of the Novel.

"IT IS DIFFERENT FOR ME"--1st published in New Leader
(16 July 1926), p. 3; reprinted in Abinger Harvest, 1936.

        Satiric verse written on the occasion of a letter to
the Times by the Dean of Durham, in which he complains of
the "vulgar profanity" of the language used by the Labour
Party in the House of Commons, and inquires whether there
is no "adequate means of preventing or punishing it." Forster's verse notes that "rudeness is only for gentlemen."

ITALIAN CHAUFFEUR--See: Angelo (HE XXV)

ITALIAN LADY, AN--Is able to comfort a child who stumbles
and falls in Santa Croce when neither Lucy nor Mr. Emerson
are successful. (RWV II)

                              J

JACK--The leader of the villagers. He demonstrates,
through word and deed, the effects of the Acts of Enclosure
on the countryside and its absolute destruction unless stern
measures are taken. He appears in all the scenes and all
the ages and is played by the same actor. He almost incites
the villagers to riot in one scene. (Act I, Sc. iii) (England's)

JACK, MR. BOSTON--The fictional sculptor of the equally
fictional statue of Forster in Kennsington Gardens. The
statue was originally designed to represent Forster pursuing
an ideal, but, as the gardens are frequented by the young, a
butterfly was substituted. (AH - My Own)

JACKSON, MR. --A teacher at Sawston School. He is a
cousin of Widdrington, Rickie's friend, and a friend of Rickie's uncle, Tony, Aunt Emily's husband. Herbert calls him
a "reactionary." He is not a disciplinarian. Herbert Pembroke suggested him for housemaster of the day boys at
Sawston. He was a failure in the position because he was a
scholar and a student rather than a director of the young.
(LJ IV)

JACKSON, MRS. --The wife of Mr. Jackson. See: Headmaster at Sawston School (LJ XVI)

JACKY--Leonard Bast's wife. Her most prominent feature
is her teeth which are of a "dazzling whiteness." Before
their marriage, she persists in asking Leonard if he loves
her. She pressures him into marriage despite his desire to
wait to come of age. She is older than he. In the garden
at Oniton, the fact that she was at one time Henry Wilcox's
mistress is revealed. (HE VI)

JAMES--A friend of Gerald Dawes at Cambridge. He received a "blue" for hockey his second term. Rickie has
never heard of him. (LJ III)

JANE--See: Margaret (Collect Ta - Co-ord)

"JANE AUSTEN, 1: The Six Novels"--1st published as
"Jane, How Shall We Ever Recollect . . ." in Nation and
Athenaeum (5 January 1924), pp. 512-514 [review of The
Novels of Jane Austen, ed. by R. W. Chapman; and Jane
Austen by Léonie Villard, trans. by Veronica Lucas];
reprinted in New Republic (30 January 1924), pp. 260-261;
reprinted [omitting the section on Villard's book] as "Jane
Austen, 1: The Six Novels" in Abinger Harvest, 1936.

        The Chapman edition of the novels, Forster holds, is
excellent on the whole except for the "grave defect" of ig-
noring Love and Friendship, The Watsons, and Lady Susan.
His "illustrations are beyond all praise." The general attraction of the text is not scholarly.

        2. "Sanditon"--1st published in Nation and Athenaeum
(21 March 1925), p. 860; reprinted as "Jane Austen, 2:
Sanditon" in Abinger Harvest, 1936.

        [Review of the fragment of a novel, Sanditon, by Jane
Austen.] Forster feels that the fragment is of "small literary merit." It is, nevertheless, of great interest because it
may serve to illuminate the last phase of Jane Austen's career.

        3. "The Letters"--1st published as "Miss Austen
and Jane Austen" in Times Literary Supplement (London),
(10 November 1932), pp. 821-822; reprinted as "Jane Austen,
3: The Letters" in Abinger Harvest, 1936.

[A review of Jane Austen's Letters, collected by R.
W. Chapman.] The letters are printed without comment.
Notes appear at the end of each volume. The editing shows
tact and good temper. Forster, however, finds a fundamental weakness in the letters: Jane Austen has "not enough
subject-matter on which to exercise her powers."

"JANE, HOW SHALL WE EVER RECOLLECT . . ." --See:
"Jane Austen, 1: The Six Novels"

JANET--Michael's wife who believed in truth. She tested all
men and all things. She had no patience with the sentimen-
talist who "shelters from the world's rough and tumble."
Michael did not like her when they first met. (Collect Ta -
Point)

JEREMIAH, MRS. --The wife of Squire Jeremiah. She has-
tens to tell everyone that whatever her husband does turns
to money. She also indicates how wonderful he is. See:
Mrs. Jerry (England's)

JEREMIAH, SQUIRE--In the last act of England's Pleasant
Land, he becomes Jerry the Builder. Like the two guests
from London, he is from the city. He calls himself a
"plain, blunt man" and "not a great gentleman as some are."
He is a self-made man and believes he has a right to speak
his own mind. He, like the two guests from town, complain
of the "shameful, disgraceful sight" of the countryside
"which no sensible man would tolerate." He tells the Squire
to turn the land into one large estate as he has done. His
lands are enclosed and he urges Squire George also to seek
an Act of Enclosure from Parliament. (England's)

JERRY--He is played by the same actor who plays Squire
Jeremiah. He appears in Act II, Sc. ii as the new owner
of Squire George's land. He orders Jack and Jill off the
land and proceeds to "develop" it. (England's)

JERRY, MRS. --She is played by the same actress who plays
Mrs. Jeremiah. She is Jerry's wife and sings his praises.
(England's)

JERRY THE BUILDER--See: Jerry (England's)

"JEW-CONSCIOUSNESS"--1st published as "Comment and
Dream: Jew-Consciousness" in New Statesman and Nation,
N.S. (7 January 1939), pp. 7-8; reprinted as "Jew-Conscious-

ness" in Two Cheers for Democracy, 1951.

Forster feels that Jew-consciousness is in the air
(1939), and it remains to be seen how far it will succeed in
poisoning it.   Those who would not ill-treat Jews themselves or even "giggle" when pogroms are instituted enjoy,
nevertheless, tittering over their misfortunes.   Anti-Semi-
tism is assailing the mind at its source and inviting it to
create false categories before exercising judgment.

JILL--One of the villagers.   Jack's wife.   (England's)

"JODHPUR"--See: "Adrift in India, 3:   Jodhpur"

JOHN--One of Margaret Schlegel's Chelsea friends whom she
dropped after marriage along with Wederkind because she
was outgrowing the need for "stimulants" and was passing
from "words to things."   (HE XXXI)

"JOHN SKELTON"--1st published in Two Cheers for Democracy, 1951.

[Originally delivered as a lecture at the Aldeburgh
Festival of 1950.]   Skelton was a "strange creature."   He
was born about 1460, probably in Norfolk, and educated at
Cambridge.   He was the tutor of the future Henry VIII and,
eventually, poet laureate.   In the early years of the reign of
Henry VIII, he voiced official policy but attacked Cardinal
Wolsey.   At that point, his influence declined.   He was ap-
pointed rector of Diss in 1503 and held that post until 1529.

Forster proceeds to examine Skelton's "Philip Spar-
row," and notes that it emphasizes the differences in taste
between the sixteenth century and our own.   Skelton was not
a precursor of the Reformation though he attacked the abuses
of the Church.   Skelton had a "feeling for rhythm" and his
work is "entertaining."

"JOSEPH CONRAD: A NOTE"--1st published as "The Pride
of Mr. Conrad" in Nation and Athenaeum (19 March 1921),
pp. 881-882; reprinted as "Joseph Conrad: A Note" in
Abinger Harvest, 1936.   A review of Notes on Life and Letters by Joseph Conrad.

Conrad had a dread of intimacy.   The difficulties one
has with him "may proceed in part from difficulties of his
own."   What is so elusive about him is that he promises to

make some general philosophic statement on the universe, and then refrains "with a gruff disclaimer."

JULEY, AUNT--See: Mrs Munt (HE II)

JULIA--Mr. Lucas's sister whom he feared and hated. She is to take care of him when his daughter marries. (Collect Ta - Road)

"JULIUS CAESAR"--1st published as "Why 'Julius Caesar' Lives" in The Listener, (7 January 1943), p. 21; reprinted as "Julius Caesar" in Two Cheers for Democracy, 1951.

[The first of a series of talks to India covering some of the set books in the B. A. course in English Literature at Calcutta University.] Were Shakespeare to have attended the performance of Julius Caesar that Forster witnessed at a primary school, he would have been surprised that the play is still alive. Why has it lived? It is exciting. It is exciting because of three, well-timed "explosions": the murder, Anthony's funeral speech, the quarrel in the tent between Brutus and Cassius. It is also exciting because of its "character-drawing."

JUNIOR RANI OF MAU--She is lax about purdah and often can be seen paddling with her handmaidens in the garden and waving her sari at the monkeys on the roof. (PI XXXV)

K

KARIM--Daughter of Aziz. See: Ahmed (PI II)

KEEPER--He appears in Act I, Sc. iii. He brings in the poacher whom he has caught on Squire George's land. (England's)

KINGCROFT, MR. --A good-natured young man, a farmer, interested in Lila Herriton. Lila confesses that she likes him extremely, but she is not "exactly engaged to him." He comes to see her off on her trip to Italy, is sent for a foot-warmer and is almost late for her departure. (WAFT I)

KRISHNA--The "peon" who should have brought Ronny Heaslop the files he had half-heartedly wanted from his office. When Krishna does not show up, Ronny starts a terrific row because it was the custom.   (PI VII)

KUNO--He is the son of Vashti.   He desires to go out into
the upper world.   He is more muscular than most and has
hair on his upper lip attesting to his atavistic tendencies.
He wants desperately to leave the machine-controlled world
and civilization to live free in the open air.   (Collect Ta -
Machine)

L

"LABOURERS' REVOLT 1830, THE"--Title of Sc. iii (Act I),
England's Pleasant Land.   For summary q. v.

LADY WHO HAD BEEN A NURSE, THE--She claims to know
the truth about Indians.   She points out that the only hope
one has is to hold sternly aloof from them.   She is later
identified as Mrs. McBryde.   (PI III)

LAL, DR. PANNA--Aziz's assistant.   He is timid and elderly.   He was in "ecstacies" at the prospect of going to the
Collector's garden party.   (PI VI)

LANDLADY OF THE STELLA D'ITALIA, THE--Has to be
awakened from her siesta to give Philip and Harriet Herriton rooms.   Harriet becomes agitated over Philip's refusal
to see Gino Carella immediately.   The landlady cautions her
in Italian to be quiet because another lady (who turns out to
be Caroline Abbot) is asleep.   (WAFT VI)

LANOLINE, MRS. --The name Jacky Bast gives when she
comes to the Schlegel home looking for her husband, Leonard.   Helen misunderstands her accent.   See: Jacky (HE
XIII)

"LAST OF ABINGER, THE"--1st published as "Abinger
Notes" in Abinger Chronicles, V (September 1944), pp. 2-5;
parts of "Abinger Notes" were incorporated into "The Last
of Abinger," in Two Cheers for Democracy, 1951.

     These random notes, Forster points out, are not
likely to please a nature-lover, nor are they documentary
enough to please the historian.   Most of them were taken
from a common-place book which he has kept for many
years.   [See: "Bishop Jebb's Book".]   They concern ideas
of the countryside: from the nature of the soil of Forster's

parish to the lack of a feeling of peace at Blind Oak Gate,
and an evening at Paddington.

"LAST MONTHS (JUNE-AUGUST 1932), THE"--Title of Chapter XV, Goldsworthy Lowes Dickinson. For summary q. v.

"LAST PARADE, THE"--1st published in New Writing, #4,
(Autumn, 1937), pp. 1-5; reprinted in Two Cheers for Democracy, 1951.

        A look at the Paris Exhibition of 1937. Forster sees
the Exhibition as samples of the Earth's "hopes and lusts."
He feels it is unlikely that they will be collected again.

LATIF, MOHAMMED--A poor, distant cousin of Hamidullah
who lives on Hamidullah's bounty having a position of neither
servant nor equal. He is a gentle, happy, dishonest old
man who never did a stroke of work in his life. He was to
serve as Aziz's major-domo for the picnic Aziz had planned
to the Marabar Caves.   (PI II)

LAURA--The "other sister" of Leonard Bast to whom he appeals for financial aid in a letter. She shows the letter to
her husband who writes a cruel, insolent reply. Nevertheless, he sends more money than Blanche, and Leonard
writes him again. (HE XLI) See: Blanche

LAURA'S HUSBAND--See: Laura (HE XLI)

LAVERSTOCK, LADY HELEN--A student of the works of
Fra Angelico whose villa the party from the Pensione Bertolini pass. Mr. Eager points out her home. (RWV VI)

LAVISH, MISS ELEANOR--A novelist whom Lucy Honeychurch and Charlotte Bartlett meet at the Pensione Bertolini
in Florence. Charlotte becomes her good friend and tells
her of the incident in which George kissed Lucy. Miss Lavish puts it in her new novel. Miss Lavish is known at the
Pensione Bertolini for her intellect. Like the Misses Alan
she opposes the Emersons. (RWV I)

LEIGHTON--Aunt Emily's butler. (LJ X)

LENNIE--The "garden-child" of the Honeychurches who helps
a "cross Mrs. Honeychurch" tie up the wind-broken dahlias.
(RWV XVIII)

LEONARD'S BROTHER--He is a lay reader. Leonard Bast
writes him for money. When no reply is forthcoming, he
writes again saying that he and Jacky would come down to
the village on foot. The brother sends him a postal order.
(HE XLI)

LEONORA--The name of the heroine in Miss Lavish's new
novel. The character is based on Lucy Honeychurch. In
the novel, two Italians quarrel over her and one is killed.
(RWV V)

LESLEY, MR. --An English civil servant who claims that
Das is more frightened of acquitting Aziz than of convicting
him because, if Das acquits him, he will lose his job as a
judge. (PI II)

LESLEY, MRS. --See: Mrs. Callendar   (PI II)

"LETTER TO THE EDITOR AND APPRECIATION OF SIR
SAYED ROSS MASOOD"--See: "Sayed Ross Masood"

LETTER TO MADAN BLANCHARD-- 1st edition, London,
The Hogarth Press, 15 October 1931 (as The Hogarth Let-
ters, Vol. I); 1st American edtion, New York, Harcourt,
Brace and Co. , 28 January 1932 (as The Hogarth Letters,
Vol. I); reprinted in Two Cheers for Democracy, 1951.

A fictional letter to a personage Forster claims is
not imaginary. The letter describes the adventures of a
group of Englishmen in the latter part of the eighteenth century and their attempts to annex the Pelew Islands in the
South Seas through the son of its king, Prince Lee Boo. He
was to have been educated in England and then returned to
the islands to rule. His death, however, intervened. As
to Madan himself, Forster warns him to be careful of the
King of the Pelews. He also inquires into his ancestry.
Madan has apparently chosen to remain on the islands and
not return to England.

"LETTERS OF 1912-13"--Section title, The Hill of Devi.
For summary see: The Hill of Devi.

"LETTERS OF 1921"--Section title, The Hill of Devi. For
summary see: The Hill of Devi.

"LETTERS OF 1921: BIRTH OF A BABY"--Section title,
The Hill of Devi. For summary see: The Hill of Devi.

"LETTERS OF 1921: COLONEL WILSON"--Section title,
The Hill of Devi. For summary see: The Hill of Devi.

"LETTERS OF 1921: DASSERA"--Section title, The Hill of
Devi. For summary see: The Hill of Devi.

"LETTERS OF 1921: GOKUL ASHTAMI"--Section title, The
Hill of Devi. For summary see: The Hill of Devi.

"LETTERS OF 1921: THE INSULT"--Section title, The Hill
of Devi. For summary see: The Hill of Devi.

"LETTERS OF 1921: NOTE ON A PASSAGE TO INDIA"--
Section title, The Hill of Devi. For summary see: The
Hill of Devi.

"LETTERS OF 1921: ON TOUR"--Section title, The Hill of
Devi. For summary see: The Hill of Devi.

"LETTERS OF 1921: THE RAINS"--Section title, The Hill
of Devi. For summary see: The Hill of Devi.

"LETTERS OF 1921: SCINDHIA'S VISIT"--Section title,
The Hill of Devi. For summary see: The Hill of Devi.

"LETTERS OF 1921: SETTLING IN"--Section title, The Hill
of Devi. For summary see: The Hill of Devi.

LEWIN, MRS.--Rickie Elliot invites her and Agnes Pembroke
to lunch at the Union. Mrs. Lewin is a typical "May-term
chaperon," always pleasant, always hungry, and always tired.
(LJ VII)

LEYLAND, COL. EDWIN--He is very much interested in
Miss Raby, the lady novelist, and wants to marry her. They
are traveling together and, when she suggests that they stay
in the same hotel in Vorta; he thinks it improper. Later,
he saves her from an awkward situation when she reminds
the Concièrge of his youthful declaration of love to her.
(Collect Ta - Eternal)

LEYLAND, MR.--A would-be artist. He is conceited and
odious. (Collect Ta - Story)

"LIBERTY IN ENGLAND"--1st published in London Mercury,
XXXII (August 1935), pp. 327-331; reprinted in Abinger Harvest, 1936.

An address delivered at the Congrès International Des Ecrivains at Paris, June 21, 1935. The essay incorporates much of "English Freedom" (Spectator, 23 November 1934, pp. 791-792). Freedom has always been praised in England. Forster is aware, nevertheless, of how "limited and open to criticism English freedom is. It is race-bound and it's class-bound. It means freedom for the Englishman, but not for the subject-races of his Empire." The most powerful blow against English freedom has been struck by the Sedition Act. It restores the right of General Search, it "impedes the moral and political education of the soldier, it encourages the informer, and it can be employed against pacifists." The law has been used to crush a book, Boy by James Hanley, as an "obscene libel." Forster wants greater freedom for writers, "both as creators and critics." He would bring this about by utilizing the "existing apparatus" and extending to all classes and races what has been confined to a "few wealthy and white-coloured people."

"LIBYAN DESERT, THE"--Title of Section viii (Part II), Alexandria.

LIESECKE, BRUNO--See: Fraulein Mosebach's young man (HE V)

LIESECKE, FRIEDA--See: Freida Mosebach

LIESECKE, VICTOR--Freida Mosebach's brother-in-law. (HE XIX)

LIONEL--Col. Leyland's brother-in-law. His sister Nelly's husband. (Collect Ta - Eternal)

LITTLE BOY, A--Henry Wilcox wants to show Oniton to Margaret Schlegel. They are blocked on the way to the pig pens by a little boy. (HE XXVI)

LITTLE BOY--See: Tom (HE XXXVII)

LITTLE FRIEND, THE--He is a friend of Emily and accompanies her, her mother, and the Curate on their "teaing-out." The Faun turns his light flirtation with Emily into love, and the Curate is angry. Later, the little friend marries Emily. (Collect Ta - Curate)

LITTLE GIRL, THE--The little girl "very smart and quiet, who figures in so many weddings" kept a watchful eye on

Margaret Schlegel, the bride-elect of Henry Wilcox. (HE
XXV)

LITTLE GIRL, A--Tells Philip Herriton that she can show
him where Gino Carella lives. (WAFT VI)

LITTLE GREEK CHILDREN--Throw stones at Mr. Graham
when he tries to lead Mr. Lucas away from the khan. (Collect Ta - Road)

LLOYD--One of the prefects at Dunwood House who made the
"matron too bright" and, as a consequence, "nearly lost his
colours."

"LONDON LIBRARY, THE"--1st published as "The Centenary
of the London Library" in New Statesman and Nation, N. S.
(10 May 1941), p. 481; reprinted as "The London Library"
in Two Cheers for Democracy, 1951.

     The London Library was inaugurated, May 1841, on
the swelling tide of Victorian prosperity. It is "on the
rocks" one hundred years later. All around are the "signs
of the progress of science" and the "retrogression of man."
Buildings are in heaps; the earth in holes. It seems now,
more than a collection of books; it is a symbol of civilization. Perhaps the Nazis will hit it with their bombs.

     But why should a subscription library arouse such ex-
alted thoughts? The answer lies in its history and its present policy. It is typically civilized and it pays homage to
seriousness and good sense. Ephemeral books have been ex-
cluded from its shelves. Technical books have not been encouraged. It caters to creatures who are trying to be human.

     It owes its origin to Thomas Carlyle. He needed
reference books while writing Cromwell. He could not af-
ford to buy all of them and the trip from Chelsea to the
British Museum Library he found vexatious. He complained
about the fact that one ought to be able to borrow books.
His complaint led to the founding of the library. He joined
with Gladstone, Grote, Hallam, Monckton Milnes to promote
a scheme for "a supply of good books in all departments of
knowledge."

     The library began in two rooms at 49 Pall Mall with
five hundred members and three thousand books. In 1845

it moved to St. James Park.   Now it has four thousand
members and four hundred, seventy thousand books.   Its success is due to its librarian, Sir Charles Hagberg Wright,
who died in 1940.

"LONDON IS A MUDDLE"--1st published as "E. M. Forster
Looks at London, The . . . [sic] City of Odd Surprises" in
Reynolds News, (9 May 1937), p. 8; reprinted as "London is
a Muddle" in Two Cheers for Democracy, 1951.

London is an untidy city which ought not to be tidied
up.   At one time, the writer loathed London, but now can
love bits of it.

LONG WALL--Tibby Schlegel's lodgings in Oxford.   (HE
XXX)

LONGEST JOURNEY, THE--1st edition, Edinburgh and London, William Blackwood and Sons, 8 April 1907; 1st American edition, New York, Alfred A. Knopf, 9 March 1922.

Rickie (Frederick) Elliot, born with a lamed foot and
practically alone in the world, has finally achieved a degree
of contentment in Cambridge after a very unhappy childhood.
While still quite young, he discovered that his mother and
father had not loved each another and that he was loved not
at all by his father and only little by his mother.   Both of
his parents, who are separated, die when he is fifteen, leaving him financially secure but without a home.   He was a
capable student at Cambridge, but non-athletic.   He spent
much of his free time in discussions of philosophy with a
small group of friends.

One of these discussions is interrupted by Agnes Pembroke and her brother, Herbert, whom he had invited for the
weekend.   They passed much of their stay trying to encourage Rickie to think about his future.

At Christmas, he spent some time with the family of
his friend, Stewart Ansell and with the Pembrokes.   Agnes is
engaged to Gerald Dawes, a handsome and a virile athlete,
who is killed in a football game during Rickie's stay.   It is
Rickie who offers the most comfort to Agnes.

Two years later when Agnes comes to visit him again
at Cambridge, he realizes that he is in love with her.   He
fears to marry because of his deformity, nevertheless, she

convinces him.   They are to wait, however, until he makes
his way in the world as a writer.

Soon after the engagement, Agnes and Rickie visit his
Aunt Emily.   There they meet Stephen Wonham whom they
learn is Rickie's half brother.   In a fit of terror, Aunt
Emily tells them of the relationship.   Later they learn that
Stephen is the illegitimate child of Rickie's mother, not of
his father as he had supposed.

Agnes and Rickie marry and live with Herbert who
has become master of a boarding house at Sawston School.
Rickie becomes the master of a Latin form.   Rickie's marriage is not happy.   The spiritual ideals he has sought were
never achieved.   Soon a child is born, a girl who is lame.
She dies.

Meanwhile, Agnes is instrumental in Stephen's ex-
pulsion from Aunt Emily's home.   Aunt Emily gives Stephen
documents concerning his birth.   Hoping to find love with his
brother, Rickie, Stephen goes to him only to be confronted
by Agnes who believes he wants money from them.   Stephen
leaves and wanders about until he gathers enough money for
a drunken spree during which he decides he will wreck Rickie's home.

In the process, he might have killed himself, but
Rickie saves him and offers him his home.   Stephen refuses
but convinces Rickie to leave Agnes with him.   Thus Rickie
begins the regeneration of his soul.   He returns to his writing and produces a long story.   Unfortunately, his regeneration is short.   He is called to his Aunt's and goes with Stephen, who insists on accompanying him promising not to
drink.   He breaks his promise and collapses on the railroad
crossing.   Rickie manages to save him from an on-coming
train, but loses his own life.   Just before he dies, he realizes that, once again, his belief in the individual has be-
trayed him.

LORD OF THE MANOR--Someone at the breakfast table
where the Wilcoxes are gathered after Mrs. Wilcox's funeral
suggests that the Lord of the Manor and not the rector was
responsible for the pollarding of the elms during the funeral.
(HE XI)

LOUISA, LADY--Miss Lavish speaks to Lucy Honeychurch
of Lady Louisa, whose family name she has forgotten, hop-

ing to find that she is a mutual acquaintance. (RWV II)

LUCAS, MR. --An old man who tried to settle into the role
of Oedipus to his daughter Emily's Antigone. He realized
he was growing old and losing interest in the affairs of other people. Yet, he led a healthy, active life. He travels
in Greece fulfilling a life-long desire. He comes upon a
khan near Colonus and has an overwhelming desire to remain there. His daughter and their party force him to leave.
On his return to England, he settles into the life of an old
man. Even the news that an earthquake has destroyed the
khan in which he had wanted to stay killing all its inhabitants on the very day of his visit does not move him. (Collect Ta - Road)

"LUNCHEON AT PRETORIA"--1st published in Abinger
Chronicle, I (January 1940), pp. 15-18; reprinted in Two
Cheers for Democracy, 1951.

Forster describes a luncheon in Pretoria, South Africa, during which a platter of chicken fricassee was spilled
on him. His answer to the apologies of the servant was a
shriek of laughter. The hostess interpreted his hysterics
as a piece of deliberate good manners though Forster assures us it was not deliberate. The suit, nevertheless, was
ruined and, on his return home, he received four pounds for
it from his insurance company.

"LYING TO CECIL"--Title of Chapter XVII, A Room with a
View.

"LYING TO GEORGE"--Title of Chapter XVI, A Room with
a View.

"LYING TO MR. BEEBE, MRS. HONEYCHURCH, FREDDY,
AND THE SERVANTS"--Title of Chapter XVIII, A Room
with a View.

"LYING TO MR. EMERSON"--Title of Chapter XIX, A
Room with a View.

M

MCBRYDE, MR. --The District Superintendent of Police in
Chandrapore. He is a fundamentally decent individual who
treats Aziz well, but is provincial in his attitudes. He su-

pervises Aziz's prosecution. (PI V)

MCBRYDE, MRS. --The wife of Mr. McBryde. She was for-
merly a nurse. See: The lady who had been a nurse (PI
III)

"MACHINE STOPS, THE"--1st published in Oxford and Cambridge Review, VIII (Michaelmas Term, 1909), pp. 83-122;
reprinted in The Eternal Moment and Other Stories, 1928;
The Collected Tales, 1947.

    In a room, hexagonal like the cell of a bee, with no
exterior lighting or lamps, yet filled with a soft radiance
sits Vashti, a swaddled lump of flesh--a woman about five
feet high with a face as white as fungus. An electric bell
rings and she answers. It is a call from her son, Kuno,
who wishes to see her to tell her of a trip he wants to make
to the surface of the Earth. Kuno is angry because she refuses to travel to him which he feels is the result of the
control the Machine has over all of them. Vashti tells him
that the surface of the Earth is a dead place and deadly.
He replies that he will take all the necessary precautions.
She rejoins that it is against the spirit of the age. "The
Machine, you mean," is his reply. He fades away. She
gives the lecture on Australian music she had planned to do
before he called. No public gathering is necessary in those
times. She talked and others heard. Then she ate, bathed
and slept, all the while thinking of the visit to her son. She
hesitated. He lived on the other side of the Earth. The
thought of leaving her comfortable room is almost too much
for her. Nevertheless, she leaves on the journey, clutching
the Book of the Machine which answers all difficulties.
When she arrives at Kuno's room, an exact duplicate of hers,
she has discovered that he has been threatened with "Homelessness" which means death. The victim of Homelessness
is exposed to the air which kills him. Kuno is threatened
because he ventured into the open air without a permit. As
he explained his adventure to her, Vashti was ashamed that
she was his mother. The hair on his upper lip proved his
atavistic tendencies.

    In the years following Kuno's escapade, respirators
were abolished to prevent anyone from living above ground.
There was a growing fear of "first hand ideas." This re-
sulted in the re-establishment of religion as an antidote.
Kuno has been transferred from the Northern to the Southern
Hemisphere. He communicates his belief to Vashti that the

Machine is stopping. She does not believe him though she
does notice gasping sighs in the music which is played and
notifies the Committee of the Mending Apparatus. The committee assures her that the problem will be solved, but it is
not. She eventually adapts herself to the difficulty. Other
things begin to go wrong: the bathwater "stinks," beds fail
to appear. Panic sets in as the Machine continues to disintegrate. Vashti, fearing to leave her cell which is breaking apart, finally leaves and finds Kuno as she crawls over
the dead and the dying. They kiss. Before they die, he
tells her of a new world for the Homeless who will live in
the free air.

"MACOLNIA SHOPS--1st published in Independent Review, I
(November 1903), pp. 311-313; reprinted in Abinger Harvest,
1936.

        Forster describes a toilet case from the Roman peri-
od in the Kirchner Museum in Rome. It is only one of
three objects "Baedeker condescends to give a special account." It is probably Greek and the design praises water
and praises friendship. Forster has the shade of Dindia Macolnia exclaim that the piece was bought because it was
pretty and stood "nicely on the chest of drawers." Forster
concludes that perhaps the spirit of the artist would be
pleased with and would value more her praise than the writer's.

MADGE--Miss Avery's niece who lives near Howards End.
She and her husband object to Helen's staying with them after
Leonard Bast's death at Howards End. (HE XLIII)

MADGE'S HUSBAND--See: Madge (HE XLIII)

MAGGS, COLONEL--The political agent for the neighborhood
of Mau and Aziz's dejected opponent. (PI XXXIV)

MAHARANI OF MUDKUL--The lady for whom Miss Derek
works. The Nawab Bahadur fears that she is uneducated and
superstitious. (PI VIII)

MAID--Interrupts the conversation of Mr. Wilcox and Margaret Schlegel who are trying to discover why both feel it best
that Paul Wilcox and Helen Schlegel should never meet.
Rather than resume the subject after the maid's departure,
they speak on more "normal lines." (HE VIII)

MAIDS--As they explore Oniton, Henry Wilcox and Margaret Schlegel "scare" unknown maids from the performance of "obscure duties." (HE XXVI)

MAJOR CALLENDAR'S SERVANT--Refuses to give Aziz any message from Callendar until he is tipped. (PI II)

MALI, A--Listens outside of the window as Mrs. Moore and Ronny quarrel over her desired appearance at the trial. (PI XXII)

MAN, A--Prepares to scythe out one of the dell holes at Howards End while Margaret talks to her sister, Helen. (HE XLIV)

MAN CARRYING A ROLL OF OILCLOTH, A--Charles Wilcox, whom Mrs. Munt believes is his brother, Paul, stops his car in front of a draper's and a man carrying a roll of oilcloth runs out. (HE III)

MAN OF FIFTY OR SIXTY YEARS OLD, A--Rescues the narrator from the moat which guards the land wherein no "progress" occurs. He serves as the narrator's guide in that land. He shows the narrator the gates of the land from which humanity left when it learned to "walk." The narrator wants to leave this land, but the man refuses to permit him to do so. Finally, the narrator's efforts to leave are successful. He spies a man carrying some liquid which he discovers is beer. He drinks to quench his thirst and realizes that the man who carried the beer is his own brother whom he thought he had left behind on the road. (Collect Ta - Other Side)

MAN WHO DROPPED THE BOOK, A--On her way into the air-ship which was to take her to her son, Vashti sees a man drop the Book of the Machine. If such a thing occurred in one's apartment, the floor would rise to receive it. But the gangway to the air-ship was not so prepared. Instead of picking up his property, he felt the muscles of his arm to see how they had failed him. He was returning home after fulfilling his duty to propagate the race. (Collect Ta - Machine)

MANAGEMENT, THE--The personage who takes care of the party leaving Paddington for Evie Wilcox's wedding at Oniton. The management's arrangements had been so thorough that the guests need only look pleasant and, where possible, pretty. (HE XXV)

MANSBRIDGE--The doctor Henry Wilcox takes to Howards
End to examine Helen Schlegel. He is a very young man
who questions Margaret about her sister's symptoms. (HE
XXXV)

MARABAR CAVES, THE--The destination of Aziz's outing
and the scene of the attempted rape of Adela Quested. "The
caves are readily described. A tunnel eight feet long, five
feet high, three feet wide, leads to a circular chamber a-
bout twenty feet in diameter. This arrangement occurs a-
gain and again throughout the group of hills, and this is all,
this is a Marabar Cave." After seeing one or a number of
them, the visitor returns to Chandrapore not certain that he
has had an interesting or a boring experience or "any experience at all." The walls of the circular chambers are
highly polished, but the sides of the tunnels are rough. (PI
XII)

MARCH, LIEUT. C. P. --The young man who rescued Martin
Whitby from certain death under the wheels of a train at
Basle Station. Had the fragment, Arctic Summer, continued
to a full-length novel, Forster had intended to portray the
lieutenant as a generous, idealistic, loyal individual. (AS)

"MARCO POLO"--1st published in Spectator, (21 December
1931), p. 186; reprinted as "Marco Polo's New Life" in
New York Herald Tribune, Section 11, Books, (13 December
1931), pp. 1, 6; reprinted as "Marco Polo" in Abinger Harvest, 1936.

[A review of The Travels of Marco Polo, translated
into English from the text of L. F. Benedetto by Aldo Ricci.]
Forster maintains that Marco Polo's recounting of his travels is not a "first rate" book because its author is interested
in "novelties" to the "exclusion of human beings." His book
reflects a somewhat unpleasant character: "shrewd, compla-
cent, and mean."

"MARCO POLO'S NEW LIFE"--See: "Marco Polo"

MARGARET--The music teacher, Miss Haddon, concludes
that Margaret and Jane play the piano duet she had assigned
worse than Rose and Enid, but not as badly as Ellen. (Collect Ta - Co-ord)

MARGARET'S NEW MAN--See: Leonard Bast. He attends a concert with Margaret and Helen Schlegel, Aunt Juley, Fraulein Mosebach, Tibby, and Herr Liesecke. He becomes uneasy when Helen inadvertently walks off with his umbrella in the middle of the concert. The act disturbs him because of his constant fear of being "had." He had been "had" in the past and now most of his energies go into defending himself. (HE V)

MARIA--The girl at Ragusa who was reported to have gone mad after bathing in the sea. When Giuseppe hears of her, he goes to Ragusa and carries her off. She is the daughter of a rich mine owner. Giuseppe's family believes that trouble will come to them because of this act. None does and the pair are married. She is very much like him, for she, too, has seen the Siren. She and her unborn child are killed by the villagers after a witch prophesies that her child would call the Siren from the sea. (Collect Ta - Siren) See also: Giuseppe.

MARIANNE THORNTON 1797-1887: A DOMESTIC BIOGRA-PHY--1st edition, London, Edward Arnold, Ltd., 10 May 1956; 1st American edition, New York, Harcourt, Brace and Co., 14 May 1956.

     Preface--Forster lists the sources he used for the biography of his great aunt: I. First Vellum Book containing Marianne's transcription of the life of her father, letters to 1815, and her "Recollections." II. Second Vellum Book letters to 1852. III. Ten Small Volumes begun for Forster by Marianne and continued by his mother. Largely a replica of the First Vellum Book. IV. The "Wigan" Book letters and all the matters in the early part of the First Vellum Book. V. Small Green Book. Some additional early letters. VI. Henry Thornton's Diary. VII. Recollections of Miss Laura Forster. VIII. Various letters and Ms. brochures, diaries, notes, etc. dating from 1750-1900.

"Daughter 1797-1815"

     1. "Battersea Rise"--A description of Battersea Rise, the home of Henry Thornton, Marianne's father, and the home in which she was born and raised. See also: "Battersea Rise."

     2. "The Parents"--Marianne's forebears with especial emphasis upon her parents: Henry Thornton and Mari-

anne Sykes Thornton.

3. "On Clapham Common"--Marianne's early life, reminiscence of her nurse, Hunter; her education; her uncles; and family friends: the Venns, Grants, Wilberforces, Macaulays, Teignmouths, Stephans (the Clapham Circle), Hannah More; her father's political life; the growing sympathy between father and daughter.

4. "The Deathbeds"--The death of Marianne's mother (October 15, 1815) and father (January 16, 1815).

"Sister 1815-1852"

1. "The Reign of Sir Robert"--Describes the guardianship of Sir Robert Inglis over the nine Thornton children. Marianne was the oldest (18) when her parents died. Descriptions of her travels on the Continent. Henry, Jr. was sent to Cambridge. A description of the nine Thornton children.

2. "The Continent"--Her trips to Paris 1816, 1817, 1818 and others which Forster admits are too many to record.

3. "The Birchin Lane Bank"--The financial difficulties of the orphaned family and its financial salvation by the eldest son, Henry. The bank he founded as a result is still in existence.

4. "May Meetings and William Wilberforce"--Marianne's involvement in the May Meetings which were held each year by The British and Foreign Bible Society to which were added organizations founded by the Clapham sect.

5. "The Marriages"--Marianne never married, but most of her family did. The marriages began with that of Laura Thornton to Forster's grandfather, Charles Forster (1833). They had nine children; their seventh, "Eddie," was Forster's father. Henry Thornton was married to Harriet Dealty on the same day as Laura Sophia to John Melville (1834). He was later to become the Earl of Leven and Melville; Henrietta to Richard Synnot, an Irish knight (1836); Charles to a Miss Harrison (1837); Watson to Frances Webb (1842); Isabella to Archdeacon Harrison.

6. "Deceased Wife's Sister"--Henry's wife's sister,

Emily Dealtry comes to live at Battersea Rise. When her
sister dies, gossip accumulates. Henry announces that he
intends to marry Emily causing a great flurry of legal and
family anguish. The couple elope to the Continent and Marianne is forced to leave Battersea Rise.

"Aunt 1852-1879"

     1. "East Side"--Marianne takes up residence in the
"Sweep" which became an asylum for nephews and nieces upon the death of her sister Henrietta (1853). Forster's father,
Eddie, became Marianne's favorite nephew after the death of
his cousin, Inglis Synnot. Forster speaks of Marianne's acquaintance with John Knowles, Florence Nightingale, and others. Gradually, she became less mobile.

     2. "Educational"--Describes her educational interests
and activities. Her educational tradition was derived from
Hannah More and her parents. Marianne had a disliking for
ignorance and an eighteenth century faith in reason. Her
educational philosophy: if children know more, they would
grow up happier, healthier and more helpful. She wrote a-
bout the duties of a governess and believed in training school-
mistresses for their positions.

     3. "Milton Bryon"--The home of the Inglis family,
guardians of the Thorntons and, for a time, Marianne's
home. By 1873 it grew in importance in her life--it became a "resort for aging ladies" of the Inglis family. In
1873, Marianne inherited it, a "pleasant countrified gabled
building," near Woburn Abbey. As she grew older, Marianne consorted with people who, in a worldly sense, were
less important than those she had known in her youth.

"Great Aunt 1879-1887"

     1. "My Arrival"--Forster was born at 6 Melcombe
Place, Dorset Square, London, January 1, 1879. By mistake he was christened Edward Morgan when he was regis-
tered as Henry Morgan. His mother was Alice Clara Whichelo, the third child and eldest daughter of Henry Mayle
Whichelo. Alice did not belong to the Thornton circle. Her
father was a painter. Marianne Thornton considered it best
that she become a governess. Soon after Alice took up her
duties, however, she married Forster's father. His father
died within four years of his marriage to Alice leaving her
a young widow with a child. Marianne was "fertile" with

plans for that child.

   2. "The Death of Henry Sykes Thornton"--Henry
Sykes Thornton, the eldest Thornton son, died in 1881 worth
330,085 pounds.   He left Battersea Rise to his daughters by
his first wife.   Marianne had hoped, however, that the house
would be returned to the "true succession."

   3. "My Recollections"--Forster remembers break-
fasting with Marianne.   He remembers growing tired of
those breakfasts, but also recalls being "nice" because of
his mother's admonitions.   He remembers that his aunt,
Henrietta Synnot (Enty) hated him.   He recalls Christmas,
that he learned to read at the age of four, tea with the servants, his cousins, his boyhood friends.

   4. "The Aylward Incident"--Mr. Aylward, old, a
widower and in trade, proposes to Mamie Inglis Synnot
(niece-in-law of Marianne, and widow of her favorite nephew) and a family battle breaks out.   Nevertheless, she marries him.   Forster recalls being invited to Homleigh, the
home of the Aylwards.   He never liked old Mr. Aylward, but
he loved the house, even though Aylward pronounced its name
"Ómleigh."

   5. "The End"--Forster transcribes all of the nine
letters which Marianne had written him.   He claims that
they show her at her best.   Marianne died during the Jubilee of Queen Victoria.   Before she died, however, she made
peace with Emily Thornton, her brother Henry's widow.
Marianne was buried at Milton Bryon.   She left Forster
some 8,000 pounds which he claims was "the financial salvation" of his life; he went to Cambridge on it and traveled for
a "couple of years."   After World War I, the value of the
money declined almost to nothing but, by then, he had begun
to sell his writings.   He has lived on their sales since.   He
ends declaring that she alone made his career possible.

MARTLETT, MRS. --Tibby Schlegel's landlady at Oxford.
(HE XXX)

MARY--A Honeychurch maid whose fault is that she leaves
the dustpans standing on the stairs.   (RWV VIII)

MATHESONS, THE--They live in the flat opposite the Schlegels in Wickham Mansions.   When Aunt Juley informs Helen
of their name, Helen replies that she never knew that the

lady who "laced too tightly" was named Matheson.   (HE VII)

MATRON, THE--After Mrs. Orr refuses to marry him,
Herbert Pembroke hires a matron and becomes master of
Dunwood House.   However, the matron is all wrong for her
job.   She is too bright and not motherly enough.   She neglected the little boys and was overly attentive to the big
ones.   She left the position abruptly.   (LJ XVI)

MATRON OF THE NURSING HOME, THE--A letter from her
is received by the Wilcoxes.   It announces that Mrs. Wilcox,
before her death, had asked the matron to send the enclosed note to Mr. Wilcox.   The note indicates that Mrs.
Wilcox wants Margaret Schlegel to have Howards End.   (HE
XI)

MAU--The native state Aziz goes to after his trial.   There
is no such state.   [Forster may have taken its name from
a ruined palace he visited while staying with the Maharajah
of Chhatarpur in 1921.) (PI XXXIII)

"ME, THEM AND YOU"--1st published as "Me, Them and
You; Sargent at the Royal Academy," in New Leader, (22
January 1926), p. 3; reprinted as "Me, Them and You" in
Abinger Harvest, 1936.

        Forster attends an exhibition of Sargent portraits at
the Royal Academy dressed in a stylish suit of clothes which
do not fit well.   The dress of the figures in the portraits
seem to accent the social difference which exists between
them and the viewer.   Forster seems more uncomfortable
until he encounters "You"--the lower classes.

"ME, THEM AND YOU: SARGENT AT THE ROYAL ACAD-
EMY"--See: "Me, Them and You"

"MEDIEVAL"--Title of Chapter VIII, A Room with a View.

"MEDITERRANEAN PROBLEM"--See: "A Whiff of D'Annunzio"

MEG--See: Margaret Schlegel (HE I)

MELLANBY, SIR GILBERT--The Lieutenant Governor of the
province.   He is not an enlightened man, but one who held
enlightened opinions.   He congratulates Fielding on the position he took in the Aziz case. (PI XXIX)

MELLANBY, LADY--The wife of the Lieutenant Governor to
whom some of the women had sent a telegram to protest against
Das as judge in Aziz's trial.   (PI XXII) See also: Das

MEMBER OF THE LOWER ORDERS, A--Presumably a clerk in
the shop in front of which Charles Wilcox has parked his motor
car. The appearance of the man with a metal funnel, a sauce
pan, and a "garden squirt" which Charles has ordered, interrupts the conversation he and Mrs. Munt are having concerning
Paul's presumed interest in Helen Schlegel.   (HE III)

"MENACE TO FREEDOM, THE"--1st published in Spectator,
(23 November 1935), pp. 861-862; reprinted in Two Cheers
for Democracy, 1951.

    Menace to freedom is usually conceived of in terms of
political or social interference and usually personified as a ty-
rant. The true menace, however, is the fact that "many people
do not believe in freedom." We must not despair, however,
because "hope . . . can spring from love."

MEPHISTOPHOLES [Sic]--Takes his case to the Judgment Seat
when he is upset by the events.   (Collect Ta - Co-ord)

MICHAEL--As a young man, he directly causes the death of
Harold. All he remembers of the young man in later years is
his saying "What is the point of it?" Michael marries Janet
who believes as much in truth as he in love. He works for the
British Museum and is not content with the official office rou-
tine. He becomes a conciliatory force in his department. He
turns to literature and produces a book of essays that proves
popular. He also has three children. In the middle of his
life, he inherits a house in Surrey from his father and Janet
turns to gardening. She ages more rapidly than he and becomes bedridden. He is knighted. She dies at sixty.
Adam, his younger son, leaves in anger. Michael does not
see the point of his leaving since he gave his children all
the freedom they had wanted. He retires and dies as the
result of being hit in the face with a fish while trying to
mediate a quarrel between two women. After death, Michael wakes to find himself on a sandy plain. He meditates
on his life until he hears a voice say, "The point of it . .
." and a weight falls off his body and he crosses mid-
stream.   (Collect Ta - Point)

MICHAEL's NEIGHBOR--After his death, Michael speaks to his
neighbor who is lying next to him and learns from him much
about the place they occupy.   (Collect Ta - Point)

"MICKEY AND MINNIE"--See: "Our Diversions, 4: Mickey and Minnie"

MIDHURST--The home Henry Wilcox is building for Margaret. (HE XXXII)

MILDRED--Complains about the music being impossible to play after Miss Hadden tells her and Ellen that "each ought to be like a string of pearls." (Collect Ta - Co-ord)

MILES, MR. EUSTACE--At Simpson's, Margaret Schlegel indicates that Mr. Wilcox should dine with her at Mr. Eustace Miles's, a friend. (HE XVII)

MILNER--The new Civil Surgeon, a young man, whom Fielding meets at the club. (PI XXXI)

MILTON--Mr. Henry Wilcox's parlor maid. (HE XVIII)

"MILTON BRYON"--See: "Aunt 1852-1879, 3: Milton Bryon"

"MIND OF THE INDIAN NATIVE STATE, THE"--1st published as "The Mind of the Indian Native State (By Our Indian Correspondent)" in Nation and Athenaeum, (29 April and 13 May 1922), pp. 146-147; 216-217; reprinted as "The Mind of the Indian Native State" in Abinger Harvest, 1936.

Government policy toward the Native States has been reversed for two reasons: 1) native princes share in the increased consideration accorded to Indians generally and 2) are encouraged as counter-weights against the new nationalism. The princes have, in their own estimation, very clear responsibilities to themselves and to their states which seem odd to the Westerner. Forster describes some of these "responsibilities." The new Chamber of Princes, and all it connotes, seems, nevertheless, absurd to the politically-minded Indian. The princes dislike being criticised by British Indian newspapers. Some of them protect themselves by granting "constitutions" to their people and by spreading education, but they would soon return to their old ways were the dangers gone. It is ironic that the most independent areas are those deprived of independence by the British. Though the natives of these areas hate the British, they would not change places with the citizens of the Native States.

MIRIAM--Irma Herriton's school chum who was "blessed

above all school girls" because she was permitted to hide
her baby brother in a "squashy place" where "none but herself could find him." (WAFT V)

"MISS AUSTEN AND JANE AUSTEN"--See: "Jane Austen,
3, The Letters"

MISS DEREK'S CHAUFFEUR--Stops the cavalcade which had
come to escort Miss Derek to Aziz's picnic with the news
that she had gone back "with the other young lady to Chandrapore." Fielding insists that he is in error. The other young
lady in question is Miss Quested. (PI XVI)

"MISSES WOODMAN'S MORNING CLASS (1872-1874), THE"--
Title of Chapter III, Goldsworthy Lowes Dickinson. For summary see: Goldsworthy Lowes Dickinson.

"MODERN PERIOD"--Title of Section V (Part I), Alexandria.

"MOHAMMED IQBAL"--1st published as "A Great Indian Poet Philosopher [sic]" in The Listener, (23 May 1946), p.
686; reprinted in Two Cheers for Democracy, 1951.

[Originated as a broadcast talk on the BBC's Home
Service.] Forster had met Iqbal only in passing and can
read him only in translation. Iqbal lies in his grave outside
the great mosque in Lahore, his own city. He was an ortho-
dox Moslem who was partly educated in Europe. His sympathies were first for a united India. In later life, however,
he changed his opinion. He believed in the "Self"--the Self
as a fighting unit. His philosophy was a recommendation on
how a fight should be accomplished. He believed that man
is God's vice-regent on Earth and, consequently, we must
be "hard." Renunciation of the Self is a form of cowardice
and, therefore, a crime. We shall see God, perhaps, but
we will never be God because God, like ourselves, has a
"Self" and He created us not out of Himself, but out of nothing. Iqbal disliked the pantheism he saw about him in India.
His philosophy is not to Forster's liking. He is, Forster
concedes, nevertheless a genius. Though Forster disagrees
with him and agrees with Tagore, he would rather read Iqbal. Forster believes him to be one of the great cultural
figures of modern India.

MOHAMMED, MR. SYED--The assistant engineer who comes
to visit Aziz when he is ill and tells him that it is a serious matter when a doctor falls ill. (PI IX)

MOHURRAN--Ronny Heaslop's assistant. Ronny tells Mrs.
Moore and Miss Quested that Mohurran is bringing extra
work for him. This is not the case. Ronny says this as a
means for ending a discussion of Indian attitudes which he
cannot explain. (PI VIII)

MONICA--An Italian by birth, she is a journalist whom Helen
Schlegel has met at Lake Garda and with whom she takes an
apartment in Munich. Margaret guesses at her type: "Ital-
iano Inglesiato" [sic], a "crude feminist of the South, whom
one respects but avoids." (HE XXXVII)

MOORE, MRS. --The mother of Ronny Heaslop and Ralph and
Stella Moore. She is a widow and accompanies Miss Quested to India to visit her son, Ronny. She is a sensitive old
woman who has a great regard for Aziz. At the Marabar
Caves, she has a strange experience, an intuitive sense that
life is empty and worthless. When she defends Aziz against
the charge that he had attempted to rape Miss Quested, Ronny sends her home to England. She dies on the way. (PI
II)

MOORE, RALPH--The son of Mrs. Moore by her second
husband. He is Ronny Heaslop's half-brother. He accompanies his sister, Stella, whom Fielding has married, and
Fielding on the inspection trip of educational facilities in
Mau. Aziz believes that Fielding has married his enemy,
Miss Quested, and that Ralph is her brother. When he
learns that Ralph is Mrs. Moore's son and that Fielding has
married her daughter, he is partially reconciled to Fielding.
(PI XXXIV)

"MORE BROWNING LETTERS"--See: " 'Snow' Wedgwood"

MOSEBACH, FREIDA--The German cousin of the Schlegels
who later marries Bruno Liescke. (HE V)

"MOSQUE"--Title of Part I, A Passage to India.

"MOSQUE, THE"--1st published in Athenaeum, (27 February
1920), pp. 270-271; reprinted in Abinger Harvest, 1936.

[A review of Moslem Architecture, by G. T. Rivoira,
translated into English by G. MacNeil Rushworth.] Forster
examines the structure and purpose of the mosque as it developed from the courtyard of the Prophet to which he went
when he wished to worship God. Moslem architecture, For-

ster concludes, faithfully expresses the central truth of the
Faith which inspired it: "that there is no god but God, and
even Mohammed is but the Prophet of God."

MOTHER--The mother of the boy who discovers the celestial omnibus. She will not take him seriously and is always
laughing at him.   (Collect Ta - Celest)

MOTHER OF THE WOODCUTTER'S SON--Claims she has
the prophetic power.   She had seen a strange look about Mrs.
Wilcox for some time and sensed that she would die.   Her
son explains to her the emotion he had felt when he had seen
the coffin of Mrs. Wilcox.   (HE XI)

"MOUNT LEBANON"--1st published in The Listener (24 May
1951), p. 845; reprinted in Two Cheers for Democracy, 1951.

        The essay details Forster's visit to Mt. Lebanon, the
Shaker settlement, during his visit to the United States.
The Shaker settlement has almost died out today.   Mount
Lebanon in Massachusetts is one of the last.   The community has shrunk to one enormous house.   Forster found the
few remaining inmates "bone idle."   The simplicity of the
other empty buildings he found impressive but not interesting.   He and his party left soon after inspecting the buildings.   He concludes that the buildings are a symbol of something "America supposes herself to have missed."

"MR. ANDREWS"--1st published in Open Window II (1 April
1911), pp. 4-13; reprinted in The Eternal Moment and Other
Stories, 1928; The Collected Tales, 1947.

        Mr. Andrews, recently deceased, is traveling to
Heaven.   He hears a voice, that of a Turk who is a Moslem, asking to accompany him in order to make the journey
shorter.   Mr. Andrews agrees only to learn and be dis-
quieted by the knowledge that the man is "so godless, law-
less, cruel."   He is shocked that the Moslem should think
that he would be admitted to Heaven.   Nevertheless, he feels
pity for the Moslem and, rather than asking "can I enter"
when he reaches the gate of Heaven, he asks "can he enter."
The Moslem asks the same question.   A voice answers that
both can enter.   Mr. Andrews enters and sees disposed on
various mountains the gods worshiped on Earth.   Some are
fainting for want of incense no longer offered to them.
Heaven seems emptier than it ought despite the number of
souls always entering.   Mr. Andrews longs to see the Mos-

lem and comes upon him surrounded by the virgins promised
him.   He tells Mr. Andrews that, even with all his wishes
fulfilled, he is not happy.   Certainly, he is not as happy as
when he prayed that Mr. Andrews would enter Heaven.   Both
desire to leave Heaven and their wish is granted for their
expectations were fulfilled, but their hopes were not.

MR. BON'S DAUGHTER--She accompanies her father to tea
at the house of the boy who has seen the celestial omnibus.
(Collect Ta - Celest)

"MR. ELIOT'S COMEDY"--See: "Two Books by T. S. Eliot,
2:   The Cocktail Party"

"MR. AND MRS. ABBEY'S DIFFICULTIES"--1st published
in London Mercury, VI (May 1922), pp. 28-33; reprinted
in Abinger Harvest, 1936.

        Forster lists the "problems" Mr. Abbey had with his
wards, the Keats children and their legacy over which he
had been given control.

"MRS. GRUNDY AT THE PARKERS"--1st published in New
Statesman and Nation, N. S. (10 September 1932), pp. 284-
285; reprinted in Abinger Harvest, 1936.

        Mrs. Grundy visits the Parkers only to be told that
Mrs. Edith Parker has a headache.   Mrs. Grundy insists
on seeing her.   When Mrs. Parker appears, they discuss
Mrs. Grundy's methods of interfering with others.   Mrs.
Parker finds these methods dated, preferring her own which
do not suppress the pleasures of others, as do Mrs. Grundy's
methods, but rather tend to spoil those pleasures.   Mr.
Parker, who excels on committee work, joins them.   He is
particularly effective because he is able to make "respectability" the ideal.   He tells the ladies that a new idea is
sweeping in from the continent.   This idea has been the
cause of Mrs. Parker's headache.   People, he tells them,
are coming to pity the Grundys and the Parkers because they
feel that their interference into the lives of others is a
clear sign that the Grundys and the Parkers envy their happiness.   Mrs. Grundy tells them that she has met this idea
before and does not fear it.   After she leaves, the Parkers
discuss their fate.   They fear for the future if people join
against them.   There is only one hope.   Committees will
have to be formed and Mr. Parker will be on them.

"Mrs. Hannah More"--1st published in New Republic, XLV
(16 December 1925), pp. 106-109; reprinted in Nation and
Athenaeum (2 January 1926), pp. 493-494; Abinger Harvest,
1936.

[A review of The Letters of Hanna More, selected
with an introduction by R. Brimley Johnson.] Forster
speaks of his family's relationship to Hannah More, the
eighteenth century authoress of spiritual and moralistic
tracts. She was the godmother of his great-aunt (Marianne
Thornton, see: Marianne Thornton: A Domestic Biography).
He gives a picture of her life and concludes by saying that
her life "ended by thinking nearly everything sinful."

"MRS. MINIVER"--1st published as "Top Drawer But One"
in New Statesman and Nation, N. S. (4 November 1939), p.
648; reprinted as "Mrs. Miniver" in Two Cheers for Democracy, 1951.

[A review of Mrs. Miniver by Jan Struther.] Mrs.
Miniver, the gifted heroine, gives the reader a sense of his
own incompetence. She is never disconcerted. She is beyond doubt a lady, but she is not an aristocrat. She lacks,
despite all her accomplishments, some grace or "grandeur,"
some fierce "eccentricity." She has her own style, but she
lacks "style." She uses dinginess as a weapon, but it is a
dangerous one. She assumes that it will work in the social
sphere as effectively as it does in the humorous and the
moral. This is the trouble with Mrs. Miniver and with the
class to which she belongs, the class which destroyed the
aristocracy in the nineteenth century. It is the class of
tradesmen, professional men and little government officials.
It has never been able to build a home for itself. The working class has something the middle class does not have and
the aristocracy once had: spontaneity, natural gaiety, reck-
lessness. The working class, however, is slowly losing
these qualities. People may still go on studying the English
national character, but this study will not be important in
the future. Just as Gloucestershire and Kent have become
all alike, so will England, Germany, Russia and Japan.

MUDIE'S--The shop into which Mrs. Honeychurch and Lucy
go to buy a guide book to Greece. (RWV XIX)

MUGGINS--When Mrs. Moore speaks to Ronny of meeting a
young doctor (Aziz), he assumes that she is speaking of
young Muggins from over the Ganges. (PI III)

MUNT, MRS. JULEY--The aunt of Margaret, Helen, and Tibby Schlegel. She is a widow, the sister of the Schlegels's mother. She considers the Schlegel girls odd. She goes to Howards End to determine the depth of attachment Helen has for Paul Wilcox, and mistakes Charles for his brother and, to Margaret's consternation, tells him all. (HE II)

"MUSIC, VIOLETS, AND THE LETTERS"--Title of Chapter III, A Room with a View.

MUSINGS OF A PENSIONER--The title of a collection of essays Michael produces in his retirement from the British Museum. (Collect Ta - Point)

"MY ARRIVAL"--See: "Great Aunt 1879-1887, 1: My Arrival"

"MY OWN CENTENARY"--See: "Our Diversions, 7: My Own Centenary"

"MY RECOLLECTIONS"--See: Great Aunt 1879-1887, 3: My Recollections"

"MY WOOD"--1st published as "My Wood, On the Effects of Property Upon Character" in New Leader (15 October 1926), p. 3; reprinted as "My Wood" in Abinger Harvest, 1936.

Forster notes that with his American royalties on his "book which dealt in part with the difficulties of the English in India" [A Passage to India] he bought a wood. As a man of property for the first time, he meditates upon the effects of property upon its owner. He indicates that ownership "makes me feel heavy." Property produces "men of weight" making it difficult to "move about." Secondly, his own property "makes me feel it ought to be larger." Thirdly, property makes an owner feel that "he ought to do something to it." Yet "he isn't sure what." Finally, Forster's property makes him think of the blackberries which are easily seen and easily gathered. They attract the public to the point where he wonders whether or not the wood really belongs to him.

"MY WOOD, ON THE EFFECTS OF PROPERTY UPON CHARACTER"--See: "My Wood"

MYRA--The daugher of Mrs. Warrington Wilcox. She is

also the niece of Henry Wilcox and a guest at her cousin
Evie's wedding at Oniton. (HE XXV)

N

NAPOLEON--When he hears the many references made to
him in Miss Haddon's school he is pleased. From Heaven
he decrees that all should take part in his victory at Auster-
litz. (Collect - Co-ord)

NARRATOR, THE--The loss of his book overboard during a
boating party leads him to discover the story of Giuseppe
and his encounter with the Siren. The story is told to him
by the Sicilian boatman who rescues the book and turns out
to be the brother of Giuseppe. (Collect Ta - Siren)

NARRATOR'S AUNT, THE--Is aboard the boat when the narrator loses his book overboard. She wants the Sicilian to
be thanked for removing his clothes preparatory to diving,
but she also wants to have him told that "perhaps another
time" would be better for the search. (Collect Ta - Siren)

NAVVIES--Tear down the Schlegel home on Wickham Place.
They "split it back into the grey." They have muscles and
"beery" good tempers. "They were not the worst of under-
takers for a house which had always been human, and had
not mistaken culture for an end." (HE XXXI)

NAWAB BAHADUR, THE--He is old and bearded and the
richest Mohammedan landowner in the district. Though kindly disposed to the English, he believes that their high officials may sympathize with the plight of the Indians, it is
easy to do so at a distance. He values more, he notes,
"the kind word that is spoken close to my ear." He turns
against the British when Aziz is brought to trial. (PI IV)

NELLY--Col. Leyland's sister who writes rather apprehen-
sively to her brother to discover if he has become engaged
to Miss Raby. She also notes that a maid is not a good
chaperon for him and Miss Raby. (Collect Ta - Eternal)

"NEMI"--A short story by Rickie Elliot. Agnes Pembroke
in a letter to Mrs. Lewin speaks of it as a story which
concerns a Roman ship that "is actually sunk in some lake."
(LJ IX)

NEW DISORDER, THE"--1st published in <u>Horizon</u> (London),
IV (December 1941), pp. 379-384; reprinted as a pamphlet,
New York, 1949 (1st and only edition. No indication of
publisher.)

From the poet-writer's standpoint, the current talk
of a New Order is a "sheer waste of time." There never
will be a new order and there never was an old one. Order
is something evolved from within. It has never existed in
the social and political category. Viewed realistically, the
past is only a "series of messes." The League of Nations
promised a new order and it never came. It will not come
after the present war [W. W. II]. The source of the difficulty lies in the fact that we continue to make scientific discoveries and apply them and thus destroy the arrangements
made on more elementary discoveries. If only "science
would discover and never apply." That is, if men were
more deeply interested in knowledge than in action, mankind
would be in a safer position. For Forster, the best chance
for the future society lies through "apathy," "uninventive-
ness," "inertia." There appear to be only two possibilities
for order in the entire universe: the divine order, and the
aesthetic order--the order which an artist can create in his
own work. Art is the only material object in the universe
which may possess internal harmony. The artist legislates
through creating and he creates through his sensitiveness
and his power to impose form. Form is important today.
Form is not tradition. It is "the surface crust of the internal harmony." [See: "Art for Art's Sake." Many of the
points made in "The New Disorder" appear in it.]

NIECE OF MISS AVERY--Miss Avery's niece looks madly
about for the keys but Miss Avery does not tell her that she
has taken them up to Howards End. See: Madge (HE
XXIV)

"NINE GEMS OF UJJAIN, THE" --See: "Adrift in India, 1:
The Nine Gems of Ujjain"

"1939 STATE, THE"--See: "Post-Munich"

NORDIC TWILIGHT--1st edition, London, Macmillan and Co.,
Ltd., 10 September 1940, (Macmillan War Pamphlet #3)

A frank piece of propaganda in which Forster brands
the Nazis as destroyers of culture. As much as he longs
for peace, he cannot see how England can come to terms

with Hitler.   Hitler never keeps his word; he tolerates no
other way of looking at things saving his own.   A peace
which has the result of a Nazi victory would not differ much
from a Nazi war.   Germans would go on killing others until
no one who criticised them survived.   In the end, they might
secure world domination and produce a culture.   The imagination reels at the thought.   They have nothing to work with.
Their culture cannot be creative because creation is disin-
terested, passionate and understanding.

In this day when so many are fearful [1940], Forster
sees comfort in the fact that violence so far has never
worked.   Even when it conquers, it fails in the long run.
This failure may be due to Divine Will.   It may also be as-
cribed to the strange nature of man who refuses to live by
bread alone.   He alone among the animals has attempted to
understand his surroundings.   [The essay is similar to "Two
Cultures: The Quick and the Dead, What has Germany Done
to the Germans?"   See: "Culture and Freedom" and "What
Has Germany Done to the Germans?"]

NORMAN GIRL--She appears in the prologue.   She looks
back at the Saxon youth with whom she had been talking.   Her
backward glance is intended to symbolize the future union of
Norman and Saxon and the foundation of the future England.
(England's)

NORMAN KNIGHT, THE--He appears in the prologue, symbolizing the Norman conquest.   (England's)

"NOT LISTENING TO MUSIC"--1st published as "How to Listen to Music" in The Listener (19 January 1939), p. 173;
reprinted as "Not Listening to Music" in Two Cheers for Democracy, 1951.

Forster finds listening to music is such a "muddle"
that one scarcely knows how to begin to describe it.   Forster finds that he is not in attendance for the greater part
of every performance.   He "wool gathers" and is surprised
others do not.   He hears two types of music during those in-
tervals when he does attend: 1) music that reminds him of
something,   2) music itself.   He used to be very fond of the
first.   Yet he recognizes the danger of such music because
it opens the door to the "imp" of the concert hall: inattention.   Consequently, Forster prefers "music itself."   Music
untrammelled and untainted by reference is obviously the
best sort of music to listen to.   Forster's own performances

upon the piano grow worse yearly, but he will never give
them up; they help him not to "wool gather."

"NOT LOOKING AT ART"--See: "Not Looking at Pictures"

"NOT LOOKING AT PICTURES"--1st published as "Not Looking at Art" in New Statesman and Nation, N. S. (15 July
1939), pp. 82-83; reprinted as "Not Looking at Pictures" in
Two Cheers for Democracy, 1951.

     Forster maintains that pictures are not easy to look
at; he admits to be "bad at looking at pictures." Roger Fry
enjoyed going to a gallery with him because he found it a-
musing to be with someone who scarcely ever saw what a
painter painted. Long years of wandering down miles of
galleries have convinced Forster that there must be something rare in pictures, something which he is incapable of
detecting for himself. One of the things which helps us to
keep looking is composition usually, in the form of diago-
nals. Unfortunately, if none appear, Forster feels that the
composition is at fault. Besides composition, the viewer
must deal with color. Forster admits that he has less success with color than with composition. On the whole, however, he is improving. He is a little more receptive. If
he can make progress, so too, he believes, can the outsider with courage and modesty.

"NOTE ON A PASSAGE TO INDIA"--See: "Letters of 1921:
Note on A Passage to India"

"NOTE ON THE WAY, A"--Originally a portion of "Notes
on the Way," Time and Tide (2, 9, 16, 23 June 1934). The
second contribution (9 June 1939), pp. 723-724 was reprinted
as "A Note on the Way" in Abinger Harvest, 1936.

     Forster discusses the sustaining quality of art, espe-
cially literature and its ability to "prop the mind" like the
work of A. E. Houseman which "because he is not writing
about us . . . can give us calm."

"NOTES ON THE ENGLISH CHARACTER"--1st published in
The Atlantic Monthly, CXXXVII (January 1936), pp. 30-37;
reprinted in Abinger Harvest, 1936.

     The English character is essentially incomplete as
are all national characters. But the English character is
incomplete in a way that is annoying to the foreign observer.

It has a bad surface--self-complacent, unsympathetic, and reserved. The Englishman is slow to give vent to his emotions. His brain power, which is abundant, is used to confirm prejudices rather than to dispel them. With such equipment, he cannot be popular. Nevertheless, there is little vice in him and no real coldness. It is the machinery which is wrong. John Bull with his top hat and his comfortable clothes, his substantial stomach and his substantial bank account is the perfect national figure. He is essentially middle class.

"NOTES ON THE WAY"--See: "A Note on the Way:" "Racial Exercise;" "Does Culture Matter?"

"NOVELS OF VIRGINIA WOOLF, THE"--See: "The Early Novels of Virginia Woolf"

NURREDIN--See: The elegant grandson of the Nawab Bahadur (PI VIII)

NURREDIN'S MOTHER--Pays a visit to Hammidulah's wife who proposes to Aziz that he and Hammidulah go behind purdah to meet them. Out of the meeting comes a discussion of the proposal made by the women during Aziz's trial to leave purdah as a protest. The proposal was never carried through. (PI XXX)

NURSE, THE--Tells Adam he is being nasty to his father, Michael who is dying, by saying that he will be forgotten and someone else will be knighted. (Collect Ta - Point)

O

"OBJECTS, THE"--See: "For the Museum's Sake"

OLD GENTLEMAN WITH A BEARD--See: The Nawab Bahadur (PI IV)

OLD MAN WITH WHITE WHISKERS, AN--Miss Lavish chases after him leaving Lucy Honeychurch unchaperoned in the square of Santa Croce. (RWV II)

OLD WITCH, AN--She prophesied that Giuseppe and the girl, Maria, had silent devils who could do little harm. She insisted, however, that their child would always be speaking and laughing and perverting and, last of all, he would go into the sea and fetch up into the air the Siren and all would hear and see her sing.   (Collect Ta - Siren)

OLD WOMAN--See: Maria Rhomaides   (Collect Ta - Road)

OLD WOMAN--See: Miss Avery (HE XXII)

"ON CRITICISM IN THE ARTS, ESPECIALLY MUSIC"--See: "The Raison D'Être of Criticism in the Arts"

"ON THE MEANING OF A MAN'S BOOKS: E. M. FORSTER, LOOKING OVER HIS LIBRARY FINDS OLD FRIENDS AND SOME STRANGERS"--See: "In My Library"

"ON TOUR"--See: "Letters of 1921: On Tour"

ONE OF A GANG OF PATHANS--Cecil Fielding suggests to Adela Quested that the individual who had tried to assault her in the cave was, perhaps, one of a gang of Pathans who were in the district at the time.   (PI XXVI)

ONITON GRANGE--See: The Grange (HE XV)

ORR, MISS--Herbert Pembroke proposes to Miss Orr two days after the Headmaster tells him that the master of Dunwood House should be married.   Herbert wants the mastership, hence the proposal.   Miss Orr is quiet, clever, kindly, capable and amusing.   She and Herbert were old acquaintances.   She refuses his proposal.   (LJ XVI)

OSGOOD, MRS.--A house guest of Mrs. Worters.   (Collect Ta - Other)

"OTHER KINGDOM"--1st published in English Review, II (July 1909), pp. 651-672; reprinted in Living Age, CCLXII (28 August 1909), pp. 547-567; The Celestial Omnibus and Other Stories, 1911; The Collected Tales, 1947. [A short story.]

Mrs. Worters, Evelyn Beaumont, and Jack Ford are being tutored in Latin by Mr. Inskip, the narrator.   Their discussion of the value of learning Latin is interrupted by Mrs. Worters's son, Harcourt, who tells them that he has bought a copse, "Other Kingdom."   They are overjoyed at the news.   He presents the copse to his fiancee, Evelyn. Tea arrives and a suggestion is made that the party should have tea in Evelyn's wood.   Evelyn leads the party in.   She

commands them to sing the line from Virgil that they had
construed earlier in the day: "Ah, you silly ass gods live
in the woods."

After tea, the group makes its departure. Harcourt
and Inskip draw apart and Harcourt asks him about Evelyn's
progress noting that, in many ways, she is practically a
child. Harcourt wonders if she ought not to turn to English
Literature since Latin is rather a luxury when she knows so
little. They agree to call a halt to the Latin lessons. When
Evelyn joins them, Harcourt suggests that Other Kingdom be
fenced in and a path through it made. She objects. Despite
her objection, Harcourt has the path made. Eventually,
Evelyn agrees to it and to the fence and the bridge he wants.

Meanwhile, Jack Ford, Harcourt's Ward, has written
something in his book which pokes fun at his guardian which
Harcourt inadvertently reads. Inskip tells Ford that he
should apologize. Evelyn, overhearing their conversation,
insists that Harcourt would not want an apology. She sees
Harcourt as he is supervising the workmen building the
bridge. In her exuberance and belief that Harcourt would
laugh the matter away, she is totally unprepared for the response she receives. Agitated, she falls into the water and
is hurried off to bed. Ford is sent away.

After his departure, the winds begin to blow so
fiercely that no one is able to leave the house. Evelyn tells
Harcourt that, while she remains in the house, the winds
will not cease to blow. One day, after luncheon, she insists that they all go to the copse. She changes her dress
for the green one and is radiantly happy. She sings a song
about Ford's love for her and dances about. Harcourt tries
to catch her, but she eludes him. Everyone thinks her lost
in the woods. Harcourt grows angry. Suddenly, the wind
rises and a violent storm breaks. Later, the Archdeacon
confides in Inskip his belief that Evelyn, who has not been
found, has eloped with Ford. Harcourt, enraged, goes to
Ford's lodgings hoping to surprise the two, only to discover
that Evelyn is not and never was there.

"OTHER SIDE OF THE HEDGE, THE"--1st published in
The Celestial Omnibus and Other Stories, 1911; reprinted in
The Collected Tales, 1947. [A short story.]

The narrator is traveling on a road. He is overcome with weariness and rests. Others pass him by as he

has passed others by including his brother. A puff of air
revives him. It seems to come from a nearby hedge. Step-
ping through, he falls into a body of water and is rescued
by an old man who has the voice of an eighteen year old.
He learns from the old man that one goes nowhere in this
landscape unlike the progression those of the "road" take for
granted. The narrator wants to leave this land, but his
wish is denied. Finally, he manages to escape and finds
himself once again on the road. He is thirsty and asks one
of the travelers for a drink. The traveler, who gives him
some beer, he discovers is the brother he had left behind.

OTWAY, SIR HARRY--A friend of Miss Lavish and a neighbor of the Honeychurches. Miss Lavish claims that he is a
radical like herself. He buys the villas, Cissie and Albert,
and rents Cissie to the Emersons.   (RWV II)

"OUR BUTTERFLIES AND BEETLES"--See: "Ronald Firbank"

"OUR CURIOSITY AND DESPAIR"--See: "Proust"

"OUR DEPUTATION"--1st published as "Comment and Dream:
On a Deputation" in New Statesman and Nation, N. S. (14
January 1939), reprinted as "Our Deputation" in Two Cheers
for Democracy, 1951.

     A description of an official visit to a government
ministry and an analysis of the "technique . . . employed
by those in high authority." Forster reflects on this technique and sums it up thusly: "they begin a sentence deeply,
gruffly, gently; it moves along like a large friendly animal;
then it twitters, turns acid and thin and passes right over-
head with a sort of whistling sound."

"OUR DIVERSIONS"

     1.   The Scallies--1st published as "Our Diversions,
[3]: The Scallies" in Egyptian Mail (18 November 1917),
p. 2; reprinted as "Our Diversions, 1: The Scallies" in
Abinger Harvest, 1936.

     Forster describes a performance presented by the
Scallies ("they were the Scallies, the black and white Scallies") in Alexandria during the First World War. The only
consolation they could give to the men in uniform was that
they were all British.

2. The Birth of an Empire--1st published as "The Birth of an Empire in Nation and Athenaeum (26 April 1924), pp. 110-11; reprinted as "Our Diversions, 2: The Birth of an Empire" in Abinger Harvest, 1936.

Forster describes the British Exhibition at Wembly. He concludes that it is a place where millions will spend money, hundreds will make money, and a few highbrows, like himself, will make fun.

3. The Doll Souse [sic]--1st published as "The Bad Fairies" in Nation and Athenaeum (2 August 1924), pp. 562-563; reprinted as "Our Diversions, 3: The Doll Souse" in Abinger Harvest, 1936.

A detailing of Forster's visit to Queen Mary's dolls's house at the British Empire Exhibition at Wembley. He finds it the "apotheosis of non-being."

4. Mickey and Minnie--1st published as "Mickey and Minnie," in Spectator (19 January 1934), pp. 81-82; reprinted as "Our Diversions, 4: Mickey and Minnie" in Abinger Harvest, 1936.

A hard look at Walt Disney's animated cartoon characters Mickey and Minnie Mouse. Forster maintains that he is a "film-fanned rather than a film-fan." Once a "fortnight" [two weeks], he attends performances. Forster finds Mickey "energetic without being elevating," and one "of the world's great lovers." Minnie is "simple, tender, brave and strong" and Mickey is her "Rajah, her Sun."

5. Chess at Cracow--1st published in Time and Tide (13 August 1932), pp. 885-886; reprinted as "Our Diversions, 5: Chess at Cracow" in Abinger Harvest, 1936.

Forster describes a chess game played with living people as chessmen in Cracow, Poland.

6. The Game of Life--1st published in Athenaeum (27 June 1919), pp. 517-518; reprinted as "Our Diversions, 6: The Game of Life" in Abinger Harvest, 1936.

Forster muses on life understanding it as a "game" in which "fate" is the umpire and "Hope" is the "ball." He concludes that life is "Piquet"--a "grim relaxation."

    7.   My Own Centenary--1st published as "My Cen-
tenary: Or Why Not?" in Nation and Athenaeum (1 October
1927), pp. 835-836; reprinted as "Our Diversions, 7: My
Own Centenary" in Abinger Harvest, 1936.

    Forster humorously notes that a statue will be
erected to his memory on his centenary. He will be shown
chasing a butterfly.

"OUR GRAVES IN GALLIPOLI"--1st published as "Our
Graves in Gallipoli: A Dialogue" in New Leader (20 Oc-
tober 1922), p. 8; reprinted as "Our Graves in Gallipoli" in
Abinger Harvest, 1936.

    Two English graves in Gallipoli speak. They talk of
the new interest [1922] in "protecting our graves in Gallipoli," and of the reasons given for war. They close their
dialogue with a question: why cannot men learn that "all
graves are one?"

"OUR GRAVES IN GALLIPOLI: A DIALOGUE"--See: "Our
Graves in Gallipoli"

"OUR PHOTOGRAPHY: SINCLAIR LEWIS"--See: "Sinclair
Lewis"

"OUR SECOND GREATEST NOVEL?"--1st published as "The
Second Greatest Novel?" in The Listener (18 April 1943),
pp. 454-455; reprinted as "Our Second Greatest Novel" in
Two Cheers for Democracy, 1951.

    [A Broadcast Talk in the BBC's Indian Service.]
Forster proposes Proust's À La Recherche du Temps Perdu
as the second greatest novel that Western Civilization has
produced. He considers that War and Peace is the greatest.
Proust's novel is not as warm-hearted or as heroic or as
great as War and Peace, but it is superior as an artistic
achievement for four reasons: 1) The hero is, more or less,
Proust himself; 2) it is not concerned with events and
people as Tolstoy's book is, but with memories of events and
people which result in a "daydream-like" quality; 3) the
brilliant depiction of a social scene: the French aristocracy;
4) Proust is a "master drawer of character;" 5) Proust's
theory of love: it is "gloomy."

"OUTSIDER ON POETRY, AN"--1st published in The Listener
(28 April 1949), p. 228; reprinted in Two Cheers for Democ-

racy, 1951.

[A review of Poetry of the Present compiled and introduced by Geoffrey Grigson.] Forster maintains that the
outsider is often ill-equipped to judge modern poetry because such poetry demands unaided opinion. The present
indifference to poetry is part of the general menace to literature. The modern poet often reflects through his poetry
a discomfort with the universe. When reading the modern
poet, it is desirable to be good tempered.

P

PAN PIPES--The title of a collection of short stories by
Rickie which was rejected by the publishers to which it was
sent. See: "Andante Pastorale" (LJ XV)

PARKER, EDITH--The wifely half of the Nosey Parkers on
whom Mrs. Grundy calls. She is clear in her criticism of
Mrs. Grundy's methods which are, she notes, based on the
mistake of "trying to suppress people's pleasures." She,
on the other hand, obviously not "nineteenth century," tries
to "spoil their pleasure." (AH - Mrs. G)

PARKER, NOSEY--Was scarcely equal to his wife and Mrs.
Grundy as a field worker. He was, however, excellent in
committees without being obtrusive, he managed to generate
that official uneasiness upon which all their work depended.
He raises the banner of respectability and calls it idealism.
He tells the ladies that they have become the objects of pity
because people believe that their efforts to improve them
are based on their envy of others. (AH - Mrs. G)

PARLOUR-MAID, A--Precedes some callers who are coming out of the house to where Henry Wilcox and Margaret
are in the castle meadow. The "unpunctual guests" turn out
to be Helen and Mr. and Mrs. Leonard Bast. (HE XXVI)

PARLOUR-MAID, THE--Tells Stephen, who has leanred that
he is Rickie's half-brother and has come to Dunwood House,
that Mrs. Elliot will see him. (LJ XXVI)

PARSIVAL--The name of Mrs. Lewin's dove. Her discuss-
ing its fate helps to overcome the awkward situation created
by Rickie's announcement that he is to marry Agnes Pembroke. (LJ VIII)

PASSAGE TO INDIA, A--1st edition, London, Edward Arnold
and Co., 4 June 1924; 1st American edition, New York, Harcourt, Brace and Company, 14 August 1924.

Dr. Aziz, returning from the house of the Civil Surgeon to which he was summoned in the midst of a dinner
party and learning that the official had gone to his club without leaving a message for him, sets out on foot to Chandrapore and his home. He stops at a mosque on the way and
there meets an Englishwoman, Mrs. Moore. At first he is
angry believing that she had entered with her shoes on.
When he perceives that she is shoeless, he is mollified. He
engages her in conversation. Mrs. Moore has newly come
from England to visit her son by her first marriage, Ronald
Heaslop, the City Magistrate. Aziz accompanies her back
to the club which he cannot enter because he is an Indian.
She has become his friend.

Adela Quested, who had come to India with Mrs.
Moore and Heaslop's prospective fiancée, declares at the
club that she wants to see the "real India," not the India
which comes through the protection of the British Colony.
To please her and Mrs. Moore, someone proposes to hold
a "bridge" party and to invite some natives for the ladies to
meet. The party is a failure. Something good comes of it,
however. Cecil Fielding, the Principal of the small Government College invites Miss Quested and Mrs. Moore to tea.
He also invites Dr. Aziz and Prof. Godbole, an instructor
at the school. The tea is a success until Ronny Heaslop
comes to call for the ladies. Fielding had taken Mrs.
Moore on a tour of the school leaving Aziz and Miss Quested alone with Godbole. Heaslop is furious. Annoyed by
his attitude, she tells him she does not wish to become his
wife. She changes her mind before the evening is over when
she and Heaslop take a drive in the Indian countryside.

Mrs. Moore and Miss Quested accept Aziz's offer to
conduct them to the district's one natural attraction: the
Marabar Caves some several miles outside of the city. The
visit is a disaster. Mrs. Moore senses from the booming,
hollow echo she hears in one of the caves that there is no
meaning to life. Miss Quested enters one of the caves alone.
Moments later she rushes out in terror claiming that she
had been nearly attacked by Dr. Aziz. He is arrested.

The trial of Dr. Aziz sharpens the division between
the Anglo-Indians and the natives. When Mrs. Moore main-

tains that Aziz could not have attempted to attack Adela
Quested, her son, Ronny, sends her home to England.
Fielding, who is of the same opinion, is ostracized at the
club.

Word goes about during the trial that Mrs. Moore
had been smuggled out of the country because she had information which could clear Aziz.   The natives, when they
hear her name, work it into a chant as though she were a
deity.   "Esmiss Esmoor," they chant.   Adela, who reacted
to the chanting of Mrs. Moore's name as if she were in a
trance, relives the whole of the crucial day.   Under the
questioning of the prosecuting attorney, she recollects each
moment until the moment of her lingering the the cave.   She
falters.   Suddenly, she withdraws all charges.

Chandrapore erupts into bedlam on the news of
Aziz's acquittal.   Anglo-Indians are downcast while the natives
are jubilant.   Heaslop will have nothing more to do with
Adela.   She accepts Fielding's hospitality for several weeks,
then returns home.   Aziz wants to press Adela for legal
damages, but Fielding persuades him not to.

Two years later, Aziz, a Moslem, is physician to the
Rajah of Mau who dies on the night of the feast of the birth
of the god Krishna.   Fielding arrives with his wife and
brother-in-law on an inspection tour of educational facilities.
Aziz thinks he has married his enemy, Adela.   He learns
that Fielding has married Mrs. Moore's daughter, Stella.
Before they part for the last time, Aziz and Fielding go out
riding.   Though the difficulties between them have come to
an end, they realize that the differences between them divide
them forever.   That their affection for each other, though
sincere, cannot bridge the gap between their races.

PASSENGERS, THE--They are aboard the airship.   They
call out angrily to the female attendant, "Are we to travel
in the dark?"   (Collect Ta - Machine)

"PATTERN AND RHYTHM"--The title of Chapter VIII, Aspects of the Novel.   For summary see: Aspects of the
Novel.

PEMBROKE, AGNES--An old friend of Rickie Elliot.   After
the death of her fiancée, Gerald Dawes, she marries Rickie.
At first she encourages him in his writing but, gradually,
forces him into a dull, conventional life at Sawston School.

When she learns that Stephen Wonham is Rickie's half-brother, she tries to alienate him from Aunt Emily and her husband. She and Rickie have a daughter who is as deformed as her father. The child dies. (LJ I)

PEMBROKE, HERBERT--An old friend of Rickie Elliot and brother of Agnes. He was nearly twenty years her senior. Though not a cleric, he had, nevertheless, the air of being on the verge of orders. His features as well as his clothing had the clerical cut. He was master of a form in the Sawston School and a born organizer. Eventually he becomes master of Dunwood House. (LJ I)

PEMBROKE, MR. --In attempting to point out the value of work to her brother, Tibby, Margaret notes that Mr. Pembroke is an example of one who, despite his defects of temper and understanding, gives her more pleasure than many who are better equipped, solely because he has worked regularly and honestly. (HE XIII)

PENNY--An old man. The Wilcox gardener. Crane, the chauffeur, tells Charles when Charles questions him that Penny had driven the Wilcox car. (HE XI)

PENSIONE BERTOLINI--The hotel on the Arno in which Lucy Honeychurch and Charlotte Bartlett have rooms during their stay in Florence. Through some mistake, they learn, when they arrive, that they have not been given the room with a view for which they had written. (RWV I)

"PEOPLE"--Title of Chapter II, Aspects of the Novel. For summary see: Aspects of the Novel.

"PEOPLE (CONTINUED)"--Title of Chapter IV, Aspects of the Novel. For summary see: Aspects of the Novel.

PERFETTA--A widowed cousin of Gino Carella. She was too humble for social aspirations. She lives with Gino and Lila as "factotum." Gino tells Lila that Perfetta is to go with her whenever she leaves the house. (WAFT III)

PERSEPHONE--See: Phaethon (RWV VI)

PHAETHON--Is the name the narrator gives to the driver of the coach which takes the party from the Pensione Bertolini into the hills of Florence to Fiesole. He begs leave of the party to pick up "Persephone" on the way telling them that

she is his sister. (RWV VI) [In classical myth, Phaeton
was the son of Phoebus (the sun). He drove his father's
chariot and could not control the horses causing Libya to be
parched and the inhabitants of Africa, blackened. He would
have set the world on fire had Zeus not stopped him with a
thunder bolt. Persephone, in classical myth, is the wife of
the god of the underworld, Hades. He surprised her one
day while she was gathering flowers and carried her away to
his kingdom. Demeter, her mother, tried to secure her
freedom, but had to be content with seeing her only half of
the year.]

"PHAROS"--Title of an essay in Pharos and Pharillon.

PHAROS AND PHARILLON--1st edition, Richmond, Surrey,
England, Hogarth Press, 15 May 1923; 1st American edition,
New York, Alfred A. Knopf, 20 July 1923.

The volume is divided into two sections: "Pharos"
and "Pharillon." "Pharos" includes the following" "Pharos,"
"The Return from Siwa," "Epiphany," "Philo's Little
Trip," "Clement of Alexandria," "St. Athanasius," "Timothy the Cat and Timothy Whitebonnet," and "The God Abandons Anthony." "Pharillon" includes: "Liza in Egypt,"
"Cotton from the Outside," "Between the Sun and the Moon,"
and "The Poetry of C. P. Cavafy."

The essays in "Pharos" treat of Alexandria in its
pre-Moslem days and "Pharillon" discusses the city after
the Moslem conquest to the present.

I.   "PHAROS"

"Pharos"--1st published, Athenaeum (28 November;
5, 12 December 1919), pp. 1250-1251; 1282-1283; 1330-1331;
reprinted in Pharos and Pharillon, 1923. The essay describes the early legendary history of the island, Pharos,
the building of the lighthouse ("[it] was made of local lime-
stone, of marble, and of reddish-purple granite from As-
souan"), how it functioned, and its eventual neglect after the
Moslems captured Alexandria.

"The Return from Siwa"--1st published as "Alexandria Vignettes: The Return from Siwa" Egyptian Mail
(14 July 1918), p. 2; reprinted as "The Return from Siwa"
in Pharos and Pharillon, 1923. A detailing of the founding
of Alexandria by Alexander the Great and planned by his

architect, Dinocrates.

"Epiphany"--1st published as "Alexandria Vignettes:
Epiphany (B. C. 204)" in Egyipitan Mail (6 October 1918), p.
2; reprinted as "Epiphany" in Pharos and Pharillon, 1923.
A discussion of the accession of Ptolemy V, Epiphanes
(B. C. 204) to the throne of Egypt, which includes a detailing of the intrigues of Agathocles, his father's Prime Min-
ister, and Agathoclea, his nurse, who tried to keep the news
of his father's death secret so that they might rule in his
name.

"Philo's Little Trip"--1st published probably in The
Egyptian Mail between 1916-1918; reprinted in Pharos and
Pharillon, 1923.   Describes a deputation of six Jews led by
Philo from Alexandria to Rome and the court of Caligula for
the purpose of relieving the Jews of Alexandria from wor-
ship of Caligula as a god.   They were successful.

"Clement of Alexandria"--1st published: Athenaeum
(1 August 1919), pp. 713-714.   A review of Clement of Alexandria, with an English translation by G. W. Butterworth;
reprinted in Pharos and Pharillon, 1923.   A short life of
Clement of Alexandria, (born in Greece c. 150 A. D.), who
became head of the theological college in Alexandria.   Forster notes that, in his writings, he may have attacked pa-
ganism but he never denounced it.   He showed his "respect
for the existing fabric" and hoped that it would pass "without catastrophe from Pagan to Christian. "   But his hopes
were to come to nought.   Christianity "hacked the ancient
world to pieces. "

"St. Athanasius" -

Part I - 1st published as "Alexandria Vignettes:
Lunch at the Bishop's (A. D. 310)" in Egyptian Mail (31 July
1918), p. 2; reprinted as "St. Athanasius (Part I)" in Pharos and Pharillon, 1923.   Details the finding of Athansius
who was to become Patriarch of Alexandria and finally a
saint of the Church playing, as a child, at baptism on the
beach of Alexandria.   The play was witnessed by the then
Patriarch who took the boy into his home, made him his pu-
pil, his deacon, his coadjutor, his successor in the see,
and finally a saint and doctor of the Church.

Part II--1st published in Athenaeum (9 May 1919), p.
6; reprinted in Pharos and Pharillon, 1923.   Details the

struggle between Athanasius and Arius over the Arian here-
sy which held that Christ was younger than God.   Athanasius
saw "that while it popularized Christ it isolated God, and
raised man no nearer to heaven in the long run."

"Timothy the Cat and Timothy Whitebonnet"--1st pub-
lished as "Timothy Whitebonnet and Timothy the Cat" in
Athenaeum (25 July 1919), pp. 646-647; reprinted in Living
Age, CCCII (6 September 1919), pp. 594-595; reprinted as
"Timothy the Cat and Timothy Whitebonnet" in Pharos and
Pharillon, 1923.   Discusses the theological struggles among
the Monophysites, Arians, Nestorians, Manichaeists, and
Donatists for control of the Patriarchate of Alexandria which
resulted in the murder of the Patriarch Proterius who was
supported by the Greeks, and the installation of Timothy
"the Cat."   "The Cat" was eventually deposed and Timothy
Whitebonnet (so called because of the headgear he wore) was
dragged from Canopus and consecrated in his place.   When
Basiliscus ascended the throne of the Caesars, Whitebonnet
was expelled and the Cat ruled again.   When Zeno became
emperor, the Cat was driven out and . . . Here Forster
breaks off to note that the controversy continued for centuries.   The Cops still hold to the single nature of Christ
while the remainder of Christendom believe in the double
Nature.   He closes by noting that all the great structures of
Alexandria are gone, but ideas still live.

"The God Abandons Anthony"--See: below, "The Poetry of C. P. Cavafy"

II.   PHARILLON -

"Eliza in Egypt"--1st published probably in The Egyp-
tian Mail between 1916 and 1919; reprinted in Pharos and
Pharillon, 1923.   Forster edited and wrote an introduction
for Original Letters from India (1779-1815) by Mrs. Eliza
Fay, London, 1925.   Part of this volume covers the materi-
al treated in the essay.   Forster details the adventures of
Mrs. Fay, her husband and their party on their trip through
Alexandria and Egypt.   Despite the dangers and "fatigues,"
Mrs. Fay bore all like a "lion."

"Cotton from the Outside"--1st published as "Alexandria Vignettes: Cotton from the Outside," Egyptian Mail
(3 February 1918), p. 2; reprinted as "Cotton from the Outside," in Pharos and Pharillon, 1923.   Forster describes a
visit to the Alexandrian cotton exchange.   The din makes

him think that someone has been killed.   What he sees reminds him of Dante's Inferno.   He then describes a visit to
Minet el Bassal where the cotton is sold on sample.   Here
there is relative peace.   But the peace is soon shattered
when he witnesses the cotton being baled.

"The Den"--1st published in Egyptian Mail (30 December 1917), p. 2; reprinted in Pharos and Pharillon, 1923.
Forster was desirous of visiting an opium den and accompanies the police of Alexandria on a "raid." He and the police were disappointed in their expectations.   Forster concludes that drugs are just not being smoked.

"The Solitary Place"--1st published as "Alexandria
Vignettes: The Solitary Place" in Egyptian Mail (10 March
1918), p. 2; reprinted as "The Solitary Place" in Pharos and
Pharillon, 1923.   Forster talks of the countryside that
"stretches westward from the expiring waters of Lake Mari-
out" which he finds difficult to describe.   Once the location
of monasteries, the land seems desolate.   There is nothing
there of "the ordered progress of the English spring."   Yet
there is the "quiet persistence of the earth" which impresses
him.

"Between the Sun and the Moon"--Probably published
first in The Egyptian Mail between 1916 and 1919; reprinted
in Pharos and Pharillon, 1923.   Forster describes the modern Alexandria noting that undoubtedly the Rue Rosette is the
most fashionable.   In ancient days it was called the Canopic
Road and was not genteel nor smart but presented "along its
length scenes of extraordinary splendour."   Legend has it
that the body of Alexander the Great lies beneath the Mosque
of Nebi Daniel.   Very little else remains of the ancient city.

"The Poetry of C. P. Cavafy"--1st published in
Athenaeum (25 April 1919), pp. 247-248.   N. B.   The article
included a translation into English of Cavafy's poem "The
God Abandons Anthony" translated by G. Vassopoulo, reprinted in Pharos and Pharillon, 1923.   "The God Abandons
Anthony" was detached from the essay and printed between
the "Pharos" and the "Pharillon" sections.   Forster finds
that Cavafy can never be "popular" because he "flies both
too slowly and too high."   He has the "strength (and of
course the limitations) of the recluse."   One mood of Cavafy
he finds "intensely subjective" and another "he stands apart
from his subject matter."

"Conclusion"--Forster notes that a serious history of Alexandria is yet to be written. He hopes that his essays have indicated "how varied, how impressive, such a history might be." Unfortunately, he finds little interesting in the modern city whose "material prosperity seems assured."

"PHILO'S LITTLE TRIP"--See: Pharos and Pharillon

PLACE--Section title in Part II, Two Cheers for Democracy.

"PLOT, THE"--Title of Chapter IV, Aspects of the Novel. For summary see: Aspects of the Novel.

PLYNLIMMON, MRS. --An Anglo-Indian lady who attends Evie Wilcox's wedding at Oniton. She is one of those women who prefer influence to rights. "The woman who can't influence her husband to vote the way she wants ought to be ashamed of herself," she declares. (HE XXV)

POACHER, A--Appears in Act I, Sc. iii. He is brought in by the keeper for poaching a rabbit on Squire George's land. The Squire orders him to trial despite the pleas of the villagers. (England's)

"POETRY OF C. P. CAVAFY, THE"--See: Pharos and Pharillon.

"POINT OF IT, THE"--1st published in The English Review, IX (November 1911), pp. 615-630; reprinted in The Eternal Moment and Other Stories, 1928; The Collected Tales, 1947.

[A short story.] Harold, an invalid, is sent to a farm to recuperate, but dies from overexertion when his friend, Micky, insists that he row harder so that they will not be late for dinner.

As he grows older, Micky, now called Michael, forgets about the incident except for Harold's words: "The point of it . . ." and goes about the business of his life. He marries Janet who believes in truth as he believes in love. They have three children and he works in the British Museum. He writes several books and is knighted. His children grow up and marry. His wife dies. He has trouble with his youngest son. He is knighted and then dies. After death, he awakens and looks at the sky thinking he could live here forever. He learns that he is in the "Heaven of the soft," and Janet is in the "Heaven of the hard."

He reviews his life: "my books forgotten; my work super-
seded. " He dies a second death and returns to the scene of
the accident which opened the story; he hears a voice say
"the point of it . . ." A weight falls from his body and he
crosses mid-stream.

"POINT OF VIEW OF THE CREATIVE ARTIST, THE"--See:
"The Challenge of Our Time"

POLE, MISS--A guest at the Pensione Bertolini. Miss Lavish tells her of her new novel. It is to be about modern
Italy. (RWV III)

POLICEMAN, A NATIVE--During the trial of Aziz, the
court is thrown into chaos when an Indian shouts out that
Adela Quested is "so uglier than Aziz" implying for that reason he could not be guilty of attempting to rape her. A native policeman, in an attempt to quell the disorder, turns
out an innocent bystander roughly. (PI XXIV)

"PONDICHERRY"--See: "Catastrophe: Pondicherry"

PORGLY-WOGGLES--The affectionate name Dolly Wilcox
gives to one of her children. (HE XXIII)

PORPHYRION FIRE INSURANCE COMPANY--The company
which Leonard Bast is a clerk. On Henry Wilcox's advice,
he leaves his position. (HE XIV)

PORTER, A--A young, handsome Italian who declared his
love for Miss Raby. Now, years later, he is the Concièrge
at the Hôtel des Grandes Alpes, the hotel owned by the son
of Signora Cantû. She claims that the Concièrge is the center of the plot to ruin her hotel. (Collect Ta - Eternal)

PORTER, A--Philip Herriton's porter at Monteriano put him
"out-of-sorts" with Italy. Instead of carrying Philip's bag,
he "ran up the line playing touch-you-last with the guard. "
(WAFT II)

PORTER, A BEARDED--Brings a parcel for Paul Wilcox to
his brother, Charles, who is about to leave the railroad station with Aunt Juley for Howards End. Charles is angered
when he is asked to sign for it. His anger is increased
when the porter has no pencil and threatens to report him to
the stationmaster. Nevertheless, as he leaves, he gives the
porter a tip. (HE III)

"POSSIBILITIES OF A PLEASANT OUTING"--Title of Chapter V, A Room with a View.

"POST-MUNICH"--1st published as "The 1939 State" in New Statesman and Nation, N. S. (10 June 1934), pp. 888-889; reprinted as "Post-Munich" in Two Cheers for Democracy, 1951.

English people today [1939] are in the state of being "half-frightened and half-thinking about something else at the same time." It is a "1939 State." The best must be made of the equivocal situation produced by the Munich agreement. Those who have money should start spending because spending settles the nerves and one should spend as if "civilization is permanent." He urges his readers to buy books, and to go to concerts and plays.

POWELL--The Honeychurch gardener who has to drive Cecil Vyse to the railway station. (RWV XVIII)

PRANK, JOSEPH EMERY--The pen name of Miss Lavish. (RWV XV)

"PRIDE OF MR. CONRAD, THE"--See: "Joseph Conrad: A Note"

PRINCIPAL, THE--She is in charge of the school in which Miss Haddon works. It is she who decrees that the curricula should be "co-ordinated." (Collect - Co-ord)

"PROLOGUE"--Section title in England's Pleasant Land. For summary see: England's Pleasant Land.

"PROPHECY"--Title of Chapter VII, Aspects of the Novel. For summary see: Aspects of the Novel.

PROPRIETORS OF THE LIVERY STABLE, THE--Tell Henry Wilcox that Helen Schlegel has arrived and taken a fly [a type of carriage] to Howards End. (HE XXXV)

"PROUST"--1st published as "Our Curiosity and Despair" in New York Herald Tribune, Section 11, Books (21 April 1929), pp. 1, 6; reprinted as "The Epic of Curiosity and Despair" in Nation and Athenaeum (27 April, 4 May 1929), pp. 107-108; 158; reprinted as "Proust" in Abinger Harvest, 1936. [A review of A la Recherche du Temps Perdus in 2 vols. by Marcel Proust, translated into English by C. K. Scott Moncrieff; and Proust by Clive Bell.]

Forster maintains that Proust is as difficult in English as he is in French. His novel, À la Recherche du Temps Perdus, is ten times as long as an ordinary novel. It is an epic of curiosity and despair. His general theory of human intercourse is that the fonder we are of people, the more we understand them.

PUNKAH WALLAH, THE--The man who pulled the rope which moves the fan [punkah] in the courtroom in which Aziz's trial is held. Adela Quested sees him and notes his splendid form. He seemed to her to be a "male fate," a winnower of souls. In reality, he is completely unaware of what is transpiring. (PI XXIV)

Q

QUESTED, ADELA--The "queer, cautious girl" whom Ronny Heaslop had commissioned Mrs. Moore, his mother, to bring to India from England to marry him. Like all newcomers to India, Adela, in Ronny's eyes cannot understand the gulf which separates the English from the Indians. She is eager to see the real India and consents to visit the Marabar Caves with Aziz. The trip proves disastrous. She believes that she has been the victim of an attempted rape by Aziz in one of the caves. Later, despite pressures, she retracts the charge at his trial. The scandal which ensues causes her to leave India for England. (PI II)

QUESTED, MISS--A guest at the luncheon given Mrs. Wilcox by Margaret Schlegel. Miss Quested "plays." (HE IX)

R

RABY, MISS--A famous lady novelist, author of The Eternal Moment, who once, twenty years before the opening of the story, was pursued by a handsome young Italian porter who declared his love for her but from whom she ran screaming. Now he has become a concièrge, is married and has children. Miss Raby reminds him of the incident which he has apparently forgotten. The memory disturbs him because he fears that he will lose his position. (Collect Ta - Eternal)

"RACIAL EXERCISE"--1st published as "Notes on the Way"

in Time and Tide (18 March 1939), pp. 335-336; reprinted
omitting the last paragraph as "Racial Exercise," in Two
Cheers for Democracy, 1951.

Most people, Forster maintains, cannot name their
eight great-grandparents and, as each of us looks back into
his or her past "doors open upon darkness." On such a
shady past "do we erect the ridiculous doctrine of Racial
Purity."

RAFI--The nephew of Syed Mohammed. He visits Aziz when
he (Aziz) is ill. He attempts to start a scandal by saying
that Prof. Godbole is also ill and that he, like Aziz, took
tea at Mr. Fielding's thus implying that their illness was
caused by something served them on that occasion. (PI IX)

"RAINS, THE"--See: "Letters of 1921: The Rains" in The
Hill of Devi

"RAISON D'ÊTRE OF CRITICISM"--See: "The Raison d'Être
of Criticism in the Arts"

"RAISON D'ÊTRE OF CRITICISM IN THE ARTS"--1st published as "On Criticism in the Arts, Especially Music" in
Harper's Magazine, CVC (European edition: CXXXIV) (July
1947), pp. 9-17; reprinted as "The Raison d'Être of Criticism" in Horizon (London), XVIII (December 1948), pp. 397-
411; reprinted as "The Raison d'Être of Criticism in the
Arts" (omitting last paragraph) in Two Cheers for Democracy, 1951.

[An address delivered at a symposium on music at
Harvard University.] Forster maintains that he loves music
and that music is the "deepest of the arts and deep beneath
the arts." Hence, he emphasizes it in this brief survey of
the raison d'être of criticism in the arts. Love of the arts
alone is not enough. Love must be clarified and controlled
to give full value and it is here that criticism might help.

The case for criticism: Most will agree that the
previous training is desirable before we approach the arts.
Untrained appreciation has a tendency to lead to the appreciation of no one but oneself. Against this problem, the critical spirit is valuable.

Except at the actual moment of contact, it is desirable to know why we like a work of art and to be able to

defend our preferences by argument. There is, nevertheless, a danger: that training may sterilize the sensitivities.

This activity [criticism], may be best employed if
one allows it to construct esthetic theories. A more practical activity for criticism is the sensitive dissection of particular works of art. Criticism can also stimulate. There
is, however, a type of criticism which has no "interpretive
value," but it should not be condemned. It can result in
"adorable literature."

We can readily agree that criticism has educational
and cultural value. Forster, however, would like it if he
could establish its raison on a higher basis than public util-
ity. There is, nevertheless, a basic difference between the
critical and the creative states of mind.

In the creative state, a man is taken out of himself
and dips a "bucket" into his subconscious and draws up
something normally beyond his reach. He mixes this with
his normal experience and out of the mixture he makes a
work of art. The creative state of mind is akin to a dream.

The critical state, on the other hand, has many mer-
its and employs some of the highest and subtlest faculties of
man. "Think before you speak is criticism's motto; speak
before you think is creation's." Criticism has two aims:
esthetic, and the relation of the object to the rest of the
world.

A work of art is a curious thing, because through it
the beholder undergoes a change analogous to creation. Unfortunately, this sense of cooperation with the artist which
the beholder has--the supremely important step in our pilgrimage through the fine arts--is the one step criticism cannot help us with even though it can prepare us for it.

The work of art is also "recalcitrant" to criticism in
that it presents itself as extremely virgin. It expects always to be heard or seen for the first time, always to cause
surprise. It expects not to be studied or examined as a
crossword puzzle. This "eternal freshness" presents a difficulty to critics. A second reading may give a just and
true opinion of the work, but critics ought to remain
startled by the work of art. This ability to be "startled" on
a second reading is usually beyond the ability of critics.
This effect--the ability to be startled even though the piece

is known "inside out"--is most often accomplished in music
because music exists in time and outside of time instantane-
ously.

The claim that criticism takes us to the heart of art
must be disallowed. Some think that criticism can help an
artist to improve his work. If this claim is correct, a
raison for its existence is immediately established. Forster,
however, has found criticism of his own writing to be totally irrelevant in improving it.

Criticism can help the artist in only two ways: 1) It
helps him keep company with the best, 2) It can help him
over details, "niggling details, minutiae of style." Forster's
conclusion, however, is generally unfavorable to criticism.
He finds that it has not given substantial help to the artists.

RAJAH OF MAU, THE--The Rajah of the native state to
which Aziz goes after his trial. The Rajah is brought to observe the festivities of the birth of the god, Krishna. This
is done against the advice of his physicians. He is old and
very ill and does not wish to be seated since this "was no
moment for human glory." He dies during the festivities.
(PI XXXIII)

RAJAH OF MAU'S CONFIDENTIAL SERVANT, THE--See:
The Rajah of Mau's private secretary

RAJAH OF MAU'S HINDU PHYSICIAN, THE--Had accompanied the Rajah to the shrine of the god to observe the festival of the birth of the god, Krishna. He briefly reports
the Rajah's symptoms to Dr. Aziz who has become the Rajah's westernized physician. (PI XXXIII)

RAJAH OF MAU'S PRIVATE SECRETARY, THE--The Rajah
of Mau has died. His Hindu physician, his private secretary
and his confidential servant remain with the body. His death
was being concealed lest the glory of the festival of the birth
of the god, Krishna, be dimmed by the event. (PI XXXV)

RALPH--Aziz asks Mrs. Moore if Mr. Heaslop is her only
child. She answers that she has two younger children:
Ralph and Stella in England. See: Ralph Moore (PI II)

RAPHAEL--Calls Mephistopholes [sic] an "innocent devil"
when he complains about the "goings-on" in Miss Haddon's
school. (Collect Ta - Co-ord).

RAVEN, THE--A Tearoom in Shrewsbury where Evie Wilcox's
wedding party stop for tea.   Margaret did not join them,
preferring to see the city.   (HE XXV)

READER OF THE PAPER, THE--The reader of the paper
at the dinner party advises Helen Schlegel that she is not
fulfilling her proper role.   She is the one to give advice that
the money is to be left to the Society for the Preservation
of Places of Historic Interest or Natural Beauty, and not
Mr. Bast.   (HE XV)   See also: The Hostess

"READING AS USUAL"--1st published in The Listener (21
September 1939), pp. 586-587; reprinted as a pamphlet, London, Tottenham Public Libraries, October, 1939. [A Broadcast Talk on the BBC.]

    War means waiting with nothing to do.   This means
that we are going to have a great deal of time for reading.
Under these circumstances, it is best to go about with a
book in one's pocket.   Now, what to read: 1) Read what you
enjoy, 2) Don't be ashamed of enjoying it, 3) If you enjoy
good and bad "stuff," give the good stuff the preference.
Beyond this, Forster finds he cannot advise on what to read
because he does not know the reader personally.   Forster
likes to read books that were written on the past which illuminate the present.   Unlike Nazi Germany wherein people
are not free to choose what they wish to read, England is
still free and it is the duty of Englishmen, even in their
reading, to keep their freedom.   Reading in war-time and
reading in peace-time are, therefore, exactly the same.

RECORDER, THE--Sets the scene, discusses the back-
grounds, points out the morals.   (England's)

RECTOR OF THE PARISH OF HILTON, THE--Charles Wilcox is angry because the rector has had the elms pollarded
during the funeral of his mother, Mrs. Wilcox.   (HE XI)

RECTOR OF THE PARISH OF ONITON, THE--Margaret discovers that he had been a friend of her father before his
father's death.   (HE XXVI)

RED-NOSED BOY, THE--Mahmoud Ali tells Aziz and Hamidullah that the red-nosed boy, an Englishman, has again in-
sulted him in court.   Mahmoud Ali, however, does not blame
him.   The boy, he claims, was told to insult him and was
quite a nice boy until the "others" got hold of him.   He uses

this incident as an argument for his belief that Indians cannot be friends with Englishmen. The incident foreshadows
the events which are to occur between Aziz and the Englishmen he tries to befriend. (PI II)

"RETURN FROM SIWA, THE"--Title of an essay in Pharos
and Pharillon. For summary, see: Pharos and Pharillon.

"REVEREND ARTHUR BEEBE, THE REVEREND CUTH-
BERT EAGER, MR. EMERSON, MR. GEORGE EMERSON,
MISS ELEANOR LAVISH, MISS CHARLOTTE BARTLETT,
AND MISS LUCY HONEYCHURCH, DRIVE OUT IN CAR-
RIAGES TO SEE A VIEW: ITALIANS DRIVE THEM, THE"--
Title of Chapter VI, A Room with a View.

RHOMAIDES, MARIA--An old woman whom Mr. Lucas sees
tending wool on the porch of the khan. She is its proprietress. She, her daughter (aged forty-six) and grandson as
well as the remainder of her family are crushed to death by
a large tree which falls during a violent storm. (Collect
Ta - Road)

RICCABOCCA, DR. --A fictitious character Forster has taken
from Bulwer Lytton's novel, My Novel. [He is used to flesh
out episode six of the pageant.] Riccabocca locks himself
into the stocks near the Abinger Church. (AH - AB)

"ROAD FROM COLONUS, THE"--1st published in The Independent Review, III (June 1904), pp. 124-134; reprinted in
The Living Age, CCXXXXII (16 July 1904), pp. 174-181;
The Celestial Omnibus and Other Stories, 1911; The Collected Tales, 1947.

     [A short story.] Mr. Lucas is in Greece having ful-
filled a life-long dream. He finds it to be just like England.
Yet, being there has done something for him. It has made
him discontented. A strange desire to die fighting has come
to possess him. Stopping near a wayside khan (inn), he sees
a hollow tree out of which a stream is gushing. He looks
inside. There are pictures of the Virgin and ex voto offer-
ings. He decides to make the place his own. Tasting the
water, he finds it sweet. He falls asleep only to be a-
wakened by a young man singing and the arrival of his
daughter, Emily, Mrs. Forman, Mr. Graham and the English-speaking dragoman. Mrs. Forman, after they settle
for tea, remarks that the area reminds her of the Colonus
of Sophocles. Mr. Lucas realizes that his happiness depends

upon his remaining there. He believes that he has his
daughter on his side when the tea things are gathered and
the party prepares to leave for Olympia. Mr. Lucas is
adamant about his desire to remain in the khan. He is lifted
forcibly upon his mule. The little Greek children throw
stones at Mr. Graham while he is apologizing to Mr. Lucas
who does not resist being led away.

        Back in London, Mr. Lucas complains that he had a
bad hight's sleep. A parcel comes from Greece sent by
Mrs. Forman and wrapped in a Greek newspaper which Ethel
reads. She reads a story which describes the death of the
family who owned the khan where Mr. Lucas has insisted on
staying. The family were killed in a storm which felled the
large tree Mr. Lucas had admired. The tree, in turn,
crushed the khan and its inhabitants. Mr. Lucas does not
seem to hear. He is absorbed in the letter he wants to
write to his neighbors complaining of the noise they are making at night.

ROBERT--A young farmer of some education who falls in
love with Rickie Elliot's mother and by whom she has Stephen illegitimately. (LJ XXIX)

ROBERTS, MAJOR--Aziz is certain that Major Roberts will
give him leave to take his children back to Mussoorie. During his absence, he believed, Fielding would leave for England. (PI XXXI)

ROBINSON, JULIA--See: The Two Miss Robinsons (Collect
Ta - Story)

ROBINSON, MARY--See: The Two Miss Robinsons (Collect
Ta - Story)

"ROGER FRY"--See: "Roger Fry: An Obituary Note"

"ROGER FRY: AN OBITUARY NOTE"--1st published as
"Roger Fry" in The London Mercury, XXX (October 1934),
pp. 495-496; reprinted as "Roger Fry: An Obituary Notice"
in Abinger Harvest, 1936.

        Forster writes of Roger Fry as one who "rejected
authority, mistrusted intuition" and, as a result, his loss to
the world is incalculable. Yet, "somehow he cannot be
mourned," because there is something "anti-funereal" about
him.

"ROMAIN ROLLAND AND THE HERO"--1st published in The
Listener (8 March 1945), pp. 269-270; reprinted in Two
Cheers for Democracy, 1951.

[A Broadcast Talk in the BBC's Eastern Service.]
Romain Rolland was a French writer of international importance. Whether he was a great writer is debatable. He is
not as celebrated today as he was a quarter of a century a-
go [1920], when he had almost the stature of a Tolstoy. He
did not fulfill his early promise as a novelist and the world
did not fulfill his hopes.

Born in 1866, he became a professor at Paris. He
had strong Teutonic sympathies and an enormous admiration
for German music and literature. He cherished the Teutonic cult of the great man. His life-long insistence on the
"Hero" is not French. He combined hero worship with belief in "the people." By "the people" he does not mean the
common man, but the people as a fiery, instinctive emotion-
al force. His most important work, John Christopher [sic],
the theme of which is the hero as musician, was awarded
the Nobel Prize for Literature in 1916.

He was shattered by W. W. I; he became, as a result,
an internationalist and a "pre-cursor of the League of Nations." Rolland became unpopular in France and spent the
war years in Switzerland. He worked in the drama, and
knew and understood a great deal about music.

His novel, John Christopher, will probably not live
like that of Proust. It is too episodic and diffuse.

"RONALD FIRBANK"--1st published as "Our Butterflies and
Beetles" in The New York Herald Tribune, Section 11,
Books, (5 May 1929), pp. 1, 6; reprinted (with the same
title) in Life and Letters, III (July 1929), pp. 1-9; reprinted
as "Ronald Firbank" in Abinger Harvest, 1936.

[Originally written as a review of the collected edition of the works of Ronald Firbank, with an introduction by
Arthur Waley; and a review of No Love by Donald Garnett.
The version of the essay printed in Abinger Harvest omits
much of the references to No Love.]

Ronald Firbank is "fin de siècle" and "fundamentally
unserious." To the historian, he is an interesting example
of literary "conservatism." Nevertheless, he is a "genius"

in his "flit about fashion."

"RONALD KIDD"--1st published in New Statesman and Nation
(23 May 1942), p. 336; reprinted in Two Cheers for Democracy, 1951.

[An address delivered at the funeral of Ronald Kidd.]
The public side of Kidd which served humanity was superbly
developed. He must have had an enthusiasm for liberty all
his life, but it became noticeable in 1934 when he founded
the Council for Civil Liberty which Forster joined soon after
its establishment. The protest against the Sedition Bill first
brought the council to public notice. Kidd gave to his work
all his strength and literally died that "we" may be free.
Even in his last illness, he still concentrated on the Council
and its work. He knew that freedom is not the prerequisite
of any one section of the community. He was active whenever he saw the possibility of promoting and extending civil
liberty.

ROOM WITH A VIEW, A--1st edition, London, Edward Arnold, 14 October 1908; 1st American edition, New York,
G. P. Putnam's Sons, 6 May 1911.

    In Florence, Lucy Honeychurch and Charlotte Bart-
lett, her cousin and chaperon, find themselves at the Pensione Bertolini without the room with a view for which they
had written. At dinner, Mr. Emerson embarrasses them by
offering them his and his son's rooms which have the re-
quired view. The ladies are persuaded to accept the offer
when the Rev. Arthur Beebe, their friend and rector of
Lucy's parish, tells them they would be under no obligation
to Mr. Emerson if they accepted. Charlotte nevertheless
considers the Emersons ill-bred.

    At Santa Croce, Lucy meets Mr. Emerson who leads
her to the Giotto frescoes. His ideas about art and the position he takes about living life honestly confuse her, yet she
finds herself more at ease with him than she had expected.

    Late one afternoon, Lucy decides that she would go
for a walk alone. She walks through the Piazza Signoria
and, as she does so, she passes two men who are arguing.
One, in a rage, stabs the other and he dies at her feet
staining with blood the pictures she had bought previously.
At the same moment, she sees George Emerson watching
from across the square. She faints as he reaches her side.

After she recovers, she sends him to retrieve her pictures.
He throws them into the Arno because they are covered with
blood. He feels something very significant has happened to
him in the Piazza. Lucy forces him not to tell anyone what
had occurred. She is disturbed when he tells her that the
murder would make him want to live.

A large party from the pensione, including Lucy and
George Emerson, drive out to Fiesole in the hills above Florence. During a stop, Lucy discovers a terrace covered
with violets. She is alone. George steps forward and kisses her. Charlotte, who has come to call her back to the
carriage, sees George kiss her. She tells her cousin that
George is a cad, and Lucy has her promise to tell no one.
In the morning, they leave for Rome.

Back at Windy Corner, her home in Surrey, Cecil
Vyse and Lucy become engaged. When she learns that Sir
Harry Otway intends to lease the houses he has recently
bought, Lucy suggests the Misses Alan whom she had met
in the Pensione Bertolini. After seeing the houses, Cecil
and Lucy walk on through a wood. By a pond, Cecil asks
her if he could kiss her. The kiss is not a success. It
causes Lucy to think of the Emersons.

Cecil meets Mr. Emerson in the National Gallery in
London shortly before the Miss Alans are to take possession
of Sir Harry Otway's house. Her persuades Mr. Emerson
and George to take it instead. He did not, of course, connect them in any way to Lucy. He hoped that the social order of the neighborhood would be disrupted with them in possession of the house.

After the Emersons move in, Mr. Beebe takes Freddy, Lucy's brother, to meet them. Freddy asks George to
go swimming. The three choose the pond in the wood for
their swim. Meanwhile, Lucy, her mother and Cecil take
the shorter route through the wood for their visit to an old
neighbor. They come upon the three. George greets Lucy
joyously and she merely bows stiffly.

One Sunday, George is visiting Windy Corner. He,
Freddy, and Freddy's friend ask Cecil to join them in a
game of tennis. Cecil refuses preferring to read a novel
by Miss Lavish whom Lucy had met at the Pension Bertolini. The novel contains a scene which, thinly disguised,
recounts George's kissing Lucy. Cecil, of course, does not

connect the situation, but George and Lucy are profoundly
moved. On the way into the house, George again kisses her.
Charlotte, a house guest at the time, and Lucy go to George
and ask him to leave. Before he obeys, he tells Lucy that
he loves her and that it would be unthinkable for her to
marry Cecil.

That evening she breaks her engagement to Cecil
though she denies to herself her love for George. She learns
that the Miss Alans are planning a trip to Greece. She decides to go with them to escape her confusion. After a day
in London with her mother, Lucy stops off at Mr. Beebe's
house rather than go with Charlotte to church. There she
meets Mr. Emerson. She learns from him that George has
gone to London. She reveals that she has broken her engagement to Cecil. Mr. Emerson tells her that he has an
intuition that she loves his son; Lucy begins to cry. She
gradually recognizes that his assumption is true. She marries George and they spend their honeymoon in the Pensione
Bertolini. They realize that Charlotte was subtly on their
side. She knew that Mr. Emerson was in Mr. Beebe's
house and, consequently, was instrumental in their meeting.

ROSE--At four o'clock, she and Enid take the places of Mildred and Ellen at the piano. They play the duet Miss Haddon gives them worse than Mildred but not as badly as
Emily. (Collect Ta - Co-ord)

ROSE--See: Rose Tyler (Collect Ta - Story)

ROTHENSTEIN--A guest at the luncheon Margaret Schlegel
gives for Mrs. Wilcox. She is too busy placing him at the
table to answer Mrs. Wilcox's query of news from Helen
who is visiting her cousin in Stettin. (HE IX)

RUSSIAN PRINCE, A--He is a guest at the Grand Hôtel des
Alpes. He falls asleep in its lobby in a prominent and un-
graceful position. (Collector Ta - Eternal)

RUTH--Mrs. Worters's sister and a guest in her home.
She is also one of the party who goes to the wood given
Evelyn Beaumont by Harcourt Worters. (Collect Ta - Other)

S

"ST. ATHANASIUS"--Title of an essay in Pharos and Pharillon.   For summary see: Pharos and Pharillon.

"SALUTE TO THE ORIENT"--1st published in The London
Mercury, IV (July 1921), pp. 271-281; reprinted in Abinger
Harvest, 1936.

      An attempt to understand the East by referring to nov-
els written about it by Europeans: Pickthall and Loti, and
by Egyptians: Adès and Josipici.   The attempt ends when
Forster asks: "What is the use of generalizing?"

SANDBACH, MR.--Had held a curacy in the North of England which he resigned because of ill health.   While recuperating at Ravello, he had become tutor to the boy, Eustace.
He is one of the party at the picnic during the course of
which the panic occurs.   (Collect Ta - Story)

"SANDITON"--See: Jane Austen, 2: Sanditon"

"SAWSTON"--Title of Part II, The Longest Journey.

SAWSTON--The location of Rickie Elliot's home after marriage to Agnes Pembroke.   (LJ IV)

SAWSTON--The location of the Herriton home within easy
reach of London.   (WAFT I)

SAWSTON SCHOOL--Is near the Pembroke house.   Herbert
Pembroke was master of a form there.   The school was
founded in the seventeenth century as a tiny grammar school
for poor day-boys.   Then, in the nineteenth century, it began to educate the children of the welathy and produced a
large number of bishops.   (LJ IV)

"SAYED ROSS MASOOD"--1st published as a letter to the
editor and appreciation of Sir Sayed Ross Masood, Urdu,
XVII (October 1937), pp. 853-860; reprinted omitting the letter as "Sayed Ross Masood" in Two Cheers for Democracy,
1951.

      Forster claims to have been the oldest and most inti-
mate of Masood's many English friends.   Masood opened
Forster's eyes to new horizons and a new civilization.   So
great was his influence on Forster that Forster dedicated his
A Passage to India to him for it would never have been written without him.

Masood was essentially an artist though his career was of a practical character. His standards were those of good taste. He had little use for logical and ethical consistency. He overwhelmed Anglo Saxons by his energy and unconventionality of address. He did not really dislike the English as rulers of India; he pitied them. His real work, of course, lay within his own community in his own country. When that career is described, it must not be forgotten that he was essentially an artist.

SAXON YOUTH, A--He appears in the play's prologue. He speaks to the Norman girl. After they part, she looks back at him, symbolizing the future union of Norman and Saxon and the foundation of England. (England's)

"SCALLIES, THE"--See: "Our Diversions, 1: The Scallies"

"SCINDHIA'S VISIT"--See: "Letters of 1921: Scindhia's Visit"

SCHLEGEL, EMILY--The mother of Margaret, Helen, and Tibby (Theobald). She was English. She died when Tibby was born. Helen was five at her death and Margaret, thirteen. (HE III)

SCHLEGEL, ERNEST--The father of Margaret, Helen, and Tibby (Theobald). He died five years after his wife when Tibby was five, Helen ten, and Margaret eighteen. Mrs. Munt, his wife's sister, who offers to keep house for the family after his wife's death, refers to him as "peculiar and a German." He classed himself as an idealist, inclined to be dreary. He had fought against Denmark, Austria, and France. He worked in a provincial university. There he had married Emily. Because of her money, the couple were able to live in London. (HE III)

SCHLEGEL, HELEN--The sister of Margaret and the second child of the Schlegels. She was "rather apt to entice people, and, in enticing them, to be herself enticed." She thought she was in love with Paul, the youngest Wilcox son. It is because of this early attachment that Margaret meets Mrs. Wilcox and eventually becomes the second Mrs. Wilcox. Helen is attracted by the situation confronting Leonard Bast. She has an affair with him which results in an illegitimate child. (HE I)

SCHLEGEL, MARGARET--She is "not beautiful, not supremely brilliant, but filled with something that took the place of both qualities." That something is "best described has profound vivacity, a continual and sincere response to all that she encountered in her path through life." Though inexperienced in life, she presumes to advise Helen. She was capable of accepting occasional failure as part of the game. She becomes friendly with Mrs. Wilcox who wills Howards End to her. She marries Mr. Wilcox and is a good wife to him. (HE I)

SCHLEGEL, TIBBY (THEOBALD)--See: Tibby

SCREAMING GIRL, A--She is the owner of the dog (which turns out to be a cat) run over by one of the cars in Evie Wilcox's wedding party. (HE XXV)

SECOND DARKNESS, THE--Title of Part II, Two Cheers for Democracy.

SECOND GRAVE--One of the two graves in "Our Graves in Gallipoli." Through their conversation, Forster stresses the futility of war. (AH - Our)

"SECOND GREATEST NOVEL? THE"--See: "Our Second Greatest Novel?"

SERVANT, A--A servant at Oniton shouts for the key to the bathing shed which Charles Wilcox wants. He is misunderstood by another servant in the garden. (HE XXVI)

SERVANT IN THE GARDEN, A--See: A servant (HE XXVI)

SERVANT OF THE CLUB--He is a man who is encouraged by Mahmoud Ali to tell all he overhears the Englishmen say at the club. He speaks English. It is from what he reports that the false rumor grows that Miss Quested and Mrs. Moore are offended with Aziz's failure to take them to the Marabar Caves as he had promised. (PI XIII)

"SETTLING IN"--See: "Letters of 1921: Settling In"

SHADES, THE--Tell the intruder from Hell to return there. (Collect Ta - Point)

"SHELLEY, PLATO, GOETHE"--Title, Chap. VII, Goldsworthy Lowes Dickinson. For summary see: Goldsworthy Lowes Dickinson.

SHELTHORPE--The house of the Pembrokes in Sawston.
(LJ III)

SHOOLBRED AND MAPLE--Furniture dealers in Tottenham
Court Road, London, whom Cecil Vyse holds in disdain. He
could almost see, as he stood in the drawing-room of Windy
Corner, their vans delivering furniture.   (RWV VIII)

SIGNOR CANTÙ'S WIFE--Signor Cantù's mother claims that
her daughter-in-law is at the center of the plot, joined by
the Concièrge, to ruin her and her hotel, the Biscione.
(Collect Ta - Eternal)

SILTS, THE--Seedy cousins of Rickie Elliot's father who kept
house for him after the death of Rickie's mother. He visits
them at Christmas, but is eager to leave for the Ansell's.
(LJ III)

"SINCLAIR LEWIS"--1st published as "Our Photography:
Sinclair Lewis" in New York Herald Tribune, Section II,
Books (28 April 1929) pp. 1, 6; reprinted as "A Camera
Man" in Life and Letters, II (May 1929), pp. 336-343; Sin-
clair Lewis Interprets America, Cambridge, Mass., Harvard
Press, 1932; "Sinclair Lewis," in Abinger Harvest, 1936.

        Lewis has made thousands all over the globe alive to
the existence of America's Middle West. The method he
uses to do so is "throughout photographic." He has a freshness and vigor. He is a novelist of the instinctive sort.
Though ironic and "even denunciatory" at times, he has
"nothing of the aseptic awfulness of the seer."

"SINCLAIR LEWIS INTERPRETS AMERICA"--See: "Sinclair
Lewis"

"SISTER 1815-1852"--Section title, Marianne Thornton: A
Domestic Biography. For summary see: Marianne Thornton: A Domestic Biography.

"SISTER 1815-1852, 1: THE REIGN OF SIR ROBERT"--
Section title, Marianne Thornton: A Domestic Biography.
For summary see: Marianne Thornton: A Domestic Biog-
raphy.

"SISTER 1815-1852, 2: THE CONTINENT"--Section title,
Marianne Thornton: A Domestic Biography. For summary
see: Marianne Thornton: A Domestic Biography.

"SISTER 1815-1852, 3: THE BIRCHIN LANE BANK"--Section title, Marianne Thornton: A Domestic Biography. For summary see: Marianne Thornton: A Domestic Biography.

"SISTER 1815-1852, 4: MAY MEETING AND WILLIAM WILBERFORCE"--Section title, Marianne Thornton: A Domestic Biography. For summary see: Marianne Thornton: A Domestic Biography.

"SISTER 1815-1852, 5: THE MARRIAGES"--Section title, Marianne Thornton: A Domestic Biography. For summary see: Marianne Thornton: A Domestic Biography.

"SISTER 1815-1852, 6: DECEASED WIFE'S SISTER"--Section title, Marianne Thornton: A Domestic Biography. For summary see: Marianne Thornton: A Domestic Biography.

SMALL BOY, A--Stephen tries to hire his trap by offering to pay for his railway ticket back and giving him sixpence. (HE XXXIII)

" 'SNOW' WEDGWOOD"--1st published as "More Browning Letters" in The Listener, Supplement #36 (13 October 1937), p. xv; reprinted as " 'Snow' Wedgwood" in Two Cheers for Democracy, 1951.

[A review of Robert Browning and Julia Wedgwood by Richard Curle.] Forster comments on the Julia Wedgwood-Robert Browning correspondence which began in 1864 shortly after the death of his wife, Elizabeth Barett. There is no exact indication of why they eventually quarreled. Curle, the editor, seems to credit it to the fact that she was much too "portentious and bleak a female," but Forster, who had known her, disagrees.

SOLDIER, A PRIVATE--A guest of Gino Carella at the performance of Lucia di Lammermoor also attended by Philip and Harriet Herriton and Caroline Abbot. (WAFT VI)

"SOLITARY PLACE, THE"--Title of an essay in Pharos and Pharillon. For summary see: Pharos and Pharillon.

"SOME OF OUR DIFFICULTIES"--See: "T. S. Eliot"

SOMEONE--On the gangway leading up to the airship, someone says "We shall be late." (Collect Ta - Machine)

SOMETHING, MR. SOMEONE--Mr. Eager wants to display his knowledge of the foreign residents of Florence to Lucy Honeychurch on the carriage trip to Fiesole. He points out the home of Mr. Someone Something, an American of the best type--"so rare." (RWV VI)

SON OF A WOOD-CUTTER, THE--One of the villagers of Hilton who is thrilled by the prospect of Mrs. Wilcox's funeral. He is pollarding one of the churchyard elms when he witnesses the scene which he later describes to his mother. What he sees awes him so that he cannot continue his work even though he knows that he should. His mind, after the funeral, turns to thoughts of love. He looks at the grave and sees some colored flowers which he notes shouldn't be used "at buryings." Furtively, he wrenches a chrysanthemum from a sheaf and puts it in his pocket for his girl. (HE XI)

SORLEY, MR. --See: Mr. Graysford (PI IV)

SPINSTER, A--Margaret Schlegel thinks of a spinster she had once visited who though poor, silly, and unattractive, had a mania that every man who approached her fell in love with her. She thinks how like that spinster she is in believing that Mr. Wilcox was courting her. (HE XVIII)

"SPIRITUAL CITY, THE"--Title of Section iii (Part I), Alexandria.

"SPRING COTTAGE, THE"--Title of Chapter II, Goldsworthy Lowes Dickinson. For summary see: Goldsworthy Lowes Dickinson.

"SQUIRE GEORGE'S DIFFICULTIES A. D. 1760"--Title of Scene i, (Act I), England's Pleasant Land. For summary see: England's Pleasant Land.

"STATE AND ITS RULER, THE"--Section title, The Hill of Devi. For summary see: The Hill of Devi.

STELLA--The daughter of Mrs. Moore. She later marries Fielding. See also: Ralph (PI II)

STELLA D'ITALIA--The hotel in which Caroline Abbot and Lila Herriton stay in Monteriano. It is there that Lila meets Gino Carella whom she marries. (WAFT I)

STEPHEN'S WIFE--See: a voice   (LJ XXXV)

"STORY, THE"--Title of Chapter II, Aspects of the Novel.
For summary see: Aspects of the Novel.

"STORY OF A PANIC, THE"--1st published in The Independent Review, III (August 1904), pp. 453-472; reprinted in
The Celestial Omnibus, 1911; The Collected Tales, 1947.

[Forster's first short story.]   A party of English
visitors to Ravello decide to have a picnic.   They go to a
hill overlooking the Vallone Fontana Caroso.   Eustace, a
young, rather petulant boy sits carving a pan pipe which he
plays.   During a lull after their lunch when the group speak
of the death of Pan, a terrible fear overtakes them and a
compulsion forces them to run pell mell down the hill.
When they stop their mad dash, they realize that one of their
number, Eustace, has been left behind.   They slowly make
their way back up the hill and discover him on his back
seemingly unconscious.   They ask him what he has been doing.   As he begins to tell his tale, they notice the footprints
of goats in the moist earth beneath the trees.

The clergyman in the party announces what they all
feel: the Evil One has visited the area.   A change comes
over Eustace as the party returns to its hotel.   He begins
acting "like a real boy."   He scurries in front of the group
"like a goat."   Sighting three old Italian ladies, Eustace
kisses one and gives her flowers.   All are astonished save
the old woman.   When the party reach the hotel, Eustace
greets Gennaro, the "stop-gap" waiter, wildly.

That night, Tyler, the narrator, awakens to discover
Eustace behaving wildly in the garden.   Gennaro is enticed
into capturing Eustace and bringing him into the hotel.
Eustace is locked in his room despite his protests.   Gennaro
tells Tyler that Eustace will die if kept indoors.   The light
in the room is dropped accidentally and, in the darkness,
Gennaro sets Eustace free only to die himself.

"STORY OF THE SIREN, THE"--1st published as a pamphlet, Richmond, England, The Hogarth Press, 2 July 1920;
reprinted in The Eternal Moment and Other Stories, 1928;
The Collected Tales, 1947.

[A short story.]   The narrator, boating near Capri,
loses the manuscript of his thesis on the Deist controversy

overboard. One of the boatmen, a Sicilian, prepares to re-
move his clothes to dive for it. One of the women in the
boat suggests that the Sicilian and the narrator be landed on
the shore and the boat return for them after the volume has
been retrieved. The scene is beautiful. After the Sicilian
retrieves the book, he tells the narrator that the Siren might
appear in such a scene. He tells the narrator that his brother, Giuseppe, had seen the Siren one day while diving for
coins. He was never the same after. He carried off and
married a girl, Maria, who like him had also seen the Siren
one day while bathing. It was prophesied that their child
would call the Siren from the sea. The townspeople were
fearful of the couple and their unborn child. Maria is pushed
over a cliff and dies. Giuseppe roamed far and wide looking
for another who has seen the Siren, only to die of consump-
tion in Liverpool.

"STRATFORD JUBILEE, THE"--1st published in The Spectator, (23 April 1932), p. 586; reprinted in Two Cheers for
Democracy, 1951.

    Half-way through the eighteenth century, a clergyman
in Stratford named Gastrell chopped down a mulberry tree
which had been planted by Shakespeare. He was hounded out
of town for the deed and the tree was made into relics some
of which, including a casket, was sent to Garrick, the actor.
As a result of that gift, he decided to organize a celebration
at Stratford, a thirty-day jubilee, in the Autumn of 1769.
The affair included everything but the performance of a
Shakespearean play. The "greater and graver minds" of the
day held aloof from "Garrick's Vagary." They suspected
frivolity and self-advertisement. Boswell came, nevertheless, dressed as a Corsican and Garrick carried Shakespeare's glove. And it rained wildly. The townspeople were
frightened believing that the flood was God's judgment against
them. Those who weren't afraid fleeced the visitors. Garrick managed to recite his ode--"an empty piece"--despite
the cut on his chin "delivered" by his drunken barber. He
lost heavily over the fiasco, but gained a great deal when the
jubilee was presented the following winter on the boards of
Drury Lane.

STUDENTS--Hysterical boys, Indians, who had gathered in
front of the City Magistrate's Court and jeered when Ronny
Heaslop and Adela Quested drove up. (PI XXIV)

SUBALTERN, THE--Aziz meets him on the Maidan when he

decides to go there rather than to the Collector's garden
party.   The subaltern liked anyone who could ride a horse.
For a time, their polo match erases the differences in their
races.   (PI VI) Later, the subaltern, who is from a Gurkha
regiment, is present in the smoking room at the club when
the Collector considers the course of action to be taken in
the face of the possible riot brewing over Aziz's trial.   The
aubaltern, a bit drunk, suggests that Gurkhas be called in
claiming that English troops are no good in such a delicate
situation.   He feels that the sporting type of native is best:
Jats, Punjabi, Sikhs, Marathas, Bhils, Afidis, Pathars.
(PI XX)

"SUPPLIANT, THE"--See: "Adrift in India, 4: The Suppliant"

T

"TAGORE AS A NOVELIST"--See: "Two Books by Tagore,
2: The Home and the World"

"T. E. "--See: "T. E. Lawrence"

"T. E. LAWRENCE"--1st published as "T. E. " in The Listener (31 July 1935), pp. 211-212; reprinted as "T. E.
Lawrence" in Abinger Harvest, 1936.

[A review of Seven Pillars of Wisdom by T. E. Lawrence.]   Forster notes that Lawrence hated to be called
"Lawrence of Arabia. " Lawrence disliked his Seven Pillars
of Wisdom, but the edition, edited by A. W. Lawrence, is
"already a joy for experts. " [Note: Forster was a personal friend of Lawrence. See: "Clouds Hill. "]

"TEMPLE"--Title of Part III, A Passage to India.

"TERCENTENARY OF THE 'AREOPAGITICA, ' THE"--1st
published as "A Tercentenary of Freedom" in The Listener,
(17 December 1944), pp. 633-634; reprinted as "The Tercentenary of the 'Aeropagitica' " in Two Cheers for Democracy, 1951.

[A Broadcast Talk in the BBC's Home Service.]
Forster notes that the essay was written to commemorate
the third century of the publication of Milton's Areopagitica.
The Parliament, at the time of its composition, was fighting

the King.   Milton upheld the Parliament, but it had passed
a defense regulation for the control of literature and had
placed all printed matter under a censorship.   Milton was
shocked and wrote the Areopagitica as a protest.

Milton makes many very good points in it.   Among
the smaller is the inconvenience censorship presents to a
creative or scholarly writer.   The larger problems it deals
with include the fact that censorship means uniformity and
monotony and ultimately spiritual death.   Milton, Forster
points out, held that it is preferable that bad books should
be published rather than that all books be censored.   He was
liable to prosecution after the publication.

Milton would disapprove of the indirect censorship applied through war-time "paper control."   At present, most
of the paper available goes to government departments and,
as a consequence, most of the great English classics have
gone out of print.   Milton would not have liked the "ap-
proved script" from which broadcasters are obliged to read
for the reason of security.

In places, the Areopagitica is a disturbance to our
self-complacency.   In others, however, it is an encourage-
ment.   Forster was intensely patriotic, and he was proud
of the variety of opinions available in England.

"TERCENTENARY OF FREEDOM, A"--See: "The Tercentenary of the 'Areopagitica' "

TESSI, SPIRIDONE--Gino Carella's best friend who worked
in the custom house at Chiasso.   Gino had not seen him for
two years.   (WAFT III)

TEWSON--A prefect at Dunwood House.   He was "a saintly
child" in spectacles who had risen to this height by reason
of his immense learning.   (LJ XVI)

THEOBALD, MRS. --Lila Herriton's mother.   She comes to
see Lila off to Italy, cries and thinks her daughter is in
"high spirits to begin so long a journey."   (WAFT I)

THEY--The females at the dinner party Margaret and Helen
Schlegel attend after meeting Leonard Bast.   "They" argue
with Margaret and Helen about "ideals."   They insist that
Margaret is wrong in believing that Mr. Bast "would not
gain his soul until he had gained a little of the world."   The

narrator observes that the female mind, though "cruelly practical in daily life, cannot bear to hear ideals belittled in conversation." (HE XV)

"THEY HOLD THEIR TONGUES"--1st published in New Statesmen and Nation, N. S. (30 September 1939), p. 453; reprinted in Two Cheers for Democracy, 1951.

The old order, when "Fate advanced slowly," and tragedies were "manageable," and human dignity "possible," has vanished. Those who chronicle this age [1939], and its silliness and look upon the "tongue-holders" will not only pity us but disdain us.

"THEY RETURN"--Title of Chapter VII, A Room with a View.

THOMAS--A soldier Stephen and Rickie meet on their ride. Stephen drinks with him and recites some off-color verse to him about Aunt Emily. (LJ XII)

THOMPSON, FLEA (FLEANCE)--A shepherd on the estate of Aunt Emily. For four hours in the rain, Stephen guards his sheep while Flea goes courting his girl. (LJ X)

"THREE ANTI-NAZI BROADCASTS"--See: "What has Germany Done to the Germans?" "What Would Germany do to Us?" "Culture and Freedom."

THREE OLD ITALIAN LADIES--After his experience on the mountainside, Eustace sees three old Italian ladies. He kisses one and gives her some flowers. (Collect Ta - Road)

"THREE STORIES BY TOLSTOY"--1st published as "Tolstoy's Birthday" in Talking to India by E. M. Forster, Ritchie Calder, Cedric Dover, Hisa Ch'ien and Others, London, George Allen and Unwin, Ltd., 1943; reprinted as "Three Stories by Tolstoy" in Two Cheers for Democracy, 1951.

Forster maintains that the three stories by Tolstoy, "The Cossacks," "The Death of Ivan Ilyitch," and "The Three Hermits," may help us to understand Tolstoy. Though all different, they have one thing in common: they all teach that the simple people are the best, though Tolstoy was far from simple. He was an aristocrat, an intellectual, a landowner who thought property wrong. He was ravaged by in-

trospection and remorse.   In "The Death of Ivan Ilyitch,"
Tolstoy criticizes modern civilization; in "The Three Hermits," he shows what civilization needs.   The independent,
simple life of the Cossacks charmed Tolstoy and warmed his
imagination, resulting in his first masterpiece, "The Cossacks."

        At different phases of his life, Tolstoy believed in a
different type of simplicity.   When he was young, he believed in the Cossacks because they were spontaneous and
loved animal violence and pleasure.   In "The Death of Ivan
Ilyitch," he shifted his love to the Russian peasant, and in
"The Three Hermits," he turned to the saint who, in the
eyes of the world, is an imbecile but is capable of walking
on water.   Though inconsistent, he never wavered in his
central faith: simplicity.

"THREE T. S. ELIOTS, THE"--See: "Two Books by T. S.
Eliot, 1: Notes Toward the Definition of Culture"

TIBBY (THEOBALD SCHLEGEL)--The brother of Margaret
and Helen Schlegel.   He suffers from hay fever.   He is an
"intelligent young man" but "dyspeptic" and "difficult."
From babyhood, something has driven him to the unwelcome
and the unexpected.   (HE I)

TICKET BOY--Mrs. Munt (Aunt Juley) asks him for the di-
rections to "Howards Lodge" when she arrives at Hilton.
The boy corrects her by indicating that the name of the Wilcox home is Howards End.   (HE III)

TILLIARD--A student-philosopher and a friend of Rickie at
Cambridge.   He holds the view that things exist only when
there is someone to look at them.   Rickie thinks that his
view is attractive.   (LJ I)

"TIMOTHY THE CAT AND TIMOTHY WHITEBONNET"--
Title of essay in Pharos and Pharillon.   For summary see:
Pharos and Pharillon.

"TIMOTHY WHITEBONNET AND TIMOTHY THE CAT"--
See: "Timothy the Cat and Timothy Whitebonnet"

"TOLERANCE"--1st published as "The Unsung Virtue of
Tolerance" in The Listener (31 July 1941), pp. 160-161; re-
printed as "The Unsung Virtue of Tolerance: It is Very
Easy to See Fanaticism in Other People" in Vital Speeches

of the Day, VIII (15 October 1941), pp. 12-14; reprinted as
"Tolerance" in Two Cheers for Democracy, 1951.

[A Broadcast Talk in the BBC's Overseas Service.]
The only sound foundation for a civilization is a sound state
of mind. Tolerance is that state of mind. This state is developed from negative virtues: "not being touchy, irritable,
revengeful." It is just a "makeshift" suitable for an "over-
crowded and overheated planet." Tolerance is not the same
as weakness. Putting up with people is not the same as
giving in to them.

"TOLSTOY'S BIRTHDAY"--See: "Three Stories by Tolstoy"

TOM (LITTLE BOY)--Comes with a tin can of milk sent by
Miss Avery who hopes to have Howards End occupied. He
tells Margaret and Helen Schlegel that he will come again in
the morning for the can and bring some eggs. (HE XXXVII)

TOM'S FATHER--Is mowing the big meadow at Howards End.
He wants to know if Helen's baby is old enough to play with
hay. Tom, his son, becomes the baby's "nursemaid." (HE
XLIV)

TOMPKIN--The son of Charles and Dolly Wilcox. He serves
as a distraction for Dolly when Charles accuses her of bringing about the marriage of her father to Margaret Schlegel.
(HE XXI)

"TOP DRAWER BUT ONE, THE"--See: "Mrs. Miniver"

"TOURISM V. THUGGISM"--1st published in The Listener
(17 January 1957), p. 124; reprinted as a pamphlet, London
and Dunstable, Waterloo and Sons, Ltd., sometime after 17
January 1957.

[A review of Portrait of Greece by Lord Kinross.]
For the sake of tourists (who are a set of "softies") zones
of peacefulness must be established. Tourism is a feature
of our age. It spreads "vulgarity," but violence does too.
Forster recalls his visits to Greece. His mixture of old
memories and recent ones make browsing in Helenic travel
books very agreeable. He finds the photographs in Lord Kinross's book make him wish to tour Greece again. Shall he
visit a third time? It is in the lap of the gods.

TRAVELER--Gives the narrator some beer. The narrator

learns that they are brothers.   (Collect - Other Side)

"TRIBUTE TO DESMOND MACCARTHY"--1st published in
The Listener (26 June 1952), p. 1031; reprinted as a pamphlet, Stanford Dingley, The Mill House Press, late summer
1952.

          Forster met MacCarthy about fifty years previously
[1902] at Cambridge at one of "those little discussion-socie-
ties, the Apennines."   Forster had to read a paper to the
group and was pulled to pieces.   One of the critics was
MacCarthy who, for all his gentleness, knew exactly what he
wanted to say and in the end, how to say it.   That was Forster's first and lasting impression of him.   In London some
of his friends formed a society to help him get his novel
written, but he eluded the group.   He never did write it.
After World War I, the group was reconstituted, but with a
new goal: to write reminiscences.   Here, MacCarthy was
supreme.   In the midst of the group which included Lytton
Strachey, Virginia Woolf, and Maynard Keynes, he stood out.

"TRIGGER, THE"--See: "Gerald Heard"

"TROOPER SILAS TOMKYN COMERBACKE"--1st published
as "Incongruities: 'Comerbacke' " in New York Herald Tribune, Section II, Books (6 September 1931), pp. 1, 4; revised and reprinted as: "Incongruities: S. T. C." in Spectator (19, 26 September 1931), pp. 348-349, 381-382; reprinted as "Trooper Silas Tomkyn Comerbacke" in Abinger
Harvest, 1936.

          Forster details the early military career of one Silas
Tomkyn Comerbacke--Samuel Taylor Coleridge--as a trooper
and a general problem at Cambridge having left that school
under a cloud.   "He had disgraced himself irretrievably, and
three years later wrote The Ancient Mariner."

"TRUCE (1926-1933), THE"--Title of Chapter XIV, Goldsworthy Lowes Dickinson.   For summary see: Goldsworthy
Lowes Dickinson.

TRUE PATRIOT, THE--The title of one of Anthony Failing's
books out of which Aunt Emily, his wife, asks Rickie Elliot
to read something he likes.   (LJ XXXIV)

"T. S. ELIOT"--1st published as "Some of Our Difficulties"
in The New York Herald Tribune, Section II, Books, (12

May 1929), pp. 1, 6; reprinted as "T. S. Eliot and His Difficulties" in Life and Letters, II (June 1929), pp. 417-425;
reprinted as "T. S. Eliot" in Abinger Harvest, 1936.

Eliot is a difficult writer because of our own incompetence or inattention. The Wasteland is his "greatest a-
chievement" which Forster interprets as being about "the
fertilizing waters that arrived too late. It is a poem of
horror."

"T. S. ELIOT AND HIS DIFFICULTIES"--See: "T. S. Eliot"

TURK, A--See: A Voice. (Collect Ta - Mr.)

TURTON, LADY--A character Forster invents to unveil his
statue in Kennsington Gardens. (AH - My Own)

TURTON, MR.--The Collector at Chandrapore. He is an
Englishman who is willing to extend courtesy to the natives
but will go no further. (PI III)

TURTON, MRS. MARY--The wife of Mr. Turton, the Collector. Mahmoud Ali notes that she takes bribes to influence
her husband. Some Rajah, he indicates, gave her a solid
gold sewing machine in order that water could be made to
flow through his state. (PI II)

"TWELFTH CHAPTER"--Title of Chapter XII, A Room with
a View.

"TWO BOOKS BY T. S. ELIOT"

1: Notes Toward the Definition of Culture--1st published as "The Three T. S. Eliots" in The Listener, (20 January 1949), p. 111; reprinted as "Two Books by T. S. Eliot,
1: Notes Toward the Definition of Culture" in Two Cheers
for Democracy, 1951.   .

[A review of Notes Toward the Definition of Culture
by T. S. Eliot.] Forster finds that most of the book is dedicated to sophisticated and highly educated people. On the
whole it is not "satisfactory." The three broadcasts, are,
however, successful. In the first of these, Eliot speaks of
the unity of European culture; the second describes the break-
up of that unity; the third is the least satisfactory because he
advances in it toward a definition of culture and retires without making it clear. His interest is in "polemical Chris-

tianity. "

    2: The Cocktail Party--A Comedy, 1st published as "Mr. Eliot's 'Comedy' " in The Listener, (23 March 1950), p. 533; reprinted as "Two Books by T. S. Eliot, 2: The Cocktail Party" in Two Cheers for Democracy, 1951.

    [A review of The Cocktail Party by T. S. Eliot.] Forster feels that a comedy where one of the characters is crucified on an ant hill is not comic in the usual sense of the word and the reader will do well to arm himself against difficulties which may diminish on the stage. The reader finds himself in a spiritual operating theatre. The difficulties of the play do not extend to its diction which is lucid and beautiful. The diction--a demure, chatty verse--full of turns and subtle echoes, may place affairs on the stage in a less puzzling perspective.

"TWO BOOKS BY TAGORE"

    1: Chitra--1st published in New Weekly, I (13 June 1914), p. 403; reprinted as "Two Books by Tagore, 1: Chitra" in Abinger Harvest, 1936.

    [A review of Chitra by Rabindranath Tagore.] Chitra is a "fairy play" in nine scenes which demonstrates that Tagore is not a seer or a thinker. He is "consideration and charm and tenderness." The essay includes a summary of the play.

    2: The Home and The World--1st published as "Tagore as a Novelist" in Athenaeum (I August 1919), p. 687; reprinted as "Two Books by Tagore, 2: The Home and the World" in Abinger Harvest, 1936.

    In his novel, Tagore indicates that the home is "a retreat for seemly meditation," and the world is a sphere for a "boarding-house fluctuation that masks itself in mystic or patriotic talk."

"TWO CHEERS FOR DEMOCRACY"--See: "What I Believe"

TWO CHEERS FOR DEMOCRACY--1st edition, London, Edward Arnold and Co., 1 November 1951; 1st American edition, New York, Harcourt Brace and Co., 1 November 1951.

    A collection of essays on various topics. The vol-

ume is divided into two parts: I. The Second Darkness and
II. What I Believe. Part II in turn is sub-divided into:
"What I Believe," "Art in General," "The Arts in Action,"
and "Places."

Contents: Part I--The Second Darkness: "The Last
Parade;" "The Menace to Freedom;" "Jew-Consciousness;"
"Our Deputation;" "Racial Exercise;" "Post-Munich;" "Ger-
ald Heard;" "They Hold Their Tongues;" "Three Anti-Nazi
Broadcasts: 1. Culture and Freedom, 2. What has Ger-
many Done to the Germans? 3. What Would Germany do to
Us?"; "Tolerance;" "Ronald Kidd;" "The Tercentenary of
the 'Areopagitica';" "The Challenge of Our Time;" "George
Orwell;" Part II--First Section, What I Believe: "What I
Believe." Second Section--Art in General: "Anonymity: An
Enquiry;" "Art for Art's Sake;" "The Duty of Society to
the Artist;" "Does Culture Matter?" "The Raison D'Être
of Criticism in the Arts;" "The C Minor of That Life;"
"Not Listening to Music;" "Not Looking at Pictures;" Third
Section--The Arts in Action: "John Skelton;" " 'Julius
Caesar';" "The Stratford Jubilee of 1769;" "Gibbon and
His 'Autobiography';" "Voltaire and Frederick the Great;"
"George Crabbe and Peter Grimes;" "Bishop Jebb's Book;"
"Henry Thornton;" "William Arnold;" " 'Snow' Wedgewood;"
"William Barnes;" "Three Stories by Tolstoy;" "Edward
Carpenter;" "Webb and Webb;" "A Book that Influenced
Me;" "Our Second Greatest Novel?" "Gide and George;"
"Gide's Death;" "Romain Rolland and the Hero;" "A Whiff
of D'Annunzio;" "Virginia Woolf;" "Two Books by T. S.
Eliot;" "The Ascent of F. 6;" " 'The Enchanged Flood';"
"Forrest Reid;" "English Prose Between 1918 and 1939;"
"An Outsider on Poetry;" "Mohammed Iqbal;" "Sayed Ross
Masood;" "A Duke Remembers;" "Mrs. Miniver;" "In My
Library;" "The London Library." Fourth Section--Places:
"A Letter to Madan Blanchard;" "India Again;" "Luncheon
at Pretoria;" "The United States;" "Mount Lebanon;" "Fer-
ney;" "Clouds Hill;" "Cambridge;" "London is a Muddle;"
"The Last of Abinger." For summaries and publication in-
formation see: individual titles.

"TWO CULTURES: THE QUICK AND THE DEAD"--See:
"Culture and Freedom"

"TWO CULTURES: THE QUICK AND THE DEAD, THE
NAZI BLIND ALLEY"--See: "Culture and Freedom"

TWO GUESTS FROM TOWN--Elegant ladies who are visiting

the Georges.   They deplore the countryside and point out all
of its shortcomings.   They yearn for the Mall, in London,
and talk about how coarsened Mrs. George has become since
her marriage to the Squire and her move to the country.
Young George, they feel, has become a country bumpkin,
and Miss George nothing more than a hoyden.   Later, in
Act II, they reappear only to note how attractive the country
is.   (England's)

TWO HE-BABY PAPISTS AND A SHE-BABY--Souse each
other with holy water in Santa Croce in Lucy Honeychurch's
presence.   She observes them touching the memorial to
Machiavelli with their handkerchiefs, their fingers, and their
heads.   Lucy is puzzled by their behavior until she realizes
that they think it is the shrine to some saint and by "continual contact with his shrine were hoping to acquire virtue."
(RWV II)

TWO ITALIANS BY THE LOGGIA--Lucy Honeychurch sees
them argue and one stabs the other.   (RWV IV)

TWO LITTLE OLD LADIES--The Misses Catherine and
Teresa Alan.   Lucy Honeychurch meets them in the Pensione
Bertolini.   Later Lucy recommends that they rent one of Sir
Harry Otway's villas.   Still later, Lucy intends to go to
Greece with them.   At the pensione they stood for good
breeding.   (RWV I)

TWO MISS ROBINSONS, THE--The aunts of Eustace.   One
is named Mary.   (Collect Ta - Story)

TWO PARTING GUESTS--Of the Grand Hôtel des Alpes.   The
Concièrge interrupts his discussion with Miss Raby to speed
them on their way.   One of them tips him.   (Collect Ta -
Eternal)

TWO SMALL CHILDREN--Fielding thinks that they may have
overheard Adela Quested say that Aziz is innocent.   (PI
XXII)

TYLER--The narrator.   He dislikes Eustace.   (Collect Ta -
Story)

TYLER, JANET--Daughter of the narrator.   (Collect Ta -
Story)

TYLER, MRS. --Wife of the narrator.   (Collect Ta - Story)

TYLER, ROSE--One of two daughters of the narrator, Mr.
Tyler. (Collect Ta - Story)

U

"UNITED STATES, THE"--1st published as "Impressions of
the United States" in The Listener (4 September 1947), pp.
347-348; reprinted as "The United States" in Two Cheers for
Democracy, 1951.

[A Broadcast Talk in the BBC's Home Service.]
America is rather like life. You can usually find in it what
you look for. Forster describes his first visit when he was
sixty-eight years old. He wanted America to provide him
with scenery and individuals. The visit was a complete success. After a "respectful glance at New York," he went to
the Berkshires. They made him realize that America is not
all town. The Grand Canyon was the most astounding natural "object" he had ever seen. The second item he had
sought in America, individuals, he found in universities. He
had not expected so much tact, charm, and sensitiveness.
Though the people he met were full of "Charity" for Britain,
they did not display much interest in it. Russia, on the other hand, roused almost "hysteria." Forster did encounter
hints of "oppression, violence, snobbery." He ended his
three-month visit in the Berkshires.

UNKNOWN SICILIAN, THE--The boatman who attempts to
rescue the narrator's book from the water. As he swam for
it, his "effect was that of a silver statue alive beneath the
sea. . . Something infinitely happy, infinitely wise." It was
he who tells the narrator of Giuseppe, his brother, and his
meeting with the Siren. (Collect Ta - Siren)

UNPOPULAR PARSI, THE--Fielding cannot give his total at-
tention to Aziz's problem because of affairs at the college,
notably, the affair of the Russell's viper which one of the
masters, an unpopular Parsi, had found "nosing around his
classroom." (PI XIX)

"UNSUNG VIRTUE OF TOLERANCE, THE"--See: "Tolerance"

"UNSUNG VIRTUE OF TOLERANCE: IT IS VERY EASY TO
SEE FANATICISM IN OTHERS"--See: "Tolerance"

URIZEN--See: Enicharmon (Collect Ta - Machine)

V

VARDEN--A boy in Rickie Eliot's form whom Herbert Pembroke insists be "dropped on heavily" because he is attend-
ing as a day-boy but does not reside with parents or guardians but at Mrs. Orr's.   He is an unattractive boy with pro-
truding ears.   (LJ XVII)

VASHTI--A woman of the future about five feet tall with a
face as white as fungus.   She is the mother of Kuno of
whom she is ashamed because of his desire to leave the
Machine-dominated world for life above ground.   (Collect
Ta - Machine)

VENDER OF PHOTOGRAPHS, THE--Mr. Eager, in brushing
aside the vender's wares, tears one of Fra Angelico's angels.
The vender utters a shrill cry and appeals to Lucy for help.
(RWV V)

VICAR, THE--Aunt Emily goes to church with Agnes, Rickie
and Stephen.   The vicar preached on hurrying from one dis-
sipation to another.   (LJ XIII)

VICAR, THE--Mr. Beebe asks the Vicar about Lucy and is
told that she is the cousin of one of his parishioners who
praised Mr. Beebe's sermon.   (RWV III)

VICTORIER [sic]--The daughter of Signora Bertolini, the
owner of the Pensione Bertolini in Florence.   (RWV I)

"VIRGINIA WOOLF"--1st published as a pamphlet, Cambridge, The University Press, 22 May 1942; 1st American
edition, New York, Harcourt, Brace and Co. , 24 September,
1942; reprinted as "The Art of Virginia Woolf" in The Atlantic Monthly, CLXX (September 1942), pp. 82-90; reprinted
as "Virginia Woof's 'Enlightened Greediness' " in Wine and
Food, #37 (Spring 1943), pp. 60-61; reprinted as "Virginia
Woolf" in Two Cheers for Democracy, 1951.

[The Rede Lecture delivered in the Senate House,
Cambridge, 29 May 1941.]   There is difficulty summing up
the work of Virginia Woolf: its richness and its complexity.
Another obstacle is that 1941 is a bad year to sum up anything.   Consequently, Forster intends merely to "speak on"
her and her works.

She liked writing with an intensity which few writers have ever attained or desired. She was not interested in improving the world which she considered made by men and that she, a woman, had no responsibility for it. She is not a great creator of character, yet she did not fall into that pitfall of many authors, that "bottomless chasm of dullness, the 'Palace of Art'." She escaped the pitfall because she liked writing "for fun." This quality makes her amusing to read. She was master of her complicated equipment.

She began writing in 1915 with a strange, tragic, inspired novel about English tourists in an "impossible" South American hotel: The Voyage Out. Its successor, Night and Day, disappointed those few who read it and the first novel. This was followed by Kew Gardens and The Mark on the Wall, "lovely things" which did not prepare the readers for Jacob's Room (1922). The style and sensitiveness of Kew Gardens remained but was applied to human relationships and the structure of society. The improbable had occurred: an essentially "poetical, apparently trifling" method had been applied to fiction. Not entirely successful, the novel, nevertheless, leads on to her genius and its "fullness:" Mrs. Dalloway (1925), To the Lighthouse (1927), and The Waves (1931). These were followed by The Years. Like Night and Day, it is an experiment in the realistic tradition. In her posthumous novel, Between the Acts, she returns to the method she understood. Orlando is an original book. Flush is a complete success. In Roger Fry, one artist writes with affection of another. Finally, there are the feminist books: A Room of One's Own and Three Guineas. The problem in her work is "could she create character?" She could give life on the page, but not eternal life, save perhaps, for Mr. and Mrs. Ramsey, Rachel, and Clarissa Dalloway.

She is especially good when she writes about eating, the intellect, society--essentially a detachment from the working classes, which resulted, because of her feminism, into an aloof and angular attitude.

Like all her friends, Forster misses her greatly. She "got through" an immense amount of work and gave pleasure in new ways.

"VIRGINIA WOOLF'S 'ENLIGHTENED GREEDINESS' "--See: "Virginia Woolf"

VOICE, A--Stephen's wife who calls to him not to take their

daughter to sleep out with him. (LJ XXXV)

VOICE, A (A TURK)--Asks to accompany Mr. Andrews on
his journey to Heaven to make the trip seem shorter.   In
life he was a Moslem and died fighting the infidel.   He grew
up in the slums of Salonika and had three wives.   He pleads
for Mr. Andrews's entry into Heaven.   Like his companion,
he is dissatisfied with the place.   (Collect Ta - Mr.)

VOICE 1--Appears in Act I, Sc. iii.   A villager who cries
"shame" and demands that the Keeper release the poacher.
(England's)

VOICE 2--Appears in Act I, Sc. iii.   A villager who points
out that the poacher can be hung for poaching even though he
cannot live on seven pence a day.   (England's)

VOICE 3--Appears in Act I, Sc. iii.   Points out that steal-
ing is evil and against the Scriptures.   She is called Granny
by Voice 1.   (England's)

"VOLTAIRE AND FREDERICK THE GREAT"--1st published
as "But. . ." in The Listener (23 January 1941), pp. 120-
121; revised and reprinted as "When Voltaire Met Frederick
the Great" in London Calling, #73 (30 January 1941), pp. 2,
4; reprinted as "Voltaire and Frederick the Great" in Two
Cheers for Democracy, 1951.

Two hundred years ago, Voltaire had visited Frederick
the Great.   The two were enthusiastic on their meeting, yet,
the visit was a disaster.   Voltaire was one of the greatest
men of his age.   He wrote enormously, in particular the
masterpiece, Candide; he was a journalist, a pamphleteer,
he dabbled in science and philosophy, he was a good "popular historian," he compiled a dictionary and wrote hundreds
of letters.   He was not a great creative artist, but was a
great man.   He did not have a perfect character.   He was
a "bundle of contradictions and nerves."

Frederick is one of the founders of modern Germany.
He believed in force and fraud and cruelty and in doing
everything himself.   He did not believe in humanity.   He was
a cynic but also a "cultivated, sensitive gentleman, a good
musician and well-read."

The visit began well.   Voltaire became embroiled in
a shady business transaction.   He laughed at the King's

French poems. After two years, he left Berlin. The "bust up" came at Frankfurt. The city did not belong to Frederick, but Frederick had learned that Voltaire had taken a copy of his French poems. He went into a passion and ordered Voltaire's luggage searched. The searchers imprisoned Voltaire and bullied him night and day. Finally, he and his niece, Mme. Dennis, were released. In later years, Frederick and Voltaire corresponded almost as enthusiastically as before, but they were careful not to meet.

"VOLTAIRE'S LABORATORY"

1: How They Weighed Fire--1st published as "Incongruities: Weighing Fire" in The New York Herald Tribune, Section II, Books, (23 August 1931), pp. 1, 4; reprinted as "Voltaire's Laboratory, 1: How They Weighed Fire" in Abinger Harvest, 1936.

Voltaire took pleasure in the complexity of the universe. He believed in God, provided that God is given nothing to do. He conducted primitive scientific experiments, with his mistress, Mme. de Châtelet, which were essentially the "visual representation of what they felt." They saw "a new world opening in every direction and asking to be interpreted." They failed, nevertheless, in their attempts to weigh fire.

2: Troublesome Molluscs--1st published as "Incongruities Voltaire's Slugs" in The New York Herald Tribune, Section II, Books, (30 August 1931), pp. 1, 4; reprinted as "Voltaire's Laboratory, 2: Troublesome Molluscs" in Life and Letters, VII (September 1931), pp. 165-173; reprinted in Abinger Harvest, 1936.

Voltaire snipped off the heads of slugs in an attempt to determine if they would grow back. No conclusive proof was obtained. Voltaire was delighted, but puzzled. Deposits of mollusc shells in Touraine annoyed him because they seem to support the flood in Genesis. Voltaire, in the last analysis, loved freedom, not truth.

VORTA--The scene of the short story, "The Eternal Moment." (Collect Ta - Ternal)

"VOTER'S DILEMMA, A"--1st published in New Leader (30 November 1923), p. 8; reprinted in Abinger Harvest, 1936; reprinted omitting ten lines in The New Republic (19 January 1948), p. 7.

      Satiric verse in which a voter cannot make up his mind on whom to choose between two candidates for Parliament. Both candidates are very much alike and both represent "The way of blood and fire and tears."

VYSE, CECIL--The fiancé of Lucy Honeychurch who has finally consented to marry him after he has asked her for the third time. Mrs. Honeychurch thinks him good, clever, rich and well-connected and with beautiful manners. He is "medieval like a Gothic statue" tall and refined. But a "Gothic statue implies celibacy." (RWV VIII)

VYSE, MR. --Margaret asks her brother Tibby, who is home for the Easter vacation and who has completed his first year at Oxford, what he hoped to do with himself. Tibby wants nothing to do with a profession. Margaret points out that Mr. Vyse, who has no profession, does not strike her as particularly happy. Helen notes that Mr. Vyse is "rather a wretched, weedy man." (HE XIII)

VYSE, MRS. --The mother of Cecil. She is a "nice woman" but "her personality like many another's, had been swamped by London." She had seen "too many seasons, too many cities, too many men for her abilities." Even with her son she was "mechanical. Mrs. Honeychurch notes that she does not look after her maids well. (RWV V)

W

WANTON DAIRYMAIDS OF BRINDABAN, THE--Those who had witnessed the festivities of the birth of the god Krishna, simulate his "sports with the wanton dairymaids of Brindaban." (PI XXIII)

"WAR AND THE LEAGUE (1914-1926), THE"--Title of Chapter XII, Goldsworthy Lowes Dickinson. For summary see: Goldsworthy Lowes Dickinson.

WATERS AND ADAMSON--Lila Herriton's solicitors who write the Herritons that Lila has had a baby by Gino Carella. (WAFT V)

"WEBB AND WEBB"--1st published in Two Cheers for Democracy, 1951.

[A revised version of a broadcast in the BBC's Far
Eastern Service delivered 26 May 1943 in the series "Some
Books."] In order to give homage to Beatrice Webb, Forster felt that he must begin with a summary of her work
which dealt with the investigation of society. This investigation led to many important volumes. The daughter of a
successful railway director, she lived a pleasant life.
Though her family was rich, some of her relatives were not.

She did not believe in a local and sentimental pity.
Nor did she believe that poverty could be cured by charity;
she believed that it could be cured by altering the conditions in which the poor lived. Her conversion to socialism
and her marriage occurred at the same time. From the
moment of their marriage, husband and wife worked as one
person. Forster recalls his only meeting with the Webbs.
They were "attentive, courteous to the last."

WEDERKIND--One of Margaret Schlegel's Chelsea friends
whom she dropped after her marriage to Mr. Wilcox. (HE
XXXI)

"WHAT HAS GERMANY DONE TO THE GERMANS?"--1st
published in The Listener (3 October 1940), pp. 447-448;
reprinted as "Three Anti-Nazi Broadcasts, 2: What Has
Germany Done to the Germans?" in Two Cheers for Democracy, 1951.

Before she could attack Europe, Germany was com-
pelled to subjugate her own people. The writers, painters,
sculptors, architects, musicians, philosophers, scientists,
and theologians--the creators and the thinkers--all were attacked. Artistic expression was denied the individual. Forster recalls the burning of books which took place May 13,
1933. The burning was followed by a systematic control of
literature. Heine's works, because he was a Jew, were denounced and banned as "soul-devastating, soul-poisoning."
Goethe was treated with more respect. When Germany had
finished with her own people, she turned against the English,
but it was all part of a single movement which had as its
aim the fettering of the writer, the scientist, the artist all
over the world.

"WHAT I BELIEVE"--1st published as "Two Cheers for Democracy" in The Nation (N. Y.) (16 July 1938), pp. 65-68;
reprinted with some additions as "Credo" in The London
Mercury, XXXVIII (September 1938), pp. 397-404; reprinted

as a pamphlet, London, Hogarth Press, 1939; reprinted in
Two Cheers for Democracy, 1951.

      Tolerance, good temper, and sympathy are what mat-
ter really but they are not enough today. Forster's law
givers are Erasmus and Montaigne and his "temple" stands
in the Elysian Fields. His motto is "Lord, I disbelieve--
help thou my disbelief." Forster believes in personal relationships. Democracy, he feels, is less hateful than other
contemporary forms of government and to that extent it de-
serves support. It is sensitive, admits variety, and allows
criticism which is to its merit. Forster believes in the
"Press." He believes that force exists and it is one of our
jobs to see that it does not get out "of its box." Force is
the ultimate reality. Its "absences are civilization." No
millenium seems likely to descend upon humanity, yet there
is no need to despair. Forster distrusts great men. They
produce a "desert of uniformity" about them. He believes
in aristocracy: an aristocracy of the sensitive, the consid-
erate, and the plucky. He is against "asceticism." He is
an individualist and a liberal.

"WHAT I BELIEVE"--The title of Part II, Two Cheers for
Democracy.

"WHAT WOULD GERMANY DO TO BRITAIN IF SHE WON?"
--See: "What Would Germany Do to Us?"

"WHAT WOULD GERMANY DO TO US?"--1st published in
The Listener, (3 October 1940), pp. 477-478; revised and
reprinted as "What Would Germany Do to Britain if She
Won?" in London Calling, #57 (10 October 1940), p. 2; re-
printed as "Three Anti-Nazi Broadcasts, 2: What Would
Germany Do to Us?" in Two Cheers for Democracy, 1951.

      In this article Forster says that cultural conditions,
though not perfect in the British Isles, are paradise when
compared with those in Germany, and heaven compared with
those conditions Germany would impose were she to win the
war. Forster believes that he knows what these conditions
would be like because he knows what Germany has done in
other countries, notably Czechoslovakia and Poland. Destruction of national culture is part of its program of conquest.

      He goes on to theorize that the fate of the British
Isles would be the same as Poland's. The Nazis would re-

organize and restaff the educational system. Theatres,
cinemas, and the wireless would be converted to the ends of
the Nazis. The British government would be held responsible for any acts which annoyed Berlin. A maximum of
brutality would be used to remodel life completely. The fate
of individual writers would be hard. The young writers
would be intimidated. Books would probably not be burned--
the blaze would be too big. However, a different interpre-
tation of English Literature would be attempted. The inter-
pretation would insist that the best writers are Nazis at
heart. Though Forster longs for peace, he cannot see how
terms can be made with Hitler. A peace with the Nazis
could not differ much from a Nazi war.

"WHEN VOLTAIRE MET FREDERICK THE GREAT"--See:
"Voltaire and Frederick the Great"

WHERE ANGELS FEAR TO TREAD--1st edition, Edinburgh
and London: William Blackwood, 4 October 1905; American
edition, New York, Alfred A. Knopf, 10 January 1920.

Lila Herriton, a widow for several years, is living
near her husband's family since his death. She agrees to
leave Sawston for an extended stay in Italy. The trip had
been suggested by her brother-in-law, Philip, and seconded
by her mother-in-law and her sister-in-law, Harriet, because they feared Lila's increasing interest in a man they
considered unsuitable for her. They are also eager to have
the freedom to train Lila's daughter, Irma, without her
mother's interference. Lila is accompanied by Caroline
Abbot, who is younger but considerably more sensible. The
winter passes peacefully and everyone believes that the trip
is a success. The spring comes and with it word from
Lila's mother that Lila has written of her engagement to an
Italian. Mrs. Herriton immediately wires Caroline for information only to receive word which she senses is false.
Caroline wires that Lila's fiance is an Italian nobleman.
Mrs. Herriton insists that Philip go at once to prevent the
wedding. Caroline meets him at the station and, on their
way to Monteriano, confesses that Gino, the man in question,
is merely the son of a dentist. He is twelve years younger
than Lila whose language he does not speak well. He is
little more than a peasant. Philip is appalled when they
meet. Gino's manners are vulgar though he is physically
handsome. He attempts to bribe Gino into breaking with
Lila only to discover that the marriage has already taken
place. There is nothing more for Philip to do but to return

home with Caroline.

The Herritons refuse to have any more to do with
Lila. She has already become disillusioned with the man she
has married. She can neither understand him or his social
customs; nor can he understand her. Gino's one ambition
is to have a son. And, even though he has an affair with
another woman, he convinces Lila, whom he treats shabbily,
that a child will bring her the happiness for which she longs.
Her hopes are short lived; she dies in childbirth.

The Herritons contrive to conceal the birth from Irma
though they tell her of her mother's death. Before her
death, Lila had written a passionate letter to Irma filled
with the bitterness of her life with Gino. This, too, the
Herritons keep from Irma. Their efforts prove futile, however, when Irma begins to receive postcards from Gino.
Soon all Sawston discovers the news.

Mrs. Herriton becomes convinced that she should have
Gino's child to raise to prevent it from becoming a Roman
Catholic. Once again she sends Philip to Italy accompanied
this time by his sister, Harriet. Caroline has the same
idea; she believes Gino a brute and hopes to raise the child
herself. Their efforts fail and Harriet, resorting to more
dramatic methods, kidnaps the child and joins Philip who
has hired a carriage to take them to the railroad station.
In the dark and the rain, the carriage overturns, killing the
baby and breaking Philip's arm. When Philip tells Gino
what has happened, Gino almost kills him in his grief and
rage. Caroline, whom Gino respects, calms him and pre-
vents a second tragedy. By the time Philip recuperates, the
two men are friends. On the way back to England, Philip
wants to declare his love for Caroline only to discover that
she loves Gino and is resolved never to see him again. All
his life Philip thought that he had understood the world only
to discover that he understood nothing.

"WHIFF OF D'ANNUNZIO, A"--1st published as "A Mediterranean Problem" in The Spectator, (22 April 1938), pp. 201-
202; reprinted as "A Whiff of D'Annunzio" in Two Cheers for
Democracy, 1951.

[A review of D'Annunzio by Tom Antongini.] Poet,
hero, and cad, D'Annunzio presents a test problem to the
Englishman. Byron, to whom he has been compared, was
difficult enough, but D'Annunzio's work is even more so

since his poetry is more poetical, his heroism more histrion-
ic, his caddishness innate in his bones and bowels and he
has no sense of humor.   His leading passion was a passion
for earthly immortality.   He was successful to a degree,
leaving a number of books, a larger number of mistresses
and the city of Fiume behind to save him from oblivion.
He was always heralding, always heading some sumptuous
embassy of his own creation, clothing his actions in a gor-
geous rhetoric.   His contacts with life were sensuous and
local in their character.   Nothing he writes is profound, yet
he is never superficial.   His courage is unquestionable; he
possessed gut and dash.   He could write like music, like
scents, like religion, like blood.   There has been nobody
like him.   He can be hailed as a poet and hero.

WHITBY, MARTIN--An English tourist at Basle Station who
is almost killed under a train.   Strangers always patronized
him.   He was a clerk in the Treasury and a civilized man
who hoped for an "arctic summer."   (AS)

WHITBY, VENETIA--The wife of Martin Whitby who never
thought of herself being anything other than that which she is
presently.   (AS)

"WHY 'JULIUS CAESAR' LIVES"--See: "Julius Caesar"

WICKHAM MANSIONS--The London home of the Schlegels.
(HE VII)

WICKHAM PLACE--The London street on which is located
the home of Margaret, Helen, and Tibby Schlegel.   The
house is quiet, and separated from the main thoroughfare.
One had the sense of a backwater.   (HE II)

WIDDRINGTON--A friend of Rickie Elliot at Cambridge who
goes with him and Ansell to the dell which Rickie has discovered.   (LJ II)

WILBRAHAM, MR.--Aunt Emily's agent.   He knew his place
and kept others to theirs.   "All society seemed spread before him like a map."   He knew the lines between the county
and the local, the laborers and the artisans, and strength-
ened them.   He acted with graded civility toward his su-
periors and carefully graded incivility to his inferiors.   (LJ
XI)

WILCOX, CHARLES--The son of Henry and Ruth Wilcox.

As their oldest child, he objects to the marriage of his father to Margaret Schlegel.   Want was to him the only reason
for action.   He beats Leonard Bast who dies as a result of
a heart attack brought on by the beating.   Charles is con-
victed of manslaughter.   (HE I)

WILCOX, DOLLY--See: Dolly Fussell.

WILCOX, EVIE--Only daughter of Henry and Ruth Wilcox
and sister of Paul and Charles.   It is at her wedding that
Margaret Schlegel learns of the affair Henry Wilcox had had
with Jacky.   Aunt Juley calls Evie a "minx."   Evie is heavy-
browed.   (HE I)

WILCOX, HENRY--Represents all of those elements which
are "at cross purposes" with the "fetishes" of the Schlegel
girls.   He has no use for "Art and Literature, Equality,
Votes for Women, and Socialism" all of which he calls non-
sense.   His views, however, rather than offending Helen,
intrigue her.   He is an elderly man with a moustache and
a copper-colored face.   He marries Margaret Schlegel after
his wife's death.   His health is broken when his son,
Charles, is sent to prison for manslaughter.   (HE I)

WILCOX, MYRA--See: Myra

WILCOX, PAUL--The youngest son of Henry and Ruth Wilcox.   Helen thinks that she is in love with him.   Both Ruth
Wilcox and Margaret think the match unsuitable.   (HE I)

WILCOX, RUTH--Wife of Henry and mother of Charles,
Paul and Evie.   She is the last of the Howard family and
owner of Howards End.   She is a semi-invalid who spends
much of her time in bed.   Her one passion is her house.
She seems to belong to the house and the tree which over-
shadows it.   She worshipped the past and the "instinctive
wisdom of what can be bestowed only by the past had des-
cended upon her--that wisdom which we give the name of
aristocracy."   Clever talk alarmed her.   She had little to
say to strangers because her life had been passed in service
to her husband and sons.   She was not an intellectual.   She
was born at Howards End.   (HE I)

WILCOX, MRS. WARINGTON--The sister-in-law of Henry
Wilcox who had fortunately returned from her tour around
the world in time for Evie's wedding and to meet Margaret
Schlegel.   (HE XXV)

"WILFRID BLUNT"--(in two parts)

Part I--The Earlier Diaries-1888-1900--1st published
as "Gog and Magog" in The Nation (London) (19 July 1919),
pp. 429-480; reprinted as "Wilfrid Blunt, 1: The Earlier
Diaries" in Abinger Harvest, 1936.

Part II--The Later Diaries--1900-1914--1st published
as "Wilfrid Blunt and the East" in The Nation (London) (21
February 1921), pp. 712, 714; reprinted as "Wilfrid Blunt,
2: The Later Diaries" in Abinger Harvest, 1936.

[A review of My Diaries, 1888-1900 and My Diaries,
1900-1914 by Wilfrid S. Blunt.] Blunt is never ashamed of
his "inconsistencies;" he acted as he felt. He was incapable
of "cant" and was intolerant of it in others. His vision was
"aesthetic" though his career in politics was practical. He
had the power of "alluring the East." He is still remembered, though his ideas are not necessarily agreed with. He
lives in its chronicles as one of the few "really noble Englishmen." He saw World War I as essentially Oriental and
the chief villain as Islam. His birth and education destined
him to be a high official, but he spent all of his life "tilting
against officialdom."

"WILFRID BLUNT AND THE EAST"--See: "Wilfrid Blunt"

"WILLIAM ARNOLD"--1st published as "An Arnold in India"
in The Listener, (12 October 1944), pp. 410-411; reprinted
as "William Arnold" in Two Cheers for Democracy, 1951.

[A Broadcast in the BBC's Eastern Service.] Forster
had read William Arnold's novel, Oakfield, or Fellowship in
the East with intense interest because it was written by the
brother of Matthew Arnold, who is, of all Victorians, most
to his taste.

William, born in 1828, was educated at Rugby and Oxford, and spent his holidays in the Lake District. He went
to India as a soldier and remained there in the civil service
where he became director of education for the Punjab. The
novel was considered an attack upon the English in India.
The story is depressing reading. Oakfield, like Arnold,
lands in India with the best of desires but is thwarted by the
Englishmen he meets. He is unpopular in his regiment, and
is reassigned. At this point, according to Forster, the most
exciting part of the story begins. The officers, though gen-

tlemanly, are affected by the general laxity of European morals
in the East. They are unchivalrous to women. Oakfield meets
Middleton, a civil servant, and his sister. Her name comes up
in the mess and Oakfield protests only to be challenged to a du-
el. He refuses to fight. Finally, goaded by challenges of cowardice, he turns on one of his tormentors and beats him with a
horsewhip. He is court-martialed as a result, but is acquitted.
Then comes the second Sikh war in which, by an act of bravery,
he regains his reputation. He resigns his commission and becomes a magistrate, but he longs to return home to England.
Finally he does return.

Forster finds the book disquieting, even when times have
changed so much in India, because it is "sincere" in stating
"fearlessly" truths which are "unwelcome." The book is prophetic for William Arnold "fizzled" out as does his hero.

"WILLIAM BARNES"--1st published as "Homage to William
Barnes" in New Statesman and Nation, N. S. (9 December 1939),
pp. 819-820; reprinted as "William Barnes" in Two Cheers
for Democracy, 1951.

An examination of the life and poetry of William Barnes
who is most noted for his poems in the dialect of Dorset.
Forster finds his poetry excellent. Barnes never "destroys,"
and seldom "criticises."

"WILTSHIRE"--Title of Part III, The Longest Journey.

WINDY CORNER--The name of the Honeychurch home. (RWV I)

WOLVERHAMPTON--The birthplace of Anthony Failing, May
14, 1842. (LJ X)

WONHAM, STEPHEN--The illegitimate half-brother of
Rickie Elliot. (LJ X)

WOODCUTTER'S SON, THE--Explains to his mother the
emotion he felt when he saw Mrs. Wilcox's coffin. (HE XI)
See also: The Mother of the Woodcutter's Son.

WOODMAN, THE--The narrator. (AH-AB)

"WORD-MAKING AND SOUND-TAKING"--1st published in
New Statesman and Nation, N. S. (9 March 1935), p. 34;
reprinted in Abinger Harvest, 1936.

Forster feels that "the pot of art gets cracked here and there and sheds a few drops into life." Words and sounds (music) often merge and support each other.

"WORK OF FORREST REID, THE"--See: "Forrest Reid"

"WORLD OF MATTER (1884-1887), THE"--Title of Chapter VIII, Goldsworth Lowes Dickinson. For summary see: Goldsworthy Lowes Dickinson.

WORTERS, HARCOURT--The son of Mrs. Worters and the fiancé of Evelyn Beaumont. He is also the guardian of Jack Ford, and the employer of Mr. Inskip. He is tall, handsome, has a strong chin and liquid, brown eyes, a high fore-head, and hair not at all grey. He announces the fact that he has bought Other Kingdom copse to round out his estate, and as a gift for Evelyn. (Collect Ta - Other)

WORTERS, MRS.--The mother of Harcourt. (Collect Ta - Other)

Y

YOUNG LADY BEHIND THE BUREAU, A--Miss Raby can hear the "genteel sniggers" of those two "most vile creatures:" a young lady behind the bureau and a young man in a frock coat who shows new arrivals to their rooms in the hotel. (Collect Ta - Eternal)

YOUNG MAN, A--Mr. Lucas is awakened from his sleep by the song of a young man. He looks at the man and finds beauty in his pose and sincerity in his greeting. (Collect Ta - Road)

YOUNG MAN IN A FROCK COAT, A--See: A young lady behind the bureau. (Collect Ta - Eternal)

YOUNG MOTHER, A--See: Mrs. Blakiston (PI XX)

YOUTH OF ATHLETIC BUT MELANCHOLY APPEARANCE, A--He is fidgeting in the portico of the Grand Hôtel des Alpes until the Concièrge says "I told you the percentage. If you had agreed to it, I would have recommended you. Now it is too late. I have enough guides." (Collect Ta - Eternal)

"YUVRAJ, THE"--See: "Catastrophe: The Yuvraj"

Z

ZULFIQAR, MR. --The Nawab Bahadur, angered by Aziz's trial and at reports of atrocities committed against Indians in the hospital, announces to the crowd which had just "rescued" Nurredin, his grandson, from the hospital, that he would renounce the title conferred upon him by the English and retire to his country estates as a private gentleman, plain Mr. Zulfiqar.   (PI XXV)

APPENDIX I

A Listing of the Characters of E. M. Forster
in Order of the Works in which they Appear

ABINGER PAGEANT, THE
Riccabocca, Dr.
Woodman, The

ARCTIC SUMMER
Austinson
Borlase, Lady
March, Lieut. C. P.
Whitby, Martin
Whitby, Venetia

CELESTIAL OMNIBUS, THE
Achilles
Bob
Bons, Mr. Septimus
Browne, Mr. (Sir Thomas
  Browne)
Dan (Dante)
Driver, the
Mother
Mr. Bons's daughter

CO-ORDINATION
Beethoven
Dolores
Ellen
Enid
Haddon, Miss
Jane
Margaret
Mephistopholes [sic]
Mildred
Napoleon
Principal, the
Raphael
Rose

CURATE's FRIEND, THE
Curate, the (Harry)
Emily
Emily's mother
Faun
Harry (the Curate)
Little friend, the

ENGLAND'S PLEASANT LAND
Bumble, Mr.
George, Miss
George, Mrs.
George, Squire
George, Young
Granny (Voice 3)
Jack
Jeremiah, Mrs.
Jeremiah, Squire
Jerry
Jerry, Mrs.
Jill
Keeper, the
Norman Girl
Norman Knight
Peacher, a
Recorder, the
Saxon Youth
Two guests from Town
Voice 1
Voice 2
Voice 3

ETERNAL MOMENT, THE
American girl new to the
  country, an
American lady

185

American lady's father, the
Anstey, Lady
Bamburgh, Marquis of
Bishop, a
Cantù, Signor
Cantù, Signora
Concièrge, the (Feo Ginori)
Driver, the
Elizabeth
French Lady, a
German waitress, the
Ginor, Feo (the Concièrge)
Gray-haired Lady, a
Harbottle, Mrs.
Heriot, Mrs.
Lelyand, Col. Edwin
Lionel
Nelly
Porter, a (Feo Ginori)
Raby, Miss
Russian Prince
Signor Cantù's wife
Two Parting Guests

HOWARDS END
Ahab
Angelo
Annie
Another Guest
Aunt Juley's Nurses
Avery, Miss
Baby
Bast, Leonard
Bearded Porter
Bertha
Bidder, Sir James
Blanche
Blanche's husband
Bracknell
Bryce, Hamar
Burton
Cahill, Mrs. Percy
Chalkeley
Chinless Sunburnt Men, the

Chorly-Worly
Clergymen, the
Condor, Miss
Cook at Howards End, the
Cook at Oniton, the
Crane
Cunningham, Mr.
Dealty, Mr.
Diddums
Doctor, the
Driver of Helen's Cab, the
Earnest Girl, an
Edser, Lady
Forstmeister, Herr
Fraulein Mosebach's Young man (Liescke, Bruno)
Friend of Mrs. Wilcox, a
Fussell, Albert
Fussell, Colonel
Fussell, Dolly (Mrs. Charles Wilcox)
Girl who had been typing the strong letter, the
Gravediggers, the
Guy
Half a dozen gardeners
Handsome girl, a
Haughty nephew, the
Haughty nephew's wife, the
Hermit, a
Hostess, the
Howard, Tom
Italian chauffeur (Angelo)
Jacky (Mrs. Leonard Bast)
John
Juley, Aunt (Mrs. Munt)
Lanoline, Mrs. (Jacky Bast)
Laura
Laura's husband
Leonard's brother
Liescke, Bruno
Liescke, Freida (Freida Mosebach)
Liescke, Victor
Little boy, a
Little boy, a (Tom)
Little girl, the
Lord of the Manor

Madge (Niece of Miss
  Avery)
Madge's husband
Maid
Maids
Man, a
Man carrying a roll of
  oilcloth, a
Management, the
Manbridge
Margaret's new young man
  (Leonard Bast)
Martlett, Mrs.
Mathesons
Matron of the nursing
  home
Member of the lower or-
  ders, a
Miles, Mr. Eustace
Milton
Monica
Mosebach, Freida
Mother of the wood-
  cutter's son, the
Munt, Mrs. (Aunt Juley)
Myra (Myra Wilcox)
Navvies
Niece of Miss Avery
  (Madge)
Old Woman (Miss Avery)
Parlour-maid, a
Pembroke, Mr.
Penny
Plynlimmon, Mrs.
Porgly-Woggles
Porter, a bearded (see:
  a bearded porter)
Proprietors of the livery
  stable
Reader of the paper, the
Rector of the Parish of
  Hilton, the
Rector of the Parish of
  Oniton, the
Rothenstein
Quested, Miss
Schlegel, Emily
Schlegel, Ernest

Schlegel, Helen
Schlegel, Margaret
Schlegel, Tibby (Theobald)
Screaming girl, a
Servant, a
Small boy, a
Son of the woodcutter, the
Spinster, a
They
Tibby (Theobald Schlegel)
Ticket boy
Tom (little boy)
Tom's father
Tompkin
Vyse, Mr.
Wederkind
Wilcox, Charles
Wilcox Dolly (Mr. Charles
  Wilcox, Dolly Fussell)
Wilcox, Evie
Wilcox, Henry
Wilcox, Myra (Myra)
Wilcox, Paul
Wilcox, Ruth (née Howard)
Wilcox, Mrs. Warington
Woodcutter's son (see: son
  of the woodcutter)

THE LONGEST JOURNEY

Aberdeen, Mrs.
Aeneas
Anderson, Mr.
Annison, Mr.
Ansell's bedmaker
Ansell, Mary
Ansell, Maud
Ansell, Mr.
Ansell, Stewart
Appleblossom, Miss
Bystander, A
Carruthers, A. P.
Certain poor woman, a
Child, the
Chunk, Mrs. Julia P.
Coates, Mr.
Cook, the
Dawes, Gerald
Dido

Amritrao
Antony
Aryan Brother, the
Astrologers
Aziz, Dr.
Aziz's maternal grand-
    father
Aziz's wife
Bannister, Hugh
Bannister, Mrs.
Bhattacharya, Mr.
Bhattacharya, Mrs.
Blakiston, Mrs.
Brahman, a
Callendar, Major
Callendar, Mrs.
Cousins of Miss Quested
Dapple
Das
Das, Mrs.
Deccani Brahman
Derek, Miss
Elegant grandson of the
    Nawab Bahadur, the
    (Nurredin)
Esmiss Esmoor (Mrs.
    Moore)
Fielding, Cecil
Fielding's bearer
Goanese servant, the
Godbole, Narayan
Godbole's colleague
Graysford, Mr.
Graysford, Mrs.
Hamidullah
Hamidullah Begum
Haq, Mr.
Harris, Mr.
Hassan
Heaslop, Ronny
Interrupting students
Junior Rani of Mau, the
Karim
Krishna
Lady who had been a
    nurse, the (Mrs. Mc
    Bryde)
Lal, Dr. Panna

Latif, Mohammed
Lesley, Mr.
Lesley, Mrs.
McBryde, Mr.
McBryde, Mrs.
Maggs, Colonel
Maharani of Mudkul
Major Callendar's Servant
Mali, a
Mellanby, Sir Gilbert
Mellanby, Lady
Milner
Miss Derek's chauffeur
Mohammed, Syed
Mohurram
Moore, Mrs.
Moore, Ralph
Moore, Stella (Stella, Stella
    Fielding)
Muggins
Nawab Bahadur, the
Nurredin
Old Gentleman with a beard
    (Nawab Bahadur)
One of a gang of Pathans
Policeman, a native
Punkah Wallah
Quested, Adela
Rafi
Rajah of Mau, the
Rajah of Mau's confidential
    servant, the
Rajah of Mau's Hindu physi-
    cian, the
Rajah of Mau's private sec-
    retary, the
Ralph (Ralph Moore)
Red-nosed boy
Roberts, Major
Servant of the club
Sorley, Mr.
Stella (Stella Fielding)
Students
Subaltern, the
Turton, Mr.
Turton, Mrs. Mary
Two small children
Unpopular Parsi, the

Zulfiqar, Mr. (The Na-
wab Bahadur)

POINT OF IT, THE
Adam
Adam's boy
Catherine
Catherine's boy
Chand, Ram
Doctor, the
Harold
Henry
Janet
Michael
Michael's neighbor
Nurse
Shades

ROAD FROM COLONUS,
THE
Daughter of Maria Rhom-
aides
Dragoman who speaks
English
Ethel
Forman, Mrs.
Grandson of Maria
Graham, Mr.
Julia
Little Greek Children
Lucas, Mr.
Old woman (Maria Rhom-
aides)
Rhomaides, Maria
Young man, a

A ROOM WITH A VIEW
Alan, Miss Catherine
Alan, Miss Teresa
Anne
Antonio
Baroncelli, Contessa
Bartlett, Charlotte
Beebe, Mr.
Beebe, Mrs.
Bertolini, Signora
Butterworth, Mrs.
Cabman, a

Eager, Rev. Cuthbert
Elses, Somebody
Emerson, George
Emerson, Mr.
'Enry
Euphemia
Flack, Mr.
Flack, Mrs.
Floyd, Mr.
Honeychurch, Freddy
Honeychurch, Lucy
Honeychurch, Mrs.
Italian Lady, an
Laverstock, Lady Helen
Lavish, Eleanor
Lennie
Leonora
Louisa, Lady
Mary
Old man with white whiskers,
an
Otway, Sir Harry
Persephone
Phaethon
Pole, Miss
Powell
Prank, Joseph Emery
Shoolbred and Maple
Something, Mr. Someone
Two he-baby Papists and a
she-baby
Two Italians by the Loggia
Two little old ladies (Misses
Catherine and Teresa
Alan)
Venders of photographs, the
Victorier [sic]
Vyse, Cecil
Vyse, Mrs.

STORY OF A PANIC, THE
Emmanuele
Eustace
Gennaro
Leyland, Mr.
Robinson, Julia
Robinson, Mary
Sandbach

190

Three old Italian ladies
Tyler
Tyler, Janet
Tyler, Mrs.
Tyler, Rose

Soldier, a private
Tessi, Spiridone
Theobald, Mrs.
Waters and Adamson

STORY OF THE SIREN,
  THE
Chaplain, the
Chaplain's sister, the
Child, a
Giuseppe
Maria
Narrator
Narrator's aunt
Old witch, an
Unknown Sicilian

VOTER'S DILEMMA, A
Brown, Mr.
Grey, Mr.

WHERE ANGELS FEAR TO
  TREAD
Abbot, Caroline
Abbot, Mr.
Carella, Gino
Chinless curate with the
  dampest hands, the
Driver of a diligence, the
Gino's cousin
Gino's father
Gino's uncle
Herriton, Charles
Herriton, Harriet
Herriton, Irma
Herriton, Joseph
Herriton, Lila Theobald
  (Mrs. Gino Carella)
Herriton, Mrs.
Herriton, Philip
Kingcroft, Mr.
Landlady of the Stella
  d'Italia, the
Little girl, a
Miriam
Perfetta
Porter, a

APPENDIX II

A List of the Works of E. M. Forster
Summarized in the Dictionary

Omitted from this list and from the dictionary are generally those contributions not collected in Forster's three volumes of essays: Abinger Harvest, Pharos and Pharillon, and Two Cheers for Democracy. Exceptions to this rule are the fragment of a novel, Arctic Summer, six essays printed as pamphlets: Battersea Rise, Desmond MacCarthy, E. K. Bennett, I Assert that there is an Alternative in Humanism, Nordic Twilight, and Tourism V. Thuggism [see: Introduction]; and the pageant, England's Pleasant Land.

This list makes no pretensions to the label, "a complete bibliography of E. M. Forster." No such list is extant. The bibliography which comes closest to the ideal is, of course, that of B. J. Kirkpatrick (London: Rupert Hart-Davis, 1968) which has been revised twice. By her own admission, however, Miss Kirkpatrick has not been able to trace "all his signed and unsigned contributions to periodicals and newspapers." Nevertheless, the bibliography she has produced is an invaluable tool for the Forster scholar.

Abinger Harvest. London, Edward Arnold and Co. , 1936.

"Abinger Pageant, The," in Abinger Harvest, 1936.

"Adrift in India, 1: The Nine Gems of Ujjain; 2: Advance, India! 3: Jodhpur; 4: The Suppliant; 5: Pan," in Abinger Harvest, 1936.

Alexandria: A History and a Guide. Alexandria, Egypt, Whitehead and Morris, Ltd. , 1922.

"Anonymity: An Enquiry," in Two Cheers for Democracy, 1951.

"Arctic Summer," in Tribute to Benjamin Britten on His
    Fiftieth Birthday, edited by Anthon Gishfors. Lon-
    don, Faber and Faber, 1963.

"Art for Art's Sake," in Two Cheers for Democracy, 1951.

"Ascent of F. 6, The," in Two Cheers for Democracy, 1951.

Aspects of the Novel.   London, Edward Arnold and Co. ,
    1927.

Battersea Rise.   New York, Harcourt Brace and Co. , 1925.

"Between the Sun and the Moon," in Pharos and Pharillon,
    1923.

"Bishop Jebb's Book," in Two Cheers for Democracy, 1951.

"Book that Influenced Me, A," in Two Cheers for Democ-
    racy, 1951.

"C Minor of That Life, The," in Two Cheers for Democ-
    racy, 1951.

"Cambridge," in Two Cheers for Democracy, 1951.

"Captain Edward Gibbon," in Abinger Harvest, 1936.

"Cardan," in Abinger Harvest, 1936.

"The Celestial Omnibus," in The Celestial Omnibus and
    Other Stories, 1911.

The Celestial Omnibus and Other Stories.   London, Sidgwick
    and Jackson Ltd. , 1911.   (Included in The Collected
    Tales, 1947).

"Challenge of Our Time, The," in Two Cheers for Democ-
    racy, 1951.

"Clement of Alexandria," in Pharos and Pharillon, 1923.

"Clouds Hill," in Two Cheers for Democracy, 1951.

"Cnidus," in Abinger Harvest, 1936.

Collected Tales, The.   New York, Alfred A. Knopf, 1947.

"Consolations of History, The," in Abinger Harvest, 1936.

"Co-ordination," in The Eternal Moment and Other Stories, 1928.

"Cotton from the Outside," in Pharos and Pharillon, 1923.

"Culture and Freedom," in Two Cheers for Democracy, 1951.

"Den, The," in Pharos and Pharillon, 1923.

Desmond MacCarthy. Stanford Dingley, England, The Millhouse Press, 1952.

"Does Culture Matter?" in Two Cheers for Democracy, 1951.

"Duke Remembers, A," in Two Cheers for Democracy, 1951.

"Duty of Society to the Artist, The," in Two Cheers for Democracy, 1951.

"Early Novels of Virginia Woof, The," in Abinger Harvest, 1936.

"Edward Carpenter," in Two Cheers for Democracy, 1951.

Egypt. London, The Labour Research Department, 1920.

E. K. Bennett (Francis) (1887-1958). Reprinted from the Caian (Michaelmas Term, 1958) as a pamphlet, May, 1959.

"Eliza in Egypt," in Pharos and Pharillon, 1923.

"Emperor Babur, The," in Abinger Harvest, 1936.

"Enchanted Flood, The," in Two Cheers for Democracy, 1951.

England's Pleasant Land. London, The Hogarth Press, 1940.

"English Prose Between 1918 and 1939," in Two Cheers for Democracy, 1951.

"Epiphany," in Pharos and Pharillon, 1923.

"Eternal Moment, The," in The Eternal Moment and Other Stories, 1928.

Eternal Moment and Other Stories, The. London, Sidgwick and Jackson, Ltd., 1928. (Later included in The Collected Tales).

"Ferney," in Two Cheers for Democracy, 1951.

"For the Museum's Sake," in Abinger Harvest, 1936.

"Forrest Reid," in Abinger Harvest, 1936.

"Forrest Reid," in Two Cheers for Democracy, 1951.

"Gemistus Pletho," in Abinger Harvest, 1936.

"George Crabbe and Peter Grimes," in Two Cheers for Democracy, 1951.

"George Orwell," in Two Cheers for Democracy, 1951.

"Gerald Heard," in Two Cheers for Democracy, 1951.

"Gibbon and His Autobiography," in Two Cheers for Democracy, 1951.

"Gide and George," in Two Cheers for Democracy, 1951.

"Gide's Death," in Two Cheers for Democracy, 1951.

Goldsworthy Lowes Dickinson. London, Edward Arnold and Co., 1934.

"Happiness," in Abinger Harvest, 1936.

"Henry Thornton," in Two Cheers for Democracy, 1951.

"Hickey's Last Party," in Abinger Harvest, 1936.

"Howard Overing Sturgis," in Abinger Harvest, 1936.

"Hymn Before Action," in Abinger Harvest, 1936.

I Assert That There is an Alternative in Humanism. London, The Ethical Union, 1955.

195

"Ibsen the Romantic," in Abinger Harvest, 1936

"In My Library," in Two Cheers for Democracy, 1951.

"India Again," in Two Cheers for Democracy, 1951.

"It is Different for Me," in Abinger Harvest, 1936.

"Jane Austen, 1: The Six Novels; 2: Sanditon; 3: The Letters," in Abinger Harvest, 1936.

"Jew-Consciousness," in Two Cheers for Democracy, 1951.

"John Skelton," in Two Cheers for Democracy, 1951.

"Joseph Conrad: A Note," in Abinger Harvest, 1936.

"Julius Caesar," in Two Cheers for Democracy, 1951.

"Last of Abinger, The," in Two Cheers for Democracy, 1951.

"Last Parade, The," in Two Cheers for Democracy, 1951.

Letter to Madan Blanchard, A.   London, The Hogarth Press, 1931.

"Liberty in England," in Abinger Harvest, 1936.

"London Library, The," in Two Cheers for Democracy, 1951.

"London is a Muddle," in Two Cheers for Democracy, 1951.

"Luncheon at Pretoria," in Two Cheers for Democracy, 1951.

"Machine Stops, The," in The Eternal Moment and Other Stories, 1928.

"Macolnia Shops," in Abinger Harvest, 1936.

"Marco Polo," in Abinger Harvest, 1936.

"Me, Them and You," in Abinger Harvest, 1936.

"Menace to Freedom, The," in Two Cheers for Democracy, 1951.

"Mind of the Indian State, The," in Abinger Harvest, 1936.

"Mohammed Iqbal," in Two Cheers for Democracy, 1951.

"Mosque, The," in Abinger Harvest, 1936.

"Mount Lebanon," in Two Cheers for Democracy, 1951.

"Mr. Andrews," in The Eternal Moment and Other Stories, 1928.

"Mr. and Mrs. Abbey's Difficulties," in Abinger Harvest, 1936.

"Mrs. Grundy at the Parkers," in Abinger Harvest, 1936.

"Mrs. Hannah More," in Abinger Harvest, 1936.

"Mrs. Miniver," in Abinger Harvest, 1936.

"My Own Centenary," in Abinger Harvest, 1936.

"My Wood," in Abinger Harvest, 1936.

"New Disorder, The," Horizon (London), IV (December 1941), pp. 379-384. (Reprinted as a pamphlet, New York, 1949. No publisher given.)

Nordic Twilight. London, Macmillan and Co., Ltd., 1940.

"Not Listening to Music," in Two Cheers for Democracy, 1951.

"Not Looking at Pictures," in Two Cheers for Democracy, 1951.

"Note on the Way, A," in Abinger Harvest, 1936.

"Notes on the English Character," in Abinger Harvest, 1936.

"Other Kingdom," in The Celestial Omnibus and Other Stories, 1911.

"Other Side of the Hedge, The," in The Celestial Omnibus and Other Stories, 1911.

"Our Deputation," in Two Cheers for Democracy, 1951.

"Our Diversions, 1: The Scallies; 2: The Birth of an
    Empire; 3: The Doll Souse; 4: Mickey and Minnie;
    5: Chess at Cracow; 6: The Game of Life; 7: My
    Own Centenary," in Abinger Harvest, 1936.

"Our Graves in Gallipoli," in Abinger Harvest, 1936.

"Our Second Greatest Novel," in Two Cheers for Democ-
    racy, 1951.

"Outsider on Poetry, An," in Two Cheers for Democracy,
    1951.

A Passage to India. London, Edward Arnold and Co., 1924.

"Pharos," in Pharos and Pharillon, 1923.

Pharos and Pharillon. Surrey, England, The Hogarth Press,
    1923.

"Philo's Little Trip," in Pharos and Pharillon, 1923.

"Poetry of C. P. Cavafy, The," in Pharos and Pharillon,
    1923.

"Point of It, The," in The Eternal Moment and Other Sto-
    ries, 1928.

"Post-Munich," in Two Cheers for Democracy, 1951.

"Proust," in Abinger Harvest, 1936.

"Racial Exercise," in Two Cheers for Democracy, 1951.

"Raison D'Etre of Criticism in the Arts, The," in Two
    Cheers for Democracy, 1951.

"Reading as Usual," The Listener, (21 September 1939),
    pp. 586-587. (Reprinted as a pamphlet: London,
    Totenham Public Libraries, 1939.)

"Return from Siwa, The," in Pharos and Pharillon, 1923.

"Road from Colonus, The," Independent Review, III (June
    1904), pp. 124-134. (Reprinted in The Celestial Om-
    nibus and Other Stories, 1911.)

198

"Roger Fry: An Obituary Note," in Abinger Harvest, 1936.

"Romain Rolland and the Hero," in Two Cheers for Democracy, 1951.

"Ronald Firbank," in Abinger Harvest, 1936.

"Ronald Kidd," in Two Cheers for Democracy, 1951.

A Room With a View. London, Edward Arnold, 1908.

"St. Athanasius," in Pharos and Pharillon, 1923.

"Salute to the Orient," in Abinger Harvest, 1936.

"Sayed Ross Masood," in Two Cheers for Democracy, 1951.

"Sinclair Lewis," in Abinger Harvest, 1936.

" 'Snow' Wedgwood," in Two Cheers for Democracy, 1951.

"Solitary Place, The," in Pharos and Pharillon, 1923.

"Story of a Panic, The," in The Celestial Omnibus and Other Stories, 1911.

The Story of the Siren. Richmond, England, The Hogarth Press, 1920. (Reprinted in The Eternal Moment and Other Stories, 1928.)

"Stratford Jubilee, The," in Two Cheers for Democracy, 1951.

"T. E. Lawrence," in Abinger Harvest, 1936.

"Tercentenary of the 'Areopagitica', The," in Two Cheers for Democracy, 1951.

"They Hold Their Tongues," in Two Cheers for Democracy, 1951.

"Timothy the Cat and Timothy Whitebonnet," in Pharos and Pharillon, 1923.

"Tolerance," in Two Cheers for Democracy, 1951.

"Tourism V. Thuggism," The Listener, (17 January 1957),

p. 124. (Reprinted as a pamphlet: London and Dunstable, Waterloo and Sons, Ltd., 1957.)

"Tribute to Desmond MacCarthy," The Listener, (26 June 1952), p. 1031. (Reprinted as a pamphlet: Stanford Dingley, England, The Mill House Press, 1952.)

"T. S. Eliot," in Abinger Harvest, 1936.

"Trooper Silas Tomkyn Comerbacke," in Abinger Harvest, 1936.

"Two Books by T. S. Eliot," in Two Cheers for Democracy, 1951.

"Two Books by Tagore," in Abinger Harvest, 1936.

Two Cheers for Democracy. London, Edward Arnold and Co., 1951.

"United States, The," in Two Cheers for Democracy, 1951.

Virginia Woolf. Cambridge, England, The University Press, 1942.

"Voltaire and Frederick the Great," in Two Cheers for Democracy, 1951.

"Voltaire's Laboratory," in Abinger Harvest, 1936.

"Voter's Dilemma, A," in Abinger Harvest, 1936.

"Webb and Webb," in Two Cheers for Democracy, 1951.

"What Has Germany Done to the Germans?" in Two Cheers for Democracy, 1951.

"What I Believe," in Two Cheers for Democracy, 1951.

"What Would Germany Do to Us?" in Two Cheers for Democracy, 1951.

Where Angels Fear to Tread. Edinburgh and London, William Blackwood and .Sons, 1905.

"Whiff of D'Annunzio, A," in Two Cheers for Democracy, 1951.

200

"Wilfrid Blunt," in Abinger Harvest, 1936.

"William Arnold," in Two Cheers for Democracy, 1951.

"William Barnes," in Two Cheers for Democracy, 1951.

"Word-Making and Sound-Taking," in Abinger Harvest, 1936.